Desiring CHINA

.

PERVERSE MODERNITIES

A series edited by JUDITH HALBERSTAM *and* LISA LOWE

Desiring CHINA

Experiments in Neoliberalism, Sexuality,

and Public Culture

LISA ROFEL

DUKE UNIVERSITY PRESS ✳ Durham and London 2007

© 2007 Duke University Press

All rights reserved

Printed in the United States of America

on acid-free paper ∞

Designed by Katy Clove

Typeset in Sabon

by Keystone Typesetting, Inc.

Library of Congress Cataloging-in-Publication Data

appear on the last printed page of this book.

To *Graciela,*
in thanks for her love and imagination

CONTENTS

ACKNOWLEDGMENTS

*J*ntellectual endeavors are pleasurable to the extent they are engagements in collective conversations. I would not have been able to write this book without a group of interlocutors who always pushed my thinking beyond where I expected it to go: Jacqueline Brown, Gail Hershatter, Dorinne Kondo, Neferti Tadiar, Anna Tsing, Sylvia Yanagisako, and Mei Zhan. My colleagues at the University of California, Santa Cruz, offered numerous creative suggestions when I presented several of the chapters as lectures and have helped to make intellectual work meaningful: Anjali Aarondekar, Mark Anderson, James Clifford, Gina Dent, Carla Freccero, Jennifer Gonzalez, Jody Greene, Donna Haraway, David Hoy, Jocelyn Hoy, David Marriott, Rhadika Mongia, Helene Moglen, Hugh Raffles, Vanita Seth, Neferti Tadiar, Anna Tsing. Other colleagues gave generously of their moral and intellectual support: Ann Anagnost, Tani Barlow, Chris Berry, Kathleen Biddick, Steven Caton, Lawrence Cohen, Donald Donham, Judith Halberstam, Bruce Knauft, Lydia Liu, and Gayle Rubin. Many of the graduate students I have worked with at UCSC read and commented on my work and sustained my intellectual passions. They are remarkable interlocutors: Jon Anjaria, Angelina Chin, Timothy Choy, Cathryn Clayton, Ulrika Dahl, Lieba Faier, Gillian Goslinga, Anna Higgins, Wenqing Kang, Lyn Jeffery, Hiro Matsubara, Megan Moodie, Shiho Satsuka, Bettina Stoetzer, Yen-ling Tsai, Sasha Welland, and Robin Whitaker. I thank colleagues in China who have given me an intellectual home there: Cui Zi'en, Dai Jinhua, Tan Shen, and Wang Hui. Louisa Schein and Angela Zito went above and beyond with their careful reviews of the entire manuscript. I am deeply grateful. Kerry Walk continued to serve as my writing angel despite her heavy obligations. Eric Glassgold offered me his brilliant dissection of psychoanalytic theories. Robyn Wiegman created queer comradeship as the convener of a University of California Humanities Research Institute seminar on "Interdisciplinary Queer Studies." The book began there. My wonderful comrades in that group, in addition to Robyn, included Madelyn Detloff, Carla Frecerro, David Gere, George Haggerty, Eithne Lubheid, Nayan Shah, and Sandy Stone. I was fortunate to present several chapters as lectures at Emory University's Department of Anthropology, University of Washington's Humanities Center, the Women's Studies programs at the University of California, San Diego, and the University of California, Los Angeles, University of Chicago's Department of Anthropology, University of Michigan's Department of East Asian Studies, and Yale University's Department of Anthropology. I thank Bruce Knauft, Chandan Reddy, Judith Halberstam, Miriam Silverberg, Elizabeth Povinelli, Lydia Liu, and Eric Worby for those invitations. A generous grant from the Henry Luce Foundation made much of the research possible. A grant from the UCSC Committee on Research allowed me to complete the research. Angelina Chin, He Xiaopei, Erica Marcus, Mu Ahping, Billy Stewart, and Yen-ling Tsai helped with the research. Ken Wissoker of Duke University Press gave his unstinting support to this project. Katharine Baker shepherded the book to its publication. I owe my deepest debts to those in China who shared their insights with me about their lives, most of whom appear in the text with pseudonyms; to my partner Graciela Trevisan, who sustained me throughout; and to my mother, Jacqueline Rofel Berger, who first taught me the pleasures in learning about other ways of life and the dangers of American solipsism.

A version of chapter 1 appeared in *American Ethnologist* 21(4): 700–722. A version of chapter 2 appeared in *Spaces of Their Own: Women's Public Sphere in Transnational China*, edited by Mayfair Mei-hui Yang (Minneapolis: University of Minnesota Press, 1999). A version of chapter 3 appeared in *glq: A Journal of Lesbian and Gay Studies* 5(4): 451–74.

*O*ne evening in the summer of 1998, I glimpsed a new kind of human being. I was sitting with friends in a gay bar in Beijing, when a young Chinese man I had not met before struck up a conversation with me. With strong conviction in his voice, he asserted that it was absolutely human to express one's "personal feelings" (*ziji xinli hua*) and "personal affairs" (*geren shi*). He said he likes to tell people his personal story, that this is the right way to communicate. He saw the expression of wishes, yearnings, and aspirations as a "skill." He declared that all over the world people were quite capable of expressing what was in their hearts and that, in order to be part of the world, to be properly cosmopolitan, Chinese people needed to express themselves in that way as well. He made these assertions as if we were looking over the horizon; indeed, I followed him to imagine an emergent world of expressive desire. This was not, it seemed, a defense of homosexuality. In his calm, expectant gaze, he suggested that the scene around us was exemplary of a new humanity. Gay men and lesbians in China, he implied, are at the forefront of a new human era. Far from representing perversion, Chinese gay men and lesbians are leading China toward its proper place in a cosmopolitan globalized world.

This book describes how the production of desire lies at the heart of global processes. It engages with recent arguments about the relationship among liberal politics, neoliberal economics, and the formation of new subjectivities. In these postsocialist, post–Cold War times, what are the meanings and practices of becoming a different kind of citizen of the world? These matters are vital, I believe, in grasping the powerful and murderous exclusions taking shape in the world today as well as the political possibilities and passions that both undermine and reinforce those exclusions. Recent scholarship on neoliberal subjectivities, inspired by Foucault, delineates the rational techniques of the self that seem to derive from neoliberal economic life. I turn these important questions toward the social field of "desire" as that which appears to be the most explosive and powerful realm for constructing novel citizen-subjects not merely in China but in China's reconfiguration of its relationship to a postsocialist world. Sexuality is one of several sites in which desire is imagined and discussed in these encounters. In this regard, I join with theorists of sexuality who have demonstrated the centrality of sexual politics to transnational encounters (Cruz-Malavé and Manalansan 2002, Gopinath 2005, Manalansan 2003, Povinelli 2002, Povinelli and Chauncey 1999, Stoler 2002, Tadiar 2004). I build on this important work to highlight the multiplicities of desire constructed through a complex range of transnational relations of power. In so doing, I hope to further queer theory's project of delineating the historical contingencies of "desiring subjects" by broadening this project to consider global encounters that link political economies with manifestations of sexual, racial, and gendered hierarchies that are at once local and global.

Neoliberal strategies to develop post–Cold War capitalism have been influential in the transformations that Chinese citizens currently experience. My approach to these transformations, however, emphasizes the historical processes and heterogeneity of global practices fostered in the name of neoliberal capitalism. It is meant to forestall a sense that neoliberalism is a universal set of principles from which derives, in a deterministic fashion, a singular type of neoliberal subject. Like the term "globalization," "neoliberalism" has quickly come to imply a uniformity to experiences of capitalism throughout the world. Moreover, it is often used to imply a monolithic emergence of novel subjectivities. Events in China disrupt such totalizing assumptions. The Chinese state and its citizens do not merely embrace the cultural and political encounters that constitute our post–Cold War world but rather participate in creating them. Contrary to much current scholarship on neoliberalism, this book argues that neoliberalism has been an ongoing experimental project that began in the global south, in which nation-states had to remake themselves to participate in the post–Cold War order. China's ability to become a subject of neoliberalism supports a world in which every nation must do its (properly differentiated) part for the universally imagined plan to produce a new human nature. This "re-worlding," to borrow Mei Zhan's phrase (forthcoming), means crafting diverse dialogues with those in multiple other geopolitical locations about the meanings of these transformations in their lives and about the place of China and Chinese citizens in a postsocialist humanity.

A sea-change has swept through China in the last fifteen years: to replace socialist experimentation with the "universal human nature" imagined as the essential ingredient of cosmopolitan worldliness. This model of human nature has the desiring subject as its core: the individual who operates through sexual, material, and affective self-interest. I use the term "desire" to gloss a wide range of aspirations, needs, and longings. "Desire" is a key cultural practice in which both the government and its citizens reconfigure their relationship to a postsocialist world. In official, intellectual, and popular discourses, this desiring subject is portrayed as a new human being who will help to usher in a new era in China. I call the new China that this figure is supposed to produce "desiring China."

Beginning in the early 1990s and into the new millennium, I heard echoes of that young man's exegesis about the importance of "desire" for a global humanity among a diverse range of people in China. I was struck by the distinctiveness of these commentaries when compared with the recent past. In the 1980s, when I first went to live and do research in China, everyday conversation would invariably turn at some point to what politics had meant for individuals' lives. People spoke of the upheavals of the Cultural Revolution (1966–76) that had fundamentally transformed their life trajectories. Or they dissected the most recently instituted policies known as economic reform (begun in rural areas in 1978 and urban areas in 1984), wondering aloud in which ways these policies, designed to reject Maoist socialism, might yet again change the course of their lives. In the 1980s, there was, I felt, a distinctive "culture of politics" in the sense that people's passions were directed toward the significance of state-sponsored political campaigns, though that significance was cast differently by class, gender, and political cohort.[1] I often heard the term "consciousness" (*sixiang, yishi xingtai*) as people explained the importance of their "thoughts" and how their "thoughts" had either been colonized by the Cultural Revolution or "opened" by various political experiences.

In the 1990s, I returned to China to learn more about the youngest generation, who had never experienced Maoist socialism. My curiosity about their self-representations as well as the representations of them by their parents' generation arose from surprising conversations with feminists I knew well in China who had come of age under socialism. Despite public touting of the benefits of economic reform, these women often made negative remarks about how these reforms might affect their daughters. Economic reform entailed a wide range of central government policies to develop a market economy and decentralize economic planning. The term "economic reform" also evoked sweeping changes in all aspects of social, political, and economic life. Gender and sexual politics served as a central crux of economic reform.[2] In official and popular pronouncements, economic reform was supposed to eradicate what, in a revisionist view, were represented as the "unnatural" gender politics of Maoist socialism. The feminists I knew expressed concern about novel kinds of sexual vulnerability they felt their daughters faced. In reaction, one prominent feminist became a neo-Confucian advocate of "traditional" Chinese family values. She allied herself with Christian evangelical organizations from the United States searching for inroads to proselytize in China. Another feminist opened a nongovernmental sex hotline offering advice about proper sexual behavior.[3]

I decided to seek out these daughters to hear how they narrated their own lives. I found that young women — and young men — quickly turned to the importance of having wide-ranging aspirations, hopes, needs, and passions. In contrast to discussions of "consciousness," these young people described their "hearts" (xinli, xintai) and "feelings" (ganjue). They spoke of the need to embrace wide-ranging "desires," from consumption to work to sex. They explicitly contrasted what they viewed as their own life-enhancing practices with the self-sacrifices they interpreted as having dominated their parents' lives. Where in the 1980s, people spoke to me about how they sought to grapple with the effects of state policies in their lives, a decade later people excitedly showed me their home furnishings, talked to me about gay cruising or extramarital sexual affairs, shared their schemes for making money, and fantasized about travel and their desire to get to America. At times, it seemed to me that the kinds of yearnings, passions, or hopes need not be specified, so long as someone could assert she or he had the capability of embodying the figure of a "desiring subject." This act of assertion caught my attention. It seemed to go beyond itself; that is, it seemed to hold out the hope of freedom from a past that this younger generation (as well as much of public culture) viewed as one of constraints and deprivations.

But lurking behind the assertion was also a keen awareness of judgment: would that person be found to inhabit this desiring figure in the proper manner? I often heard comments reflecting this anxiety but also, attached to it, evaluations of others. Indeed, these critical appraisals created a social field that marginalized and excluded those deemed incapable of the proper embodiment of "desire." This field produced diacritics that marked novel forms of class inequality, as a burgeoning bourgeoisie attempted to create new social worlds of class segregation. These judgments also reflected the tensions of rural/urban divisions, as migrant workers from the countryside arrived in the cities seeking work while legal urban residents both depended on their labor and abhorred their presence. Finally, they amplified an unstable division between those who have sex for "love" versus those who have sex for money or financial support. Among gay men and lesbians, for example, there existed a running commentary on how to distinguish the proper embodiment of a "gay" identity and what to do about those deemed to sully that identity even as they claimed it.

These everyday conversations about aspirations, longings, and passions were not subterranean. To the contrary, a plethora of public discourse in China addressed precisely these matters. Nor did people develop their "desires" necessarily in opposition to the state. Debates about appropriate and inappropriate needs and aspirations played a central role in official discussions about the policies the government should adopt in "opening" China to transnational capitalism. These debates could also be found in the explosion of glossy magazines, the rapid spread of television, various legal cases that were publicized in popular legal media, rock music and pulp novels, and eventually conversations over the Internet. In both formal interviews I conducted and in informal conversation, young women and men explicitly invoked soap operas, letters to the editor, legal decisions, spectacular cases of official corruption, and the daily news to assess, defend, and evaluate the proper way to express their aspirations and longings. Moreover, these multiple passions and yearnings made their appearance in the context of an economy that, during the 1990s, was the fastest-growing economy in the world.

American commentators imagine Chinese people as casting off socialism to find their true inner selves — whether sexual, possessive, or otherwise cosmopolitan. Rather than begin with such naturalizing assumptions, I ask instead just how these inner selves come into being.[4] One of my main arguments is that the construction of this inner self occurs through public allegories. In watching television shows, people learn the art of "longing"; in reading about court cases, they negotiate gay and consumer identities. If human nature has changed in China, this transformation takes place in the remaking of the public spaces and stories through which human nature discovers itself.

This human nature is not one that people always successfully embody. Rather, they feel drawn or compelled toward the project of embracing it. The desiring subject functions variously as a trope, a normative ideal, and a horizon of possibility — or impossibility. It promises new freedoms even as it seems to be the only game in town. It both opens up political possibilities and establishes a different terrain for powerful and dehumanizing exclusions. If socialist power operated on the terrain of "consciousness," postsocialist power operates on the site of "desire."

This book examines these new forms of subjectivity that have developed along with postsocialist transformations, some of which are connected to neoliberalism and its associated privatizations. My argument, in brief, is that central to the meanings and practices of becoming a transnational citizen-subject in China is the historical and cultural constitution of "desire."[5] Through this argument, I address two scholarly discussions usually held apart: one on the constitution of desire and the other on the relationship between neoliberalism and technologies of subjectification. In engaging both of these conversations I hope, to paraphrase Gayatri Spivak, to "interrupt" certain tendencies in each.

My goal is ambitious: to bring together in one ethnographic frame questions of desire, sexuality, political subjectivity, postsocialism, liberal politics, and transnational capitalism with its neoliberal inflections. Although it might appear that such a framework will burst at the seams, it is the only way I have found to describe the breadth and depth of China's reconfiguration of its relationship to a postsocialist world. The wide-ranging essays in this book address a soap opera, a women's museum, the emergence of gay identities, gendered cosmopolitan longings, court cases that adjudicated gay rights, intellectual property, and consumer fraud, and debates about China's entry into the WTO. Together, they trace the specific subjectivities emerging in urban China after the end of socialism.

POSTSOCIALIST EXPERIMENTS

The conversation I had in the gay bar that evening in 1998 conveyed a sense of just how much both China and the world had changed since the end of socialism. But rather than measure China's experiences against an abstract model of neoliberalism (have they arrived at the "real" version of neoliberalism yet?) or a transhistorical figure of desire (have they learned how to have pleasure yet?) — two recurrent neocolonial questions that imply infinite deferral — we might best understand those experiences as historically and culturally situated.

The specificity of desiring practices in China lies in the efforts by the Chinese state and its citizens to overcome their socialist past. Maoist socialism ended with the Cultural Revolution (1966–76). While in the late 1970s and the early 1980s some still believed in the basic tenets of socialism, many were disillusioned by the destructive passions of two basic principles of Maoism: class struggle and continuous revolution. This disillusionment posed a crisis of legitimacy for the state. Those most adamant about rejecting the Cultural Revolution, including Deng Xiaoping and his supporters, took this opportunity to mobilize a dismantling of Cultural Revolution policies, especially central economic planning. By encouraging public criticism of the Cultural Revolution, Deng Xiaoping weakened the position of those who still supported Maoist policies, while strengthening the position of those like himself who had been ousted from power during the Cultural Revolution. The central government — far from unified — thus addressed this crisis with tentative and somewhat ad hoc policies that they made sound unified and firm by calling them "economic reform."[6] These economic reform experiments initiated the process of creating "desiring China."

Economic reform eventually entailed a rejection of collective enterprise, the gradual promotion of a market economy, and the steady move toward privatization. While the state gradually retreated from a centrally planned economy, it continued to have an intimate involvement in the means and modes of economic reform. As Wang Hui (2004) has argued, the specificity of neoliberalism in post-Mao China rests in part on the premise of a continuity in the political system of governance, coupled with a discontinuity in the state's promotion of radical marketization and privatization.[7] It would be misleading, then, to characterize the market economy in China as in opposition to the state, as that which has developed in spite of or around the state.[8] Unlike Russia or some of the Eastern European nations, for example, China never engaged in wholesale "spontaneous privatization" under the aegis of U.S. economists.[9] An experimental and gradual approach has defined the tenor of China's reforms. This cautious approach did not always guarantee an orderly process. It highlights, however, the nondeterministic content and direction of the reforms. To get ahead of my story, China did not simply follow a well-established neoliberal plan, fully laid out, based on normative principles.[10]

In retrospect, one can say economic reform in China proceeded through two phases.[11] From 1978 to 1984, the government concentrated on rural reform, and from 1984 to 1989 on urban reform. After the June 4th movement of 1989, known in the West as the Tiananmen demonstrations, Deng Xiaoping and his supporters in the central government took the opportunity of this renewed political crisis to accelerate their promotion of market-based privatization. Rural reform led to the decollectivization of communes, the partial decentralization of power to local governments, the development of rural markets and rural industrialization. These radical transformations targeted the rigid rural-urban divide created under Maoism.[12] The initial result witnessed a decline in rural-urban inequality, but a growing inequality within rural areas. Rural reform also involved several unanticipated results. Widespread corruption emerged in the transfer of control over resources from the central to local governments. The ability of local cadres to command these resources for their families facilitated their prominence in the new class of rural industrialists.[13] Second, the reforms unleashed an enormous tide of rural migrants who swept into the cities in search of work.[14]

An analogous devolution of power to local governments and to cadre-managers of state-run enterprises slowly emerged from urban reform. These reforms expanded the independence of managers to redistribute resources, retain profits, and transform relations of production, leading eventually to the end of the "iron rice bowl" (i.e., guaranteed employment) and the creation of short-term contract workers, many from the countryside. As in the rural areas, the transfer of resources reorganized social relations, advantages, and interests. Most prominent among those who benefited were a small minority, including some managers but also diverse government cadres who, as in the rural areas, eventually formed a new capitalist class. Corruption charges enlivened urban debates as well, but they reflected greater ambivalence about whether certain practices could in fact be described as "corrupt" or offered novel forms of profit-making that should be applauded.[15] Finally, the state gradually separated production from consumption. State-run enterprises, in which virtually all urban residents worked under socialism, had distributed critical consumer goods through the workplace. Many enterprises discontinued this practice after economic reform. In the early moments of reform, small "free" markets in agricultural produce and consumer goods appeared adjacent to state-run markets.

The initial reforms had contradictory effects: they enhanced ordinary citizens' sense of the new possibilities that lay within their reach but also increased frustrations with the new social inequalities that soon became evident. People drew on a wellspring of memories about socialist security as well as the recent Cultural Revolution past, in which access to special privileges based on political power had been condemned, to critique the new historical conditions in which they found themselves. These new conditions included the marketization of power, inequalities in distribution and rent-seeking behavior, increasingly polarized income levels, the abolition of security in employment, and lack of reforms in social benefits.

The eruption of nationwide protests in the June 4th movement of 1989 was a response to the legitimacy of the redistribution process and the very social transition to the market. That movement did not critique merely the holdover of the old Maoist state but also the "new" reform state and the social and economic life it had produced. Various urban strata, including intellectuals, sensed a diminution in their benefits, while rural reforms stagnated in relation to urban development, bringing a renewed urban-rural divide. Students demanded that democracy, freedom, and liberal justice replace authoritarian rule in the reform process while other citizens sought an end to official corruption, opposed the "princeling party" of cadres who now formed a privileged monied class, protested the proliferating inequalities spawned by the market's expansion, and demanded social guarantees and stable prices — in short, social justice.[16]

The state's violent suppression of the June 4th movement coincided with the disintegration of the Soviet Union and the end of the Cold War. Within these global conditions, Deng Xiaoping's followers in the central government again took the opportunity of this second crisis of legitimacy to mobilize further support for market radicalism. They pushed forward the tentative movement toward privatization begun under economic reform. In effect, the state legalized the very socioeconomic arrangements that galvanized the 1989 protests.[17]

The specificity of profit-seeking practices in China appears in the fact, for example, that a large number of profit-oriented businesses are mixtures of local government ownership and private management (Oi and Walder 1999).[18] These are joined by the vast number of state bureaucracies that, owing to budgetary constraints (as well as officials' pursuit of personal wealth), operate for-profit businesses.[19] Since the early 1990s, increasing numbers of private firms have appeared to compete with these other businesses, despite their difficulties in gaining access to capital given that the central government still monopolizes its legitimate distribution.[20] Finally, both the central and local governments have sold or leased many small- and medium-sized state-owned enterprises, often to foreign companies, while combining the remaining large ones into what they hope will be competitive cartels.[21] These profit-seeking activities are not uniform within China. Enormous differentiation exists among provinces, counties, and cities in their interpretations and sometimes outright violations of central policies. Thus, abstract concepts of "the market," "private property," and "finance" cannot merely be applied to China to see if it measures up to a normative model of neoliberal capitalism.[22]

Emphasis on consumer and mass culture has dominated urban life since the June 4th movement, even as the gap between rich and poor has widened significantly. Peasant migration to the cities expanded as urban infrastructural projects and foreign investment created labor at minimal cost.[23] Migrant labor predominates in the export and coastal industrial zones.[24] Urban governments continued to place restrictions on in-migration, in effect erecting discriminatory policies based on fixed spatial identities. No measures were instituted for labor security as state-run factories steadily decreased the number of their workers or closed, while more citizens turned to the market to find jobs. The state has also slowly extricated itself from its previous socialist obligations regarding social security, such as healthcare and housing.[25]

Only during this post–June 4th period did the state begin to encourage large-scale foreign investment into China. The liberalization of foreign direct investment (FDI) served as a driving force that occasioned the eventual demise of China's state-owned enterprises (Gallagher 2005).[26] This "opening" of China that U.S. commentators so frequently describe is more accurately understood as a turn away from post-Bandung commitments to the nonaligned and third world and toward closer involvement with the United States, Japan, and the four East Asian newly industrialized countries (Taiwan, Hong Kong, Singapore, and South Korea).[27] During the first years of economic reform, the central government had created one site, Shenzhen, adjacent to Hong Kong, as a free trade zone for multinational factories. A few years later, the government expanded to four "special economic zones," and then fourteen cities, all located along the eastern coast, for joint ventures between foreign companies and the Chinese government. The foreign-invested enterprises were kept separate from the domestic economy during these early years. But in the late 1980s the central government expanded these preferential policies to the entire eastern coast and by the early 1990s extended them to all provinces. In 1999 the prohibition on foreign-private economic cooperation in China was lifted. By 2000, the government stipulated required quotas of foreign investment that *all* areas had to fill. Foreign companies gained permission to establish wholly foreign-owned enterprises without joint Chinese state ownership. They also began to buy out failing state enterprises. Greater amounts of foreign investment translated into more local financial and political autonomy and prestige for local officials.

By 2002, China had surpassed the United States as the most favored destination for foreign direct investment (Gallagher 2005, 34). Compared to other large developing countries, China is in a league of its own.[28] The 1997 "Asian" financial crisis did not affect China directly, mainly because China's financial system was not open to foreign speculation at that time. But it did lead to the realization that globalization was not external to China but internal to it because China's economy was affected by the ties it had built with Southeast and East Asian nations. This crisis played a large role in moving China more quickly to join the World Trade Organization (WTO).

The dream of regaining China's stature as an empire and the postcolonial desire to attain material and moral parity with the West have motivated much of China's actions in the post–Cold War world. Joining the WTO has allowed foreign companies to invest in nearly all aspects of China's economy but has also lowered the barriers to Chinese entrepreneurs' investments elsewhere. China's incursions into the West have occasioned anxiety, especially in the United States, that the "outside" of the West is now finding its way into the heart of the "inside." From its recent bids to acquire U.S. corporations and its steady acquisition of the U.S. government's debt, to its search for greater sources of oil and gas, and the expansion of its share of the textile industry, China's presence in transnational capitalist endeavors has expanded. The United States is not the only Western nation-state with which China has become involved since the end of socialism. But it looms large in the public imaginary of China, in part because the United States empire has continued to expand. The United States serves as a contradictory site of identification and competition. It provides a source of critique for those within China who oppose the communist party and a source of dreams about democracy. But more recently, news about United States imperialist violence has also illuminated for Chinese citizens the hypocrisies of American claims to represent such dreams. During both the first and the second Gulf Wars, it became clear that, despite its rhetoric to the contrary, the United States government had no intention of promoting democracy in the Middle East.[29]

A revisionist history inspires these transformations: Maoist socialism had been *nothing but* destructive and obstructionist and, in the end, it had hindered rather than helped China attain its deserved status as a world power. The underlying cause, in this version of history, was Maoism's suppression of "natural" humanity and its creation of unnatural passions and interests. Postsocialist reforms are portrayed, in contrast, as setting human nature free. To foster the constitution of this postsocialist humanity, shortly after the Cultural Revolution the state abolished the class labels that had so intimately defined individual life trajectories under Maoism, declaring class struggle officially over. This radical *fanshen*, or overturning, opened up social space to explore other identities, such as sexual and ethnic identities, even as it hindered the creation of a public discourse on the marked inequalities and exclusions produced by economic reform.[30] As I have argued previously (1999), a postsocialist allegory of modernity tells a story of how Maoism deferred China's ability to reach modernity by impeding Chinese people's ability to express their gendered human natures. The allegory is an emancipatory story, holding out the promise that people can unshackle their innate gendered and sexual selves by freeing themselves from the socialist state. It is also a rejection of Maoist feminism. In popular discourse, Maoist feminism is blamed for attempts to turn men and women into unnaturally gendered beings. Women are said to have become too masculine, while men were unable to find their true masculinity.[31]

After the June 4th crisis of legitimacy, the constitution of a postsocialist humanity in China entailed not merely the demolition of those politics portrayed as hindering human nature but a positive encouragement and elaboration of people's sexual, material, and affective self-interest in order to become cosmopolitan citizens of a post–Cold War world. "Desiring China" began to take shape at this moment. And through the construction of "desiring China," neoliberalism in China appeared as if it were a unified entity that signaled a new era. My argument here is at once theoretical, historical, and ethnographic. China was not confronted with a seamless totality called neoliberalism that it merely adopted. Nor did the Chinese state impose a set of neoliberal policies that then shifted citizens' desires. Nor, finally, did an overarching apparatus called "neoliberalism" lodge itself in people's subjectivities. Rather, the 1990s in China witnessed a historically specific self-conscious enthusiasm for coherence through the search for a novel cosmopolitan humanity. This enthusiasm traversed official policies, intellectual writings, and much of public culture. Chinese citizens at multiple levels—the state, business, and everyday life—tried to piece together disparate experiences of their transnational encounters to make themselves and China appear as if they were entering a wholly new, coherent era.[32]

This book tracks these aspirations to connect transnational economic policies, only some of which we might label "neoliberal," profit-seeking activities, which were far from uniform, and new kinds of desiring subjects. The question these essays address is not how China "indigenized" a global message but how various disparate state policies and corporate strategies translate into new subjectivities. The answer, I argue throughout the book, lies largely in the realm of public culture, where the creation of "desiring China" takes place.

As I argue in chapter 5, rejection of Maoism's excessive passions has led to the constitution of "interest" as a category that connotes not merely the pursuit of wealth but additionally a means to restrain those passions of the past. Maoism, however, is portrayed in a paradoxical manner. It is said to have fostered excess and also to have repressed "human nature." Post-Mao China thus faces a complex dilemma. The formation of postsocialist subjects requires not simply temperance but the positive development of desire. The predicament for successful economic reform is to find the proper balance between interest and passion. To foster desire at once resolves this exigency and endlessly throws things off balance. For it turns out that desire can be unpredictable and difficult to control. For this reason, a great deal of ambivalence persists in China about such desires as homoeroticism. This ambivalence appears in public culture debates, such as well-known legal cases concerning homoerotic desire and gay identity, as well as in informal conversation. While certain officials and ordinary citizens feel the need to condemn homosexuality, many others feel called upon to support, or at least tolerate, the existence of homosexuality. Their ambivalence reveals the importance of bringing into existence a "desiring China."

"Desire," then, is a historically, socially, and culturally produced field of practices. These longings, aspirations, and newly experienced needs articulate with the contradictions and inequalities produced out of neoliberalism in China. They create attachments and active involvement in these transformations. Novel forms of inclusion and exclusion that arose out of economic reform rested on how its policies captured a wide array of desires produced in part out of the policies themselves.

For the sake of brevity, I have condensed this story of neoliberalism in China. But my story thus far is misleading, at least in the sense that it paints a picture of reforms that proceeded smoothly and along a predetermined path. Through the chapters in this book, I try to highlight the temporal contingencies, ambivalences, and uncertainties of neoliberalism in China, as citizens debated their import in the forms and fora of public culture.

How might we approach questions of worldly encounters in these post–Cold War times? How should we interpret novel forms of humanity and citizenship emerging through these encounters? Neoliberal policies developed by transnational organizations like the WTO play a central, though not exclusive, role. They establish certain rules of the game for transnational capitalism though they do not determine how people will manipulate those rules. As with the long histories of world systems, these neoliberal capitalist practices and their attendant ideologies intersect with other modalities of power to shape but not determine the transcultural encounters that emerge through labor relations, migration, cosmopolitanism, consumption, and various forms of "desire."

Recent work on neoliberalism raises critical questions about transformations in the relationship between capitalism, governance, and subjectivity. This important literature notes definitive ruptures as well as continuities with liberal modes of rule. These scholars remind us that capitalism is a world-transforming project that has the capacity to reach into the sinews of our bodies and the machinations of our hearts. For these scholars, neoliberalism is more than a political philosophy or economic ideology. Inspired by Foucault, they argue that it is a mode of governing citizens (Burchell et al. 1991). I choose three exemplary scholars in this field to demonstrate how we might address vital questions about novel conceptions and practices of humanity that generate exploitative exclusions as well as political possibilities. I have chosen these three scholars because they each critically interrupt one another's versions of neoliberalism, enabling me to bring new insights to the story I want to tell.

Nikolas Rose (1996, 1999) offers an evolutionary history of governmentality from liberal to "advanced liberal" (a term he uses coterminously with "neoliberal") democracies. Following Foucault, he eschews the idea that governance resides solely in a centralized state. Rose traces the assemblages of each stage of history that link "the regulation of public conduct with the subjective emotional and intellectual capacities and techniques of individuals, and the ethical regimes through which they govern their lives" (1996, 38). According to Rose, the problem of governance under nineteenth-century liberalism was how to provide a solution to the apparent opposition between the need for morality and order and the desire to restrict government in the name of liberty and economy. Rose argues that the solution lay in the development of expert knowledges in the human sciences. Experts were empowered to provide new techniques for acting upon individuals in relation to a social norm and with the goal of achieving a state of welfare. Advanced liberalism was sparked by a different set of political critiques: how to overcome the interventionist nature of the liberal welfare state.[33] These critiques led to a neoliberal mentality of government. Rose argues that neoliberal political theorists do not take the market to be a natural entity but rather believe government needs to ensure that the market functions properly by, paradoxically, governing less.[34] These neoliberal theorists further seek new ethical values; specifically, greater emphasis on the idea that individuals need more freedom for self-actualization. Advanced liberal rule thus devises new technologies of governance by reconstruing individual citizens as subjects of entrepreneurial choices. It seeks to marketize expertise within calculative regimes of competition, accountability, and consumer demand. The ideal of the "social state" gives way to the "enabling state." Advanced liberal governance thus encompasses the privatization of numerous governmental activities, including the civil service, prisons, and police, the end of welfare, and the autonomization of individual entities. Social insurance, as a liberal principle of social solidarity, gives way to a privatization of risk management, and social work gives way to the self-help manual. Individuals will become experts of themselves.

Where Rose implicitly discusses Great Britain, Wendy Brown (2003) explicitly situates her analysis in the United States. Although they share a methodology of analyzing the writings of political theorists, Rose offers an institutional analysis based on an evolutionary timeline, while Brown interrupts this evolutionary tale to argue that neoliberalism arose within the historical contingencies of U.S. political mobilizations. For Brown, neoliberalism is a response to the challenges from the left as well as a provocation to the left. In Brown's version of neoliberalism, political subjectivities arise out of concrete mobilization programs rather than the abstract progress of power. Her goal is to encourage the American left to develop a new set of political strategies.

Brown delineates the political rationality that subtends neoliberalism. When deployed as a form of governmentality, neoliberalism, according to Brown, "reaches from the soul of the citizen-subject to education policy to practices of empire" (2). Brown describes four main characteristics of neoliberal governmentality: (1) It extends and disseminates market values to all institutions and social action. Neoliberalism makes normative rather than ontological claims about the pervasiveness of market rationality and therefore advocates the institution building, policies, and discourses necessary to construct this rationality. (2) The market provides the organizing and regulative principle of the state not only because the state responds to the needs of the market but is itself rendered as an enterprise organized by market rationality. (3) Economic rationality extends to formerly noneconomic domains. Moral subjects are reconfigured as entrepreneurial subjects; individuals metamorphose into rational, calculating creatures whose moral autonomy is measured by their capacity for self-care. (4) Profitability becomes the criterion for good social policy in a liberal democracy, for it fosters the entrepreneurial principle of "equal inequality for all" (5).[35] This undermines a modest tension and ethical gap that previously existed between liberal democratic values and a capitalist economy. Brown argues that neoliberal rationality has not caused but rather facilitated the dismantling of democracy in the post-9/11 national security crisis. It also defines American imperialism, even as the terms of democracy are used to obscure neoliberal goals of instituting market rationality abroad. Market economics are offered not merely as the path to democracy but as the measure of democracy. Brown concludes with a call for the American left not to remain melancholic — and therefore attached — to the loss of liberal democracy but instead to develop a left vision of social justice that would enhance the collaborative capacity of citizens to govern themselves.

Finally, while Brown and Rose examine neoliberalism within the nation-state, Aihwa Ong (1999, 2003) interrupts both of their versions of neoliberalism by describing a global structure of sutured differences. Ong reminds us of the importance of looking across geopolitical boundaries to understand how neoliberalism is a historically produced dialogue and encounter between cultures. The corpus of Ong's work examines diasporic Hong Kong capitalists, Southeast Asian governments, and Cambodian refugees in the United States to stress the differentiations that lie at the heart of neoliberal subjectification processes. Each of these subjects occupies one niche in a variegated quilt of neoliberalisms. Ong's story about them implicitly positions Rose's experts and Brown's

U.S. leftists within a global story of articulation. Hong Kong capitalists, for example, became mobile investors in the face of Hong Kong's imminent return to China. One of their class strategies is what Ong calls "flexible citizenship," by which she means the ability of these professionals and entrepreneurs to both circumvent and benefit from various nation-state regimes by selecting distinct sites for investment, work, and family relocation. The experience of a market-driven sense of citizenship is not new for these Hong Kong elites but is rather a historical legacy of their life under British colonialism, when the British government suppressed political expression and fostered Hong Kong as a laissez-faire free port. What is new is the maneuvering for citizenship among several nation-states. Although able to buy multiple citizenships through large capital investments, these elites nonetheless cannot evade entirely the racism of immigration laws as well as everyday forms of racism.

The neoliberalism of Southeast Asian governments provides yet another story. Ong (1999) argues that the specific historical and cultural manifestations of neoliberalism in Southeast Asia derive from a history of governance that reflects the interpenetration of Asian cultures with the legacy of European rule.[36] The assertion within these neoliberal economies that problems of governmentality pertain to religion and cultural difference from the West emerges from this postcolonial legacy. Neoliberalism in Southeast Asia cultivates a rational subject shaped by the authority of the state as cultural regulator rather than the calculating subject with its precarious individualism promoted in the West. The West promotes privatized risk management as a neoliberal technology of the self, while Southeast Asian governments encourage subjects to be self-reliant but also dependent on the culturally sanctioned collectivity represented by the state.

In *Buddha Is Hiding* (2003), Ong reflects on the experiences of Cambodian refugees in the United States. In this case she demonstrates how the neoliberal economism that increasingly infiltrates social life intersects with the rationality of racial classification. Asian immigrants are categorized along a black-white continuum that has historically defined racialized citizenship and forms of exclusion in the United States. As the result of specific historic contingencies of American imperialism, global capital, Reagan-era policies, and the timing of their entry into the United States, Cambodians found themselves categorized on the "black" end of the continuum as unskilled, low-wage labor. But technologies of governance are not uniform. Welfare offices, community hospitals, court systems, and churches each have their distinctive practices to induce and inculcate Americanness. Veering away from simple determinism, Ong stresses how Cambodian refugees at times deflect and transform these normalizing modes of governance. They grapple with tensions between American individualism, pragmatism, and materialism, distillations in turn of Christian ethics, and a Khmer-Buddhist ethos of compassionate hierarchy, collectivism, and otherworldliness. Ong concludes that no singular form of citizenship is produced. Rather social integration is realized through the differentiation of citizen-subjects.

This work on neoliberalism stimulates my efforts to trace the emergence of "desiring China." By extending Rose, I ask questions about the role of public culture in fostering novel cosmopolitan subjectivities. Rose joins the idea that governance resides in multiple public institutions beyond the centralized state with the critical role of experts in extending that governance. We can adapt his questions to ask how non-expert, ordinary citizens grapple with broad-ranging public discourses and how they actively negotiate, argue about, desire, and differentiate the kinds of subjectivities they are encouraged to embody. Brown anticipates the permeation of market values into all realms of social life and into the very conceptualization of democracy. By extending Brown, we can ask questions about how differentially positioned citizens in China grapple with the market economy in their lives and how they evaluate questions of freedom and constraint in relation to it. Ong allows us to see that neoliberalism is both historically produced and culturally situated across nation-state boundaries. At the heart of these encounters lie complex negotiations of race, gender, class, and national status.

In moving forward from this work, my approach to neoliberalism brings their questions together with the one that motivates these essays: how do all of these policies, philosophies, entrepreneurial activities (some of which are more about disorderly risk than methodical rationality), and transformations in subjectivities come to appear as if they adhere to one another and even define an era? This question leads me to depart from the scholarly approaches I have examined to the extent that I do not assume the coherence of "neoliberalism." Rather than take coherence for granted, I ask after its historical and cultural creation. Rather than presume we have entered a new era, I ask about the attraction of those claims. In effect, I turn around the perspective on neoliberalism.[37] I begin with the broad and diverse constitution of desiring subjects in China to ask how this search for a postsocialist, cosmopolitan humanity encourages the piecing together of disparate policies and strategies into a "desiring China." My argument partially overlaps with David Harvey's recent discussion of neoliberalism (2005). Harvey does not take political trumpeters of neoliberalism at their word. He does not believe they describe social reality but rather that they provide ideological justification for current capitalist practices that often do not coincide with and can be in contradiction to their neoliberal ideology.[38] If this view is true, the obvious question is why anyone would accept neoliberalism as the ruling order?

Rose, Brown, and Ong do not answer this question because they all leave us with individuals responding to a general structure of power.[39] Cambodians respond from the bottom of the heap. Cosmopolitan Chinese respond from the directors' chairs. But in each case they respond as individuals. A piece of the analysis remains missing. Why should we consider neoliberalism an era-making program if it merely involves individual adjustments? My argument, in contrast, is that neoliberalism in China is a *national* project about global reordering. The project is to remake national public culture. Only because neoliberalism is a national imaginary about a post–Cold War world — not just in China but in the global south — does anyone believe that neoliberalism defines an era. Such an endeavor in the global south follows on the heels of modernization and globalization as "fantasy-productions" (Tadiar 2004) through which nation-states in the south must remake themselves to participate in the global order. After all, Latin Americans brought the term "neoliberalism" into popular use. All the key experiments occurred in the global south. Only because of these southern national projects, with their insistency and vigor, does anyone in the north even notice neoliberalism. If northern progressives worry, they have learned to do so from the world-making grasp of neoliberalism brought to their doors by north-south collaborations.[40]

The essays in this book demonstrate how forms of neoliberal subjectification, which in their own terms only address individual subjects, depend on national mobilizations that draw their dynamic energies from global encounters. In this regard, I am inspired by Brown but open up what she takes for granted: the mobilizing abilities of the nation-state and its public culture in the context of global articulations. I show

how China became the subject of neoliberalism even as only individuals who happen to be Chinese appear within this discursive frame. In turn, China's ability to become a subject of neoliberalism supports a global order in which every nation must do its part to produce these new human natures. I follow Ong, but again, I open up what she touches on obliquely: that individuals find their proper niche in the world order as subjects of national (and nationally diasporic) public cultures. National and diasporic public cultures, in their global journeys, become the major medium for creating these subjectivities.

The political and cultural upheavals of China's Cultural Revolution may have made the ensuing decades seem staid by comparison. But they were no less revolutionary for all that. China recreated its place in the world as Chinese citizens refashioned themselves. They experienced a dramatic turn away from the struggle over how to display and embody the correct class subjectivity toward diffuse lessons on how to become cosmopolitan "desiring subjects." As I came to know a diverse range of urban residents and rural migrants in Hangzhou and Beijing, I heard and felt a palpable sense of excitement about this project. Learning how to express various longings, needs, and aspirations seemed to hold out the promise of leaving behind the old dilemmas of socialism. Especially in the beginning.

Everyone I spoke with was quite conscious that they were caught up in a momentous historical moment. Simple gestures took on added weight, as the refashioning process threaded across public cultural arenas, television programs, newspaper columns, advice manuals, legal cases, window shopping, intimate relationships, and daily conversation. In this process, people altered simultaneously what it meant to be Chinese and to be a citizen of the world.

These conversations showed me that much of the work to embody a desiring subject took place through engagements with public culture. Soap operas, museums, window displays, fast-food restaurants, newspapers, legal cases, gay bars and salons, and international events created overlapping discourses that drew from myriad sources and sometimes spoke to distinctive constituencies but together served as social forces to create desires. These public cultural arenas had a generative quality.

People in China imagined, discussed, and practiced appropriate and inappropriate, licit and illicit desires as they tried out these public enactments in their daily lives. A fusion of public cultural stories and one's personal life emerged as people cited for me a particular soap opera that revealed their life's struggle or a magazine article condemning homosexuality that nonetheless taught one how to be gay. Chinese citizens have always impressed me as better informed about the world and much more savvy about how to interpret politics and government than Americans. This ability, honed under socialism, continued after the demise of socialism. In discussions with me about these public representations, people from all walks of life connected them not only to the vast and striking rearrangement of cultural power within China but to the global encounters that these changes registered.

My goal in these essays, then, is not to create origin stories of desire, nor to treat it as the universal symbolic that makes people human.[41] In my telling of their tellings, the desiring subject is not a transhistorical piece of culture, nor a cross-cultural institution with local differences but universal existence. Rather, I ask why people in China have recently begun to insist on such stories and I trace the historical and cultural processes that have produced this insistence. Perhaps I need to be blunt: I do not mean that people in China never felt any longings or passions prior to the end of socialism. To the contrary, the passions that animated socialist political battles were deeply felt and have seared individual memories. But those desires were expressed through struggles to embody an appropriate class subjectivity, which became the defining mark not just of one's humanity but of one's role in historical progress.[42] In post-Mao China, to become a "desiring subject" means a rejection of those passions and the political interpretation of moving history forward that subtended them. Other material, sexual, and affective longings have replaced those sentiments, not necessarily as something Chinese people have felt for the first time but as that which is seen at the heart of creating a new kind of world and hence a different kind of human being.[43]

Desire in China, in other words, is about public narratives and the novel grounds they constructed for knowing and speaking about a postsocialist reality. The longings, needs, emotions, and attachments these verbal and visual texts performed were simultaneously forces of production (Tadiar 2004, Yanagisako 2002) and sites for instituting as well as subverting normative ideals (Warner 1999). Yanagisako (2002), in her study of Italian family firms, argues that capitalists must have not only knowledge and skills but sentiments and desires that incite, enable, constrain, and shape their productive activities. To discern sentiments as a productive force culturally shaping capitalist practices requires, Yanagisako argues, that we abandon the long-held dichotomy between instrumental and affective action that in turn is rooted in Western European cosmology. Like Yanagisako, I am concerned with the sentiments and desires that enable and incite social action in China. I, too, try to move beyond the affective/instrumental dichotomy that echoes in discussions of neoliberal rational techniques of the self. I would add to her analysis, however, the insights from queer theory that desires normalize and, in so doing, constitute those who are also excluded and marked as non-normative. Recent work in queer theory highlights the identities and desires, the normalizations and exclusions that occur in the articulations of differences (Boellstorff 2005, Eng 2001, Ferguson 2003, Gopinath 2005, Manalansan 2003, Somerville 2000).[44]

Queer theorists have also pointed out that normalizations take a lot of work to shore up, and in that work, gaps, fissures, and ambivalences lead desires into unexpected terrains. In China, this instability manifested in constituting the social field of desire as *experimental*. To be effective, economic reform policies needed to produce and foster a wide range of desires. The policies were themselves halting, partially planned but equally ad hoc. The terrain of desire they fostered reflected this experimentation. Public discourses of desire were open-ended even as they reached for moral certitude. They treated various longings and aspirations as partially unpredictable, owing not to their ontological nature but to their ability to pave a path toward freedom beyond what was retrospectively portrayed as the constraints of the past. Discerning the appropriate way to become a desiring subject took place in a multi-dimensional and shifting field of interpretive practices. Some turned to revamped Confucian values, others to Buddhism, and still others to the pull to be middle class and cosmopolitan or to the "nature" of capitalism. Many retained a diffuse sense of social fairness they had learned from socialism, even as they rejected the historically lived version of socialism they had experienced. Others crafted a revisionist history that allowed them to feel they were moving themselves and China forward in a new way. The principles invoked to foster and regulate a wide array of desires and to decide about excess or acceptability were matters of intense discussion. They had not settled into rigid codification.

Lesbians and gay men provide a particularly compelling and ambivalent challenge to these postsocialist constructions of human nature. As exemplified in the story with which I opened this introduction, lesbians and gay men could view themselves as at the forefront of a universal humanity in the expression of their desires. This interpretation is reinforced by the fact that several public sites of lesbian and gay life in large urban areas such as Beijing are among the most visibly transnational, attracting lesbians and gay men from other parts of the world who live and work in Beijing. China has no law against homosexuality. State officials, employers, and some public opinion condemned homosexuality as against "Chinese morality." But others (who did not identify as "gay"), especially those who came of age after the end of Maoist socialism, proclaimed to me that, although they did not understand homosexuality and some even found it disgusting, they thought everyone should be free to express their desires. They defended the "right" of homosexuality to exist along with the right of all desires to flourish.

Public narrations of desire are obviously suffused with power. The power to create imaginations and make them stick. The power to produce selves who take it upon themselves to embody these knowledges, visions, and sensibilities. And the power to differentiate among those deemed appropriate subjects of these imaginations and those cast as inappropriate.[45] The Chinese state and Chinese citizens' actions that construct a postsocialist world are suffused with the imbrication of desire and power. But the instabilities inherent in the experimental nature of China's neoliberal reforms meant that these "desiring-actions," to borrow a term from Neferti Tadiar (2004), were not determined in advance. The vociferous debates about which class subjects deserve their dreams that erupted through the soap opera *Yearnings* (chapter 1) heralded later public and informal discussions about the emergent bourgeoisie, the life of rural migrants, the growing gap between the rich and the poor, and the proliferation of multinational sweatshops. The controversies over a museum to represent Chinese women (chapter 2) reflected the contentious importance of gender for neoliberal proprieties. The conversations among gay men and lesbians in China about how to be properly gay signified a transnational dialogue that translated the terms of cosmopolitanism and quality (*suzhi*) into one another even as it divided gay men along urban/rural and class lines (chapter 3). The aspirations of young unmarried and divorced women echoed these cosmopolitan yearnings as they strove to move beyond the strictures and sacrifices they reinvented for a socialist past by way of cosmopolitan consumption (chapter 4). The legal realm adjudicated noncodified norms (since Chinese law does not operate according to precedent) for the proper expression of self-interest (chapter 5), overlapping with the negotiations for China's entry into the WTO (chapter 6).

The various dreams, longings, and aspirations that Chinese citizens embodied were constitutive of their belonging in a postsocialist, neoliberal-dominated world. As anthropological writings have moved away from the notion of bounded cultures, anthropologists have presumed that culture is always emergent through power-laden interactions and encounters in different locations. Recently, anthropologists have developed conceptual tools to examine encounters that do not always entail either a teleology of transition or conventional delineations of social groups to theorize the terms and modes of cultural engagement (Faier forthcoming, Satsuka 2004, Tsing 2005, Zhan forthcoming). These writings do not assume a smooth process of translation. Instead, they examine the surprising articulations of differences and similarities, the unexpected maneuvers produced through power, and the social fields of interaction arising out of gaps and misapprehensions. This ethnographic theory does not describe practices adapting to a globalized world. Rather than assume an external structure called "globalization" or "neoliberalism" or "global capitalism" that has an a priori coherence within which cultural encounters occur, these anthropologists argue that contingent encounters constitute and situate that which in momentary figurations we might call "globalization." These circulations and displacements entail dynamic workings of power and agency that cannot be described in terms of a seamless and transcendental globe. They emerge not where common ground has already been ascertained but as much through what Anna Tsing calls "friction" (i.e., the sticky, makeshift grip of worldly encounters) (2005) as through what Lydia Liu calls "translingual practice" (1995). These encounters negotiate differentially empowered agencies as they craft new relations of value and force.

The methodological core of these essays is analysis of public culture and its sinuous and sensuous insertion in people's everyday lives and dreams. I do not assume those effects but ask after the relevance of this or that piece of public culture and the historical moment of its relevance. Nor do I presume that everyone is caught up in those moments or those specific cultural events in the same manner or with the same degree of intensity. I specify which people attributed importance to which cultural productions and why. I treat these public allegories neither as closed texts nor as structurally deterministic of life trajectories. Instead, I trace the cultural processes through which people told me of their significance.

I did not begin this project with the express intention of writing about public culture. I returned to China after writing my first book about modernity, gender, and labor to find out simply which changes excited people, what motivated people's sense of hope or anger. When I conducted fieldwork in the 1980s, television and other forms of leisure, not to mention market-driven consumerism, were just beginning to surface in social life. They did not, however, predominate in conversations about personal lives. In contrast, when I returned to China repeatedly from 1991 to 2004, people I spoke with alluded to or debated everything from a soap opera to the appearance of a shopping mall to court cases. For example, when I returned to the Hangzhou factory in which I had conducted research to visit with workers I had come to know nearly a decade earlier, they were vociferously discussing the soap opera *Yearnings*. In Beijing, gay men and lesbians I spent time with kept track of the latest government directive or court case dealing with the legalities of homoerotic activities, publications, and public spaces. Feminists debated public policy in order to deal with how economic reform had both opened up possibilities for women and also shut them down. Different kinds of consumption or public stories about China's relationships with other countries also drew attention across these social groups and positions. It thus became increasingly evident to me that to understand the changes in people's personal lives, I had to place these public forms and fora alongside personal stories. Moreover, people consistently used these public narratives and events as allegories through which to reinterpret their lives. I felt compelled to follow their lead. Doing so eventually enabled my understanding of the central importance of China's national public culture as the main medium for creating neoliberal subjectivities.

The chapters are arranged in chronological order to highlight the distinctive moments of creating "desiring China." Chapter 1, "*Yearnings:* Televisual Love and Melodramatic Politics," begins in the early 1990s, after the June 4th protests but just before the radical marketization that citizens would soon experience. *Yearnings* was the first post-Mao soap opera to air in China. It generated a nationwide controversy because it allegorized post-Tiananmen ambiguities of national identity in relation to the diverse class and gender positionings of the characters as well as the viewers. This melodrama of national and cultural identity occurred within the contradictions created by the state's early attempts to develop a market economy. *Yearnings* embodied the thwarted desires set loose by those transformations, as well as the resulting cultural dilemmas about what would count as "moral." I happened to be in China during its airing and thus was drawn into various people's vociferous commentary about which characters were the true heroes and villains, and thus which characters represented the future of China. I use the popular attention given to this soap opera to explore the first broad-based public debate about post-Mao transformations in the wake of the June 4th movement.

At the time *Yearnings* stirred debate, feminist scholars of China were developing political positions not found in the soap opera. They argued that the overarching role of class difference in providing the foundation of subjectivity and power during the Maoist era obscured ongoing gendered relations of dominance and inequality. They also criticized economic reform policies for discriminating against women. Chapter 2, "Museum as Women's Space: Displays of Gender," addresses feminist scholarship in China by focusing on a women's museum established by the controversial feminist Li Xiaojiang. Li Xiaojiang established the museum around the time of Premier Deng Xiaoping's 1992 Southern Tour, in which he encouraged local governments to pursue radical marketization. The museum obliquely as well as explicitly addresses the postsocialist allegory about the need to free human nature.

Li Xiaojiang developed a project in her writings and in the museum to encourage women to "have" their gendered natures. In thus contributing to the constitution of "desiring China," Li Xiaojiang also had to struggle with multiple gendered politics: state feminism, non-state gender politics dominated by the equation of a masculine self with the humanist self, and a transnational network of cultural communication that tends to marginalize Chinese feminist critiques. The museum theorized gender by putting it on display. It created gender identities by encouraging a visual performance of them. The museum, informed by Li Xiaojiang's feminist theory, depended on but also destabilized critical cultural borders of difference that proliferate in China: the party-state versus the oppositional humanist subject; the difference between women and men; and the constitution of China in terms of the West. Rather than create a unified vision of China, Li Xiaojiang has traced its contentious boundaries, wondering aloud whether women will ever be full subjects of the nation.

Chapter 3, "Qualities of Desire: Imagining Gay Identities," turns to the construction of sexual identities. The events described in this essay took place in the latter half of the 1990s, when increasing numbers of foreigners began to live and work in China as the Chinese state encouraged foreign investment. The essay engages with scholarly and popular assertions that a "global gay" identity now exists. The emergence of gay identities and practices in China is tied, in certain respects, to transnational networks of lesbians and gay men. Gay identities are also one of several kinds of desiring identities that contributed to the production of "desiring China." This essay argues, however, that it would be a mistake to conclude that a singular "global gay identity" has come into existence in China. Transcultural processes of sex, desire, and sexual identities shape the contours of cultural citizenship in China for gay men and lesbians. Conversely, desires for cultural belonging within "Chineseness" shape the way gay men and lesbians in China construe the meaning of these transcultural practices. Through interviews and participant-observation I analyze debates among gay men and lesbians about Chinese kinship, linguistic appropriations of affinity, and the question of "quality" (*suzhi*), a broad-ranging signifier in China that encompasses debates about class respectability. Among gay men, it is often used to castigate rural gay men, some of whom make their living through sex work. *Suzhi* creates divisions among gay men in China, even as the circles of gay life in China include men and women from all over the world.

Chapter 4, "From Sacrifice to Desire: Cosmopolitanism with Chinese Characteristics," reflects conversations and events from the end of the

1990s, when increasing numbers of Chinese citizens had either been abroad or desired to go abroad and when the powerful potential of the Chinese economy had generated both interest and anxiety among Western countries. It examines why young women embody the tensions that characterize the cultural constitution of cosmopolitanism and neoliberalism in China. This tension is expressed as one between the transcendence of locality through consumption and the domestication of neoliberalism through renegotiating China's place in the world. Women literally embody Chineseness, both reproductively and as objects of desire. But as consumers and subjects of desire, Chinese women also represent the potential to transcend Chineseness. Through analysis of interviews with young adult women, I argue that there is a dual gendered strategy in worlding China: the first is to erase the woman in order to globalize the nation. The second strategy is to recoup the woman as a defensive maneuver, thus recouping civilization. This dual strategy in turn rests on structured rememberings and forgettings about China's past.

Chapter 5, "Legislating Desire: Homosexuality, Intellectual Property Rights, and Consumer Fraud," overlaps in time with the previous essay. It examines the constitution of desire in post-Mao China through various legal cases. The legal arena became increasingly relevant as China positioned itself to enter the WTO. This essay examines several recent court cases in China that have established legal guidelines for proper sexual behavior, consumer rights, and claims to intellectual property. Rather than remain within a discussion about sexuality, the chapter demonstrates that neoliberalism in China works through a broad construction of desire, and that despite the fact that these arenas appear to be quite disparate, they are in fact intimately tied to the importance of producing citizens who have broad-ranging and infinitely expandable desires. The legal cases I address in this chapter reflect how the law attempts to adjudicate between interests, passions, and desire.

Chapter 6, "Desiring China: China's Entry into the WTO," investigates the negotiations over China's entry into the World Trade Organization during the years 1999–2001. These negotiations portray another facet of producing China as a desiring nation-state. The negotiations set the terms for licit and illicit market-based desires that China as a nation-state is allowed to pursue. They also reveal the heterogeneity of "neoliberal capitalism." More broadly, the essay addresses the following questions: How can we understand the tensions produced from the interplay of global capitalism's ubiquity with its proliferation of innumerable special cases? How can we understand the claims to universality in the wto's neoliberal discourses in relation to the plethora of detail the wto adjudicates in its welter of negotiations over specific exemptions, quotas, and tariffs? My argument is that these tensions demonstrate that capitalism is an ongoing process of fraught cultural encounters that are inherently unstable. In examining neoliberal capitalism as contingent and unstable cultural practice, I follow the trail of the wto documents to trace the global terrors as well as enticements that induced China to pursue membership; the consumer fundamentalism that defines wto-style capitalism; the endless construction of China's "difference" that serves to enable a presumption of universality in the wto's official discourse; and, finally, the proliferation of disputes targeting China, in which conflicts are expressed that reveal the undecidability of what will count as beneficial and proper or adverse, unacceptable, and even immoral capitalist practices.

I am sure it is clear by now that the title of the book, *Desiring China*, is meant as a pun to capture the multiple desires that traverse the post-Mao landscape, including the construction of China as a desiring nation-state as well as the desire of others for China. The chapters range widely. They reflect the unexpected twists and turns in my anthropological pursuit of desire in post-Mao China. The tone of these essays varies as well, as I alternately felt pessimism, irony, and respect for the creativity of young people in China as they embrace the new world order.

Those long, drawn out years
Those years, so confused;
What was true, what was illusion,
It's so hard to say.
Tragedy, joy, separation, reunion
I've been through them all.
To keep on, to persist
What's it all for?
Down the long expanse of humanity
Searching high and low,
Yearning for a genuine life.
Who can tell me,
Am I right or am I wrong?
I've asked everyone at every turn.
Forgetting all the old wrongs,
What's left are true feelings spoken anew
In thousands of homes all over the world.
The stories are few,
Like a single song of a common life.
The past, the future, I'm rethinking it all.

— Theme song, *Yearnings*

1.

Yearnings

Televisual Love and Melodramatic Politics

earnings is a heartwrenching Chinese television drama about the intertwined lives, loves, and tragedies of two ordinary families, the intellectual Wangs and the worker Lius, as the vicissitudes of their joys and sorrows unfold over the two decades from the Cultural Revolution (1966–76) through the late 1980s. A melodramatic tale of romantic loves found and lost, of a baby abandoned and raised with no one (except viewers) knowing her "true" identity, of families rent apart and tenuously held together, it is a tale that those who engage with popular culture might find moving, though other, unsympathetic critics might find it sentimental.

But *Yearnings* quickly gripped at least vast urban audiences when it aired in China in January 1991, just a year and a half after the June 4th movement (Tiananmen demonstrations). The show experienced an explosion of popularity, eclipsing other television programs. So great was *Yearnings*'s popularity, it moved from airing three times a week to airing every night for three hours, playing itself out in its entirety (fifty episodes) in one month. After dinner at a university faculty member's home, I invariably joined them in watching the show. During the day, while engaged in research in the Hangzhou silk factory where I had previously worked in the mid-1980s, I listened as workers caught one another up on episodes they had to miss because of their revolving shift system.[1] By the time I left China at the end of the month, most people I knew were heatedly debating the qualities of the heroes and villains, as they simultaneously enjoyed and critically analyzed the implications of plot and character.

How is it that a story of thwarted desires and tragic sacrifices as told through the "personal" dilemmas of family relations could stir such engaged responses in China? *Yearnings*'s use of highly conventional techniques of televisual melodrama and the love content could allow one to argue that *Yearnings* was one of the first popular programs devoid of political content in China (especially for those who do not address the politics of gender and sexuality).[2] The *New York Times*, for example, heralded *Yearnings* as the dawn of the soap opera epoch in China (WuDunn 1991). The article congratulated China for offering, at last, real entertainment that enabled escape from the dreariness of socialist politics. Indeed, how one approaches this melodrama can be encapsulated in one's translation of the title (*Kewang* in Chinese). Thus, the *New York Times* talked about the success of *Aspirations*, implying that the soap opera was a sign of aspiring hopes to inculcate more of "Western" culture. One of the Chinese state's magazines for foreign consumption, *Women of China* (Bian 1991), praised *Expectation* for its realist portrayal of everyday life and, by implication, the expectations for a better life under the post-Mao state. I have chosen to translate the title as *Yearnings* to highlight the ambiguities in what is yearned for and to capture the blend of humanist and socialist narrative tropes in the melodrama.

In what follows, I argue precisely the opposite of the idea that *Yearn-ings* was devoid of political content. The unexpected storm of contro-versy that accompanied *Yearnings*'s popularity should lead us to take its politics seriously. We must ask ourselves what it meant for this type of melodrama to have garnered so much attention in China at that moment in time. How was *Yearnings*'s popularity constituted? Why did tele-vision viewers become so seduced by this particular narrative? What can the melodrama and the controversy surrounding it tell us about the constitution of desire in the initial years of the post-Mao era? In address-ing these questions, I hope to reconfigure the relationship between the "political," the "popular," and the "personal," urging a recognition that they became historically constituted in complex ways in the initial years of economic reform experimentation in China.

The key to understanding *Yearnings*'s reception, I want to suggest, lies in the ways it was suffused with reimagined possibilities of national identity, or what Benedict Anderson famously called "nation-ness" (1983,13). These reimagined national identities were sparked by the gradual dismantling of socialism, what the central government called "socialism with Chinese characteristics." The identity of the nation, and which subjects speak for the nation, became acute dilemmas at a mo-ment when China was facing perhaps its greatest political and moral crisis since the end of the Cultural Revolution. For this melodrama of national and cultural identity occurred after the contradictions created by the state's institution of a market economy while upholding its pre-vious socialist ideology had erupted into the massive June 4th student and citizen uprisings that nearly toppled the government. *Yearnings* taught viewers how to embody the desires fostered and thwarted by those transformations. The shock of state violence at Tiananmen only heightened this sense of political and social soul-searching about which kinds of desires would count as "moral." *Yearnings*'s historically specific use of the melodramatic form bound this crisis of nation-ness to dif-ferential gender and class positionings of the characters and the viewers, thus linking it to larger debates in China about which categories of persons might stand as heroes of the nation and therefore be encouraged to express their desires formed in light of the tentative neoliberal policies then emerging.

In my analysis, I move back and forth between the narrative of *Yearn-ings* and spectators' engagement with it to raise questions about how desire as linked to national identity in a postsocialist world was created through categories of gender and class as they were constituted in this popular narrative. This, in turn, leads me to rethink the operations of public culture as a site for the constitution of political debates about issues seemingly submerged within neoliberal policies, one that offers complicated possibilities for oppositional dreams. This essay has been inspired by, and joins, anthropological reconceptualizations of cultural production in a transnational world saturated by mass media. Arjun Appadurai (1996), through his concept of "global ethnoscapes," urged anthropology to turn its attention to the intimacy of local/global interactions in the formation of cultural imaginations. Purnima Mankekar (1999) has written an incisive ethnographic analysis of the intersections of gender, class, and nation in Indian television. I owe her much of my initial inspiration. Faye Ginsburg (1991, 2002) has reminded us that indigenous people are not always the object of the media gaze but can also take up the tools of media for their own cultural productions. Lila Abu-Lughod (1993a, 2005) taught us how to interpret multiple engagements with popular media from the margins of the nation-state. My analysis of this Chinese soap opera is in dialogue with these pathbreaking works, as it brings together global consumption of media with particular national and local dilemmas.

EMERGENT CONTRADICTIONS

The 1989 June 4th movement hovered loudly in the unspoken background of *Yearnings*. This movement may have appeared from outside China to be a sudden eruption but in fact citizens' discontents with economic reform had simmered below the surface for several years. Three distinct images come to mind when I recall those early years of reform.

Image One: The summer of 1983. It was my first time in mainland China (official research exchanges between the United States and the People's Republic of China [PRC] had begun only a few years before). I was in Beijing, assessing whether it was feasible to do field research and also taking an advanced Chinese language class. One of my teachers was a gentle, middle-aged man with the bearing of an intellectual who evidently had gone through a great deal in the Cultural Revolution. I never asked and he never offered his political history. But he obviously wanted me to understand his recent past. He decided to take me on a field trip of sorts to the bookstore to find contemporary novels. Once we entered, he asked the clerk for a particular title I had never heard of and the clerk, instead of leading us to a bookshelf, promptly pulled out a book hidden underneath the front counter. The book turned out to be *Ren Ah Ren!* *(Ah, Humanity!)*. The teacher calmly explained that the book was not exactly banned but not exactly promoted, either. The book was making a big splash among intellectuals because of its humanism that, the author argued, should replace socialist class politics.

Image Two: The autumn of 1984. I am ensconced in Hangzhou, learning my way around my physical, social, and political environs. One of the graduate students from Hangzhou University's economics department kindly took me for a walk downtown. We came upon the newly opened "free market" *(ziyou shichang)*. At that time we were not talking in economic abstractions but in the literal physicality of the place. Economic reform in the cities had just begun. The market was small, the length of one city block. The fact that it was not run by the government made it "free." The market was filled with booths selling clothing for young people. Young men hawked their wares they had brought from Guangdong in the south, which in turn offered goods from Hong Kong. I was told these young men were the ones known euphemistically as "waiting for work" youth. The government still held to its socialist commitment of full employment and its belief that a major distinction between socialism and capitalism is that the former does not create a reserve army of labor to exploit. These unemployed youth were encouraged to start their own small businesses. Soon they became the envy of every factory worker, who yearned to leave what had so recently appeared to be the safety of a job in a state-run enterprise. Not yet, but a few years hence, these budding entrepreneurs would be pushed aside by government cadres who became keen on their own abilities to turn power into money. All these petty entrepreneurs in the street stalls were male. I was told that the kind of traveling they did to bring back fashionable clothing was not respectable for young women. People I knew talked about these young men in ambivalent tones. They were seen as sleazy but brave; uneducated but clever; well meaning but not quite honest. There appeared to hover over them an air of the "not quite upright." These representations stood in for the conflicted feelings people had about this type of market activity. Most people I came to know were relieved to have "free markets" where they could buy things not provided by the government-run centers — including fresh fruit and vegetables brought by peasants living nearby. But was this a respectable way to make a living? To make money off merely raising the price of goods one had moved from one place to the other?

Image Three: Spring 1986. I needed to get out of Hangzhou and out of the intensity of fieldwork as everyday life. I decide to take a road trip of sorts, actually a train trip. I had heard that the island of Hainan off the south coast of China was beautiful and so headed there. After several days on the train heading southwest I managed to get on a boat to cross over to Hainan. As soon as I debarked, I spied a large field filled with shiny, new imported cars. I was impressed with the obviousness of the wealth it signaled, though I wondered who would be driving these cars. The only people I knew with access to cars in the mid-1980s were government cadres who were driven around in their work units' cars. Of course, I did wonder at the time how so many cars came to be in one place and who was selling them. Only some months later when the scandal broke in the newspapers did I learn to call this image graft and corruption (perpetrated by government cadres).

These three distinct but overlapping images succinctly capture the early moments of economic reform. The initial experiments with economic reform in the 1980s felt momentous. Everyone I knew talked about them as historically consequential. The changes were not just about the economy but about becoming different kinds of persons. A popular allegory of the time, captured in the novel *Ah, Humanity*, was that Maoism had deferred China's ability to reach modernity by impeding Chinese people's expression of their human natures. Economic reform promised to unshackle these newly invented innate selves by emancipating the populace from Maoist socialism. But this period did not witness a wholesale rejection of socialism. Official and popular repudiation of the Cultural Revolution did not negate the widespread hope that economic reform would be a means toward socialist-inspired ideals of fairness and egalitarianism. Only after Tiananmen did a majority of the population stop believing in a socialist, reform-minded state.

Prior to that moment, most people I spoke with felt excitement and hope. Anything had to be better than the excesses of the Cultural Revolution. Most willingly embraced the reform experiments. The urban reforms decentralized some power and resources to local governments and state-run enterprises and allowed tiny "free markets" to exist in basic consumer goods. At first, many workers experienced these changes in a positive light, as it gave them some flexibility to change jobs or, for men, to add sideline jobs in the markets. They no longer had to take so seriously the political study sessions in the factories, which faded out as a hindrance to productivity. My intellectual friends were more ambivalent. They expressed interest in how socialist humanism might unshackle class identities but also complained that, although Deng Xiaoping had promised to rectify the position of intellectuals, in fact their salaries and benefits lagged behind those of even peasants selling their produce in the markets.

As the 1980s drew to a close, I heard increasing frustration with the unexpected—at least for ordinary citizens—results of the initial reforms. "Corruption" offered a rubric for expressing this discontent. Loud public grievances about cadres' misuse of power for personal gain drew ritualistic spectacles put on by the government to clean up corruption in the party (echoing Cultural Revolution political campaigns). The ire directed at state officials condensed a sense of the injustices of increased polarization in incomes, inequalities in distribution, price instabilities, and the continued rigidities in job assignments. The protests that exploded in the spring of 1989 were a response to the illegitimacy of the redistribution process and the social transition to a market economy. Students demanded an end to authoritarian rule while other citizens opposed the "princeling party" of cadres who had formed a new monied class and protested the proliferating inequalities spawned by the market economy's expansion.

Yearnings appeared in the interstices between the explosive uprisings of June 4th and the subsequent government fast-tracking of neoliberal policies. The soap opera offered an early elaboration of desire: it taught the art of longing. Longing might overcome both the repressions and passions of the Cultural Revolution (in addition to the passions of June 4th). But *Yearnings* also taught viewers that the art of longing should articulate a national identity. The explosion of controversy over *Yearnings* occurred because of the soap opera's ambivalences over which characters were deemed to deserve their longings. This ambivalence, in turn, depended on the unsettled and unfinished nature of the recent past.

Benedict Anderson's pathbreaking work on nationalism (1983) premised itself on the idea that nationalism is less a political ideology than a cultural system that, like religion, gives rise to an imagined community. Anderson argued that the model of and for what he called "nation-ness" was historically enabled by the development of print capitalism. Print capitalism, including both books and newspapers, led to an imagined sense of simultaneity not, as with Christianity, marked by prefiguring and fulfillment but by transversal temporal coincidences measured by clock, calendar, and map. Mass media production gradually created national vernaculars and a vision of belonging to a community with thousands of others one might never see face to face. Television has operated in similar respects. It, too, creates simultaneity across homogeneous, empty time and a proper vernacular for those it visually includes in the national community.

To take up the challenge Anderson posed means reconfiguring his work in three respects. First, Anderson never pursued the moment beyond which nations are initially imagined. His theory explained the origin of imagined communities, but not their plots, climaxes, or denouements. Thus, we need to move beyond treating the nation as an entity that, once imagined, exists in a unitary symbolic or sociological solidity. Rather than view nationalism as a cultural *system*, we can now pay closer attention to the different and even contradictory ways nations have been imagined.[3]

Second, Anderson drew a strong distinction between political ideologies and cultural systems. His initial effort to pull "nation-ness" out from the realm of Marxist approaches to ideology was enormously creative. However, for China, the political ideology of the Chinese Communist Party cannot be separated from the nationalism that infused it from the very beginning. The 1949 socialist revolution was simultaneously about overturning the old class order and creating a nation that could shake off the yoke of semi-colonialism. Finally, one needs to extend the basis of nationalism from print media to other media such as television. Television's simultaneity, ubiquity, and openness to state control have enabled it to supplement print media as the means through which "the national order of things" (Malkki 1992, 37; 1995) is continuously imagined.

In China, where official methods of ideological dissemination such as political study sessions and "thought work" (*sixiang gongzuo*) lay bankrupt after the Cultural Revolution, consumption of television and other forms of popular culture increasingly became the process through which people were interpellated (Althusser 1971) as subjects of the nation.[4] To understand this process — how people were moved to engage with *Yearnings* — requires going beyond the initial debates in studies of popular culture[5] that oscillated between two alternative poles: a purely textual approach that emphasized containment of viewers' desires versus a celebration of spectators', or "readers'," autonomy from and resistance to "the text." (For the full range of positions in these debates, see de Certeau 1984, Dent 1992, Fiske 1987, Foster 1983, Grossberg, Nelson, and Treichler 1992, Hall 1977, 1981, hooks 1992, Jenkins 1992, Modleski 1991, Radway 1984, Ross 1989, Rowe and Schelling 1991.) There were, of course, cross-overs between these two dichotomous positions. I have chosen to emphasize the two ends of the spectrum to highlight the analytic problems underlying the entire debate.[6]

A textual interpretation of popular culture has the advantage of emphasizing the power of signification to shape the contours of fantasy, identity, and social practice, what Teresa de Lauretis called a "mapping of social vision into subjectivity" (1984, 8). These textual studies rejected the Frankfurt school legacy (Adorno and Horkheimer 1987) that importantly recognized the ideological components of capitalist mass culture but viewed audiences as uncritical, passive consumers of it. They tended to have a more sympathetic view of how popular culture might speak to real social needs and anxieties, as well as pleasures. At the same time, they reminded us that the production of meaning is a process that never stands outside of power, so that spectators' needs are often contained within dominant political and cultural agendas.

As criticisms of this approach suggested, however, a purely textual analysis ultimately closed off the possibilities for shifting the configurations of cultural power. These studies continued to assume a single spectator position while ignoring the manner in which actual audiences interpret what they watch. The assumption remained that text-as-discourse has an existence apart from the repeated and yet always differing enactments of it.

Popular culture studies that challenged the exclusive emphasis on the text celebrated knowledgeable spectators who subvert, poach on, and rework popular texts to make their "own" meanings and put them to their "own" uses. Predominantly deriving from the disciplines of communication, media, and literature, these analyses adopted the ethnographic tools of anthropology to situate actual viewing audiences, fan communities, and romance-novel reading clubs. Their ethnographic endeavors reminded us that we still need to concern ourselves with the relation between historical subjects in the world and the positions set out for these subjects in popular discourse.

Yet emphasis on consumption of texts and reader-response methodologies betrayed assumptions of a sovereign, meaning-giving subject. The exercise of cultural power through television and other texts appeared to be a process external to spectators, whose resistance in the form of choosing the meanings they prefer possessed a referential solidity gained elsewhere, in "society," but was unattached to ongoing hegemonic processes that might shape the taken-for-grantedness of either reality or fantasy. This problem was compounded by their approach to ethnography. They focused too narrowly on "subcultures" of popular consumers based on a conception of the ethnographic world as bounded wholly by the moments of engagement with particular artifacts of popular culture.

Much anthropology of media has moved beyond the dichotomous terms of this debate (Ginsburg et al. 2002). The general binary opposition of resistance versus incorporation or opposition versus homogenization has run its course through cultural studies and anthropology (see Abu-Lughod 1990, Mitchell 1990). Popular culture in China, as elsewhere, functions as a contradictory cultural site, where domination, opposition, and cultural creation coexist.[7] By defining popular culture as a site, one can acknowledge the power of the aesthetic while also tracing a television soap opera as a place where audiences, producers, and critics shape a variety of potentially conflicting ideas. To capture this intertwined existence, one needs to proceed through ethnographic endeavor. One of the virtues of the ethnographic approach is that it looks for more active processes of making culture. Ethnography assumes that people never stand outside culture but never stand within it in taken-for-granted ways. This relationship of culture to power is often mediated through such public culture phenomena as television.

My ethnographic approach to the question of how people engaged with *Yearnings* and how it taught them that desire entails longing is to regard television viewing as part of a wide range of daily practices and discourses. The soap opera became embedded in people's quotidian lives because the producers and consumers of the program themselves were situated in and produced the cultural and discursive practices, historical context, and political and economic circumstances that gave *Yearnings* its force. The moments of immersion in a particular cultural artifact are necessarily enmeshed within these other social fields of meaning and power. In the case of China, this "conjunctural ethnography," to borrow a phrase from Purnima Mankekar (1999, 49), entails attention to the contradictions of economic reform's early years, the sense of uncertainty about China's future in the immediate aftermath of June 4th, the changing role of Chinese state power, and the ongoing and open public debates about the meanings of class and gender in a post-Mao nation. An ethnographic endeavor, then, highlights the contingent way in which all social categories emerge, become naturalized, and intersect in people's conception of themselves and their world and, further, an emphasis on how these categories are produced through everyday practice.

My analysis of *Yearnings*'s significance in people's daily lives began not by way of any intention on my part to research popular culture in China. I became interested in the soap opera because it was impossible for me to escape its tenor in the lives of everyone with whom I interacted. The techniques of media research I employed grew out of these daily interactions. *Yearnings* forced its attention on me. As it did so, I began to listen more closely to the way people took up the narrative twists and turns in the plot. I listened for how they interpreted each segment of the program, how these views shifted as the program proceeded, and how the soap opera's language and narrative became a social force in people's interpretations of its significance for their lives. Because public culture in China at that time was still considered to be closely linked to state power, everyone I knew read a great deal into the program. Thus, I pursue the generative quality of *Yearnings* by treating it not as a closed text with pre-established effects on viewers but as a shifting, open-ended, intertextual narrative whose meaning was created in the spaces between the soap opera and viewers' retellings of it. Viewers had strong feelings about which interpretations dominated, as these became transferable truths about their lives. How exactly did *Yearnings*, then, teach viewers the art of longing?

To understand how a nationwide phenomenon could be built from *Yearnings*, it might be best to begin by addressing the mechanics and politics of its production. *Yearnings*, as both a narrative and an event, is inseparable from the apparatus of Chinese television as a site for the objectification of "state desires" in post-Mao China. The consumption of television on a large scale was relatively new to China when *Yearnings* aired. While television production and transmission began in the late 1950s, it was not until the first decade of economic reform that the number of television stations as well as the number of television sets proliferated. By the end of the 1980s, nearly every urban household had its own set, with China's television network estimated to reach 78 percent of the population (Li 1991).

Both the institutionalization and the ideological contours of state power are implicated in the decision-making process determining what will be aired on television and how a television series such as *Yearnings* becomes constituted as "popular." *Yearnings* was far removed from those themes most facilely associated with the state — the celebration of the communist party, the heroics of communist revolutionaries, or the joyous embrace of the latest party directives. One could have changed the channel on any night *Yearnings* aired and found just that — tears shed by revolutionary underground peasants who had finally found their way back to the New Fourth Army on its road to socialist victory. Yet in the first decade of economic reform, the state instituted visions of the modern national body politic that resonated in this drama. These visions imperceptibly framed the heated arguments surrounding *Yearnings*.

As with all state-run work units in China, each television station has a party structure that parallels its administrative structure. Yet a simple description of the institutionalization of the party-state in China is woefully inadequate for comprehending how official power works in the post-Mao era and thus how decisions get made about what will be aired on television. First, it is crucial to acknowledge that the "Chinese state" is not a coherent entity that acts in a unified fashion. Anyone who has lived or worked in China, both Chinese and foreign, recognizes the multifaceted character of state power, the simultaneously centralized and decentered nature of state politics, and, to paraphrase Wendy

Brown about the U.S. state, the way it exists as "an ensemble of discourses . . . and practices, cohabiting in . . . contradictory relation to one another" (1992, 12). The fact of *Yearnings*'s appearance on television had as much to do with the microtechniques of power located in the Beijing Television Art Center where it was conceived as with any politburo policy about mass culture.

Second, state power operates in China, as elsewhere, not just through its institutions but through the way the state creates itself as an imagined entity.[8] As Anagnost (1997) has argued about the Chinese state, the symbolic images and cultural practices by which the state is signified in China portray a unified and unifying political power. The attention given to *Yearnings* was the result, in part, of the party's efforts to further a claim, somewhat after the fact, to the terrain of *Yearnings* as yet another site upon which it speaks in the name of the people's desires for socialist morality.

Yet this state project of portraying itself as the embodiment of the will of the masses became enormously complicated in the post-Mao, post–June 4th era. The rejection of Maoist socialism and the introduction of a market economy meant that the state may have been clear about speaking in the name *of* a social body but was much less sure about what it was speaking *for*. The goals and desires of the state were never more fraught with ambiguity and uncertainty. At one moment, productivity and the pursuit of wealth were lauded by party bureaucrats; in the next moment, "socialist morality" was applauded as the antidote to undue worship of money. The Chinese party-state further complicated its ability to control social life and mass-mediated images by its decrease in funding to many work units, accompanied by the insistence that they make themselves profitable. Accordingly, advertising became ubiquitous on Chinese television.

Television is part of the commodification of Chinese social relations, as the imagined vision of economic reform instituted by the state in 1978 led to a heightened consumer-oriented social life mediated through the burgeoning market. The desire to transform China into a wealthy nation on a par with the West, official rejection of Maoist asceticism, the promotion of a market economy, and the need to overcome the visceral unpopularity of the party all met in the state's encouragement of consumption. *Yearnings* must be viewed in that domain of mass culture in which the party consciously made an effort to revamp its look, with songs about the communist party sung on other television programs by sequin-gowned young women to a disco beat and endowed with a quality verging on eroticism.[9] After June 4th the party, with even more reason, appeared to be scrambling to find the site on which it could claim to represent the common people.

Drawing the contours of this broad context is necessary for illuminating the politics of *Yearnings*'s production and the constitution of its popularity. *Yearnings* was the brainchild of a group of five scriptwriters, including two well-known and respected novelists, Wang Shuo and Zheng Wanlong. They worked under the aegis of the Beijing Television Art Center, in turn under the purview of the Beijing Broadcasting Enterprise Bureau (in turn under the aegis of the central government's Ministry of Radio and Television). According to Jianying Zha (1992), who conducted extensive research on the production process of *Yearnings*, the serial was written under the twin pressures of market-driven appeal and national pride. The Beijing Television Art Center needed a commercial success to recuperate the cost of a new studio.[10] Young writers at the studio watched the success of soap operas, known as "in-door dramas" in China, imported from Latin America and Taiwan. Several of them admitted to Zha that desire to save "face" for China figured in their decision to write what became China's first "in-door" drama. This assertion of national identity involved in *Yearnings*'s production lends further support to an argument that *Yearnings* is precisely about the meaning of nation-ness.

The scriptwriters seemed to have in mind an apolitical audience-pleaser that adapted Taiwan's dramas about the difficulties of family unity to mainland social life. The authors' intentions, as stated in public, nonetheless do not encompass the totality of meanings available in *Yearnings*. Most writers in China have honed their skills at indirect political criticism to such a fine point that audiences and readers often find pleasure in the mere act of ferreting them out. One of the scriptwriters, Wang Shuo, for example, is well known for popular novels that, while satirical, do not contain direct political criticism and therefore have eluded official censure.[11] One must wonder, at least, about the timing of this type of melodrama, produced not long after Tiananmen, when all other films and television programs were paeans to the lives of Mao Zedong and Deng Xiaoping. With popular cultural forms in China, therefore, it is critical to adopt an ethnographic approach, for the question of textual meaning is often one of how readers or spectators attribute intentionality to authors. Rather than analyze an artifact of popular culture through the dichotomy of production and reception (or consumption), it seems to make more sense, especially for a richer understanding of how *Yearnings* became a national phenomenon, to think of "production" as *including* the discussions and disagreements about the program among people as they went about their daily lives, as well as the continued promotion of the drama by the television studio (which included highly publicized visits by the stars to various cities), the media, and high-level state bureaucrats. What *Yearnings* finally signified lies in this arena.

One final point about the social context of television viewing should be noted. For many in China, the activity of television viewing signifies a quest for modernity, that elusive and ever-changing trope whose meaning is itself continuously reproduced in the larger context of an unequally balanced world system (see Rofel 1999). Television speaks of that quintessentially good life, reflected in the multitude of programs from those countries, such as the United States, that stand as icons of modernity. The television set itself is a piece of cultural capital in Bourdieu's sense (1984), through which households mark their claims to prestige. Thus, at least in the first decade of economic reform, television viewing as an activity and the acquisition of a television set, in addition to the advertisements on television, already established a social field of longing. The relocation of television viewing into the home (from official and public spaces where the few sets previously existed) turned that longing toward material and affective self-interest rather than toward the politics of the state.

For most in China, the television is also experienced as at least the partial withdrawal of the state from the realm of domestic life, which reverberated with heightened political struggles during the Cultural Revolution. I suspect that the way urban residents discuss a "hot" program reflects attempts to speak to one another as a nation around the edges of the state. Yet this relationship is complicated, for the state is involved not simply in approving programs but more essentially in creating representations that find their way into programs.[12] This context, especially the construction of the nation in an ambiguous relationship to socialism, already sets the stage for *Yearnings*'s successful debut.

Yearnings begins in 1969, the height of Cultural Revolution fervor. The Wangs, an elite intellectual family, are under attack. The family crumbles, as the father is sent down (*xiafang*) to the countryside to learn manual labor from the peasants; the mother, frail with heart trouble resulting from the attacks on her household, slowly sinks to her death; the daughter, Yaru, a doctor, loses her fiancé to a Red Guard labor camp after she has become pregnant by him; and the son, Husheng, is sent down to a local factory, bringing his college education to an abrupt end. Yaru, with all else lost, longs only to have her baby. She gives birth to a baby girl. But she loses her baby shortly thereafter when her fiancé furtively returns for a brief visit, is pursued by the Red Guards while she is out, and flees with the baby but must abandon her to an unknown woman at the bus station.

Meanwhile Husheng is befriended by a co-worker, a young woman named Liu Huifang, who comes from a humble worker background. Huifang is engaged to an older co-worker, Song Dacheng, who longs for nothing more than to be with Huifang. But Huifang is alienated by Dacheng's use of a traditional matchmaker. Aware of Husheng's desire for his fiancée, Dacheng smashes the marriage furniture he had so happily built. Huifang then marries Husheng, as much out of his yearnings for emotional sustenance as her search for genuine love.

Shortly before the marriage, Huifang's little sister returns home with an abandoned baby. (The viewers see the unknown woman at the bus station ask the young girl to hold the baby and then disappear.) Huifang begins to nurture this unknown baby, though she lives in straitened circumstances and though her husband refuses to acknowledge the baby. After the Cultural Revolution, Yaru and Husheng have their father and their house restored to them. Husheng would like to move his family into the spacious home, but Yaru adamantly refuses to allow him to bring in the child of unknown origins, insisting she is not of the Wang family blood. (The viewers' sense of irony here serves to heighten the drama.) Huifang refuses to abandon the child. She returns to her mother's cramped home with Little Fang, while her husband lives in his home with the son they also have.

A serious accident leaves Little Fang without the use of her legs and, at the tender age of seven, she becomes a disabled child. Huifang then sacrifices her secure job at the factory to attend to her. She eventually decides to divorce Husheng not only because of their irreconcilable differences about Little Fang but also over the return of Husheng's old college girlfriend, with whom he renews a passionate friendship.

Huifang is rescued in the final segments by Yaru's former fiancé, Luo Gang, now restored to his position as assistant professor of literature at Beijing University. Luo Gang longs to renew his relationship with Yaru, but her fury at his losing her baby knows no bounds. In his pain and loneliness, Luo Gang writes the story of his bitter experiences in the Cultural Revolution. His book becomes a bestseller, and his students are full of adulation. One of his students is Huifang's sister. She unburdens her heartache to her professor about her older sister's troubles. The story of the adopted child piques his interest. Luo Gang befriends the family, becoming a devoted uncle to the daughter Little Fang. Disillusioned with Yaru's hardened ways, he takes an interest in the fragile Huifang.

Luo Gang and Huifang together eventually discover the child is the baby he lost. Huifang insists he take the child and form a family with Yaru, refusing Luo Gang's expressions of attachment. Yaru, not yet knowing the child is hers, had a change of heart after the child's accident and travels to America to learn the latest surgical procedures that will restore to Little Fang the use of her legs. Little Fang recovers, only to have Huifang fall victim to a car accident and become permanently disabled. Little Fang learns of her "true" parents and declares she will be their filial daughter, but only after she cares for her adopted mother Huifang for a time.

Yearnings ends here, with everyone longing to fulfill his or her desires, but not able to do so. Clearly, *Yearnings* carries many of the formal signs of what Peter Brooks called the "melodramatic imagination" (1985), especially those to which we are so attuned in the West. *Yearnings* is a grandiose ethical superdrama constantly tensed to momentous turns of events that will reveal the essential Manichaean conflicts of good and evil (Gledhill 1987, 20ff.). It is filled with the conventional melodramatic repertoire, including coincidences of fate, hyperbolic figures, mysterious parentage, romance and tragedy, and the quintessential location in domestic space. Finally, it addresses the semiotic construction of woman, the maternal, and the feminine through stories of "personal" desire, intimate relations, and daily family life.

These formal aesthetic features certainly account, in part, for viewers' continuous involvement in the drama. *Yearnings* created an active spectatorship through the simultaneous creation of hope for the fulfillment of desire along with forebodings of impending tragedy. Yet this melodrama, as with all melodramas, has its specific cultural and historical location. *Yearnings* speaks not just to other dramas of women in the home. To assume that *Yearnings* spells the arrival of melodrama to China is to indulge in narcissistic and orientalist cultural hegemony in defining the genre, for soap opera and melodrama proved vital forms of socialist aesthetic production after the 1949 revolution. However, they revolved around heightened dramas of landlord exploitation (whether the young woman who suffers at the hands of her landlord and flees to the mountains will be rescued in time by the Red Army [*White-Haired Girl*]); and dramas of economic development (whether the forward-looking young man just returned from the city will be able to fight the lethargy and corruption of his elder cadres in the village to institute much needed modern reforms [*New Star*]).[13] The question, then, becomes not simply the emergence of melodrama in China but how it moved into the space of the home. How did these aesthetic productions turn away from stories about workers *qua* workers and into stories about domestic life and personal fates? Above all, how did the symbol of the nation become associated first with the longings of a domesticated woman and then with those of an intellectual rather than a working-class hero? To comprehend the power of *Yearnings*, one must examine the manner in which it weaves cultural form with meanings from a broader social context, for it is in and through this social/textual field that people expressed what Barthes (1975) called that "passion for meaning" that animated their interpretation of *Yearnings*.

NARRATIVES OF NATIONAL IDENTITY

Yearnings trafficked in icons of national identity. Narrative form provides the critical clue to this theme.[14] The form that pervades the drama is one known as "speaking bitterness" (*suku*). Speaking bitterness is a genre that the communist party honed and popularized in the early days of revolutionary òrganizing. It is generally approached in the secondary literature on China as a political and social phenomenon (Chan et al. 1984), and often is assumed to exist only in the 1940s and 1950s. By emphasizing its narrative qualities, however, one can begin to grasp its powerful effectiveness and to draw out the similarities in form between what otherwise seem like disparate styles of political speech.

Speaking bitterness entailed encouraging oppressed groups to tell stories of the bitterness they had eaten under the previous system. In the land reform campaigns both before and after the socialist revolution of 1949, for example, party cadres mobilized poor peasants to "speak pains to recall pains" (Hinton 1966, 157) in the form of public accusations against the gentry. These life stories were then used to move others to action in building the new nation through adoption of a class analysis that led to the redistribution of land (Belden 1949, Chen 1980, Hinton 1966).[15] Thus, narrative was an essential part of revolutionary praxis through which the party shaped socialist subjects and then linked them to the project of building the nation.[16]

I would argue that we find this genre again during the Cultural Revolution. Analogous to the earlier land reform movement, struggle sessions witnessed factions of workers and students screaming their bitter accusations against former capitalists, managers, and intellectuals (Liang and Shapiro 1983, Luo 1990, Rofel 1999).[17] Finally, in the initial years after the Cultural Revolution, intellectuals poured out their bitterness about the sufferings they had endured as they reconstructed themselves as victims of what, in its post-Mao guise, was officially labelled "the ten years of chaos." They wrote a form that came to be known as literature of the wounded, or "scar literature" (see Barme and Lee 1979, Siu and Stern 1983).[18] It created intellectuals as pure, undeserving victims of Maoist politics. The post-Mao state encouraged and used scar stories to interpellate intellectuals into an imagined vision of economic reform designed to lead China into its deserved place as a nondependent, powerful nation in the world of nations.[19] The state thus officially shaped these stories as tales of redemption and progress in which intellectuals found resolution by offering to build the nation out of the ashes of Maoism.[20] *Yearnings* puts intellectuals' written version of speaking bitterness into visual form. Thus, we find the hero writing his scar story after Yaru rejects him.

The importance of speaking bitterness in relation to the controversy over *Yearnings* is that the conception and construction of China as a modern socialist nation occurred through this aesthetic and sociopolitical practice.[21] For, if nations are imagined political communities, then we must distinguish them by the style in which they are imagined. Thus, speaking bitterness developed into a process of political *resolution* in which subjects were called upon to articulate their oppression in order to embrace new subjectivities and claim heroic stature in the eyes of the nation. It acted as a genre that allowed one to identify which social group stood as the national heroes of a particular political moment. For the greater part of the 1980s, the voices of intellectuals predominated as they claimed to speak for the nation as a result of their bitter lives in the previous era. Some did so in an attempt to wrest the nation away from socialism. But the state generally provided the ideological space for those voices as it recuperated them into projects of economic reform. At least until June 4th.

INTELLECTUALS (RE)SPEAK THEIR BITTERNESS

The weaving of these narratives of national identity through the formal elements of melodrama created a powerfully seductive visual discourse that stirred viewers' desires to make claims on the meanings of various characters' actions. The popularity of *Yearnings* was fueled, in part, by questions concerning which characters' tragedies counted as *real* tragedies, whose sacrifices *meant something*, and therefore *whose* longings deserved to be fulfilled — tragedy, sacrifice, and longing measured in terms of their isomorphism with nation-ness. These questions remained unresolved in the program because, to get ahead of my argument, the melodrama contained a certain crucible of ambivalence that, in turn, derived from the historical moment in which *Yearnings* aired. In what follows, I bring together these three elements of ambivalence, narratives of national identity, and the melodramatic form by analyzing the three overlapping parts into which *Yearnings* divided along these lines, each of which told a divergent tale of nation-ness and longing.

The opening episodes of *Yearnings* once again created a space for intellectuals, reinvigorating their memories of old traumas, pulling them into implicit support for the current regime by replaying images of those bad old days — worse, it implied, than these post–June 4th times. The mise-en-scène intimates that the drama will follow the conventional tale of intellectuals' senseless sufferings during the Cultural Revolution. We see the intellectual Wang family precariously living in their two-story Beijing home. Their home has become an architectural palimpsest, its surface layered over with Cultural Revolution graffiti denouncing the

Wangs as class enemies. The camera's sweep over the careless destruction of the family library operates to draw on the viewers' sympathies. For, through economic reform eyes, this constitutes an ignorant attack against knowledge that could build China's wealth and power. The appearance of the Wangs—the youthful innocence of the children and the frailty of the mother—along with the quotidian quality of their activities —shopping, working in a hospital and a factory—further served to establish the Wang family as undeserving victims who happen to be intellectuals but who otherwise share with other human beings the same desires for love, personal fulfillment, and family.

Just as these speak bitterness stories have always done, those in *Yearnings* interpellated intellectuals into once again constructing their lives in this genre: to claim themselves as victims of history and therefore rightful heirs to the national mantle. One night, I watched several episodes of *Yearnings* at the home of Lao Du, an older "backbone" party cadre associated with Hangzhou University.[22] Lao Du came from the north; she and her husband had followed party directives to move south just after the revolution to secure Zhejiang province for the communists (Hangzhou is the capital of Zhejiang). I had come to know Lao Du in the early 1980s in her capacity as the cadre overseeing the university's foreign guest house—a sensitive and weighty appointment. Lao Du still missed the north and so she had offered to make me northern dumplings for dinner. Lao Du and her husband had little formal education but they made sure their children attended college. Over dinner with her son, daughter, and daughter's fiancé, Lao Du proudly described her children's achievements and their hopes to go abroad to America. After stuffing ourselves on dumplings, Lao Du suggested we watch *Yearnings*. She described the program as a good way to learn about the past. As she and her daughter's fiancé walked me to the bus stop after the show, they began, in a tone of bittersweet irony, to tell me the story of the fiancé's family troubles during the Cultural Revolution, how his father was denounced, his schooling interrupted, and his home destroyed. His own story, he insisted, was exactly like that of the Wangs in *Yearnings*.

The story of *Yearnings* became the story of intellectual viewers, its history their history, its "facts" their "facts." It discursively recreated positions of identity for intellectuals that they had begun to leave behind after June 4th. It constituted them as subjects who needed to remember why they should support the post-Mao nation-state by transferring narrative authority to them as they actively watched the drama; that is, the ability and desire to speak bitterness. This narrative desire in turn fed their expectations of *Yearnings*, creating in them, as it were, a "yearning" for more of the melodrama through which they could construct meaning out of their current, post–June 4th lives.[23]

Yet, as *Yearnings* further unfolded its tale, an unexpected twist occurred. If the story had faithfully recapitulated a speak bitterness tale of intellectuals, then the Wang family would be the only victims-cum-heroes. Their characters would remain sympathetic, their motives avenged, the tragedy all theirs. As the episodes progressed, however, the drama jarringly brushed against the grain of this expectation. Yaru, the Wang family daughter and the nemesis of Huifang (our budding heroine), and Husheng, the Wang family son and Huifang's husband, appeared to become increasingly selfish, arrogant, temperamental, and petty. They appeared to transform into the villains, as they emerged in juxtaposition to the selfless, if crude, characters of the simple town folk.[24] *Yearnings*, then, begins with the sufferings of intellectuals but turns away, at least in part, from the post–Cultural Revolution project of constituting them as icons of the nation. That was a socialist realist project of pre-Tiananmen days. *Yearnings* as socialist realism would have portrayed the Wang family as larger-than-life heroes with no ambiguity. Instead, a narrative tension and ambivalence builds at this point, between the sufferings the Wang family endures and their selfish and arrogant behavior. This paradox is unacceptable for socialist realist stories and therefore must burst out of that form.

This paradox, or rather ambivalence, is created through the inscription of what might be identified as a humanist discourse into the melodrama that begins to collide with and overpower the conventional storyline of class victimization. The foreground of the melodrama becomes occupied by the painful "personal" dilemmas resulting (presumably) from that class history (or do they?): Husheng's relationship with his college girlfriend torn asunder and his subsequent longing for emotional sustenance; Yaru, separated from her fiancé, giving birth to their child out of wedlock and in secrecy; Huifang, fragmented by opposing moral claims on her affection as she searches for true love.

The introduction of a humanist discourse into China in the 1980s was fraught with political tension. The state vilified certain aesthetic productions as examples of "bourgeois humanism," creating this as a position of resistance to its power.[25] Yet I would argue that the state also enabled a discursive space for the individual. Through the imagined vision of economic reform, the individual body replaced the collective body as the unit of measurement for productivity and deserved wealth (see Anagnost 1997, Rofel 1999). Talent and even fate appeared in official discourse as suitable explanations for social inequities.

Yearnings was the unacknowledged popular stepchild of these post-Mao high culture and statist representations. The "personal" in *Yearnings*, however, is not that of the bounded, unified subject of Western humanism (Foucault 1978 [1976]). The personal is signaled rather by the shifting meanings of family relations: highlighting the importance of spousal relations over the residual hegemony of filial obligation to parents; romantic love over the ideology of marriage as a means to reproduce family status.[26] Thus, we find the heroine Huifang castigating the traditional matchmaking means of her mother and Dacheng, as she insists on making up her mind according to her heart.

With such humanist representations brought to the fore as the melodrama proceeded, viewers experienced the first unexpected turn of narrative tension. Intertwined with icons of nation-ness and class, these humanist tropes created an ambivalence about whether the Wang family dilemmas were personal or historical. Were Husheng and Yaru, as they developed into self-serving, nasty people, the bitter harvest of the Cultural Revolution generation, with whom we should empathize, or were they the bearers of bad human natures? Were intellectuals prone to these types of selves or was Yaru's exaggerated mean-spiritedness the natural emotions of a mother's inconsolable grief?[27] Were intellectuals' longings justified or not?

Kobena Mercer (1991) has argued in reference to another form of ambivalent aesthetic pleasure — Robert Mapplethorpe's photographs — that ambivalence occurs across the relations of authors, texts, and readers, because "reading" cultural meanings depends on the historical contingency of context.[28] As the intellectual protagonists did not represent the conventional socialist realist types, some of the people I knew became committed to the idea that the show was about fate. Yu Shifu, a retired silk factory worker and long-committed party member insisted, somewhat self-consciously, that the drama had little to do with class. I was surprised by her analysis, for in my previous stints in the factory where she had worked, she had relentlessly done "thought work" with me to convince me of the glories of the revolution and the party. She had suffused all of our conversations with party rhetoric, even seemingly apolitical topics such as buying shoes. Unexpectedly, we had developed a friendship. On my return to Hangzhou that winter, Yu Shifu invited me to her home for lunch but when I arrived, greeted me at the gate with much embarrassment. She lived in her husband's work unit, an army base on the famous West Lake. They did not allow foreigners inside. We decided to take a long walk around the lake toward the Buddhist temple and have lunch there. Yu Shifu described her life of retirement and before too long, turned to an animated discussion of *Yearnings*. Catching me up on episodes she had watched ahead of me, she offered the opinion that Yaru was to be pitied her poor fate. Self-deprecating laughter followed this comment, for we had just left the inside of the temple where she had explained to me that praying for one's fate was the stuff of superstition.

But others had a different critique. One evening, I had dinner with a group of economics professors from Hangzhou University. They were all men, some emeritus while others were just beginning to teach. I had first met the younger professors eight years previously when we were all graduate students. All foreigners living in China were assigned to a work unit to be responsible for them. Given my research interests in the silk industry, I had been assigned to the economics department. The atmosphere over dinner was relaxed, as our conversation roamed from our teaching lives to problems in China after June 4th. Not too long into dinner, the conversation, as it often seemed to do at that time, turned to *Yearnings*. One of the young men exploded. He declared emphatically that he was no longer going to watch the program. "This," he exclaimed, "is a show about how intellectuals have pretty words on the outside but bad hearts on the inside and how workers might have coarse words on the outside but good hearts on the inside." This program, he continued, was seriously detrimental to intellectuals. In post-Tiananmen China, the stakes for the icons of national heroism remained high, in part because they translated into systems of privilege levered in important ways by the state.

Yearnings's middle episodes witness the emergence of the heroine, Hui-fang. Fragile in build—a post-Mao visual sign of female heroine mate-rial—Huifang is a paragon of good conscience (*liangxin*) and the quin-tessence of self-sacrifice. She sacrifices her future for her family when she enters the factory after her father's death; courageously ignores the dan-ger to her reputation when she cares for Husheng while engaged to another; leaves behind the comfortable life she would have had married to a man of her own working-class background;[29] and gives up her son (it is never construed as abandon) when her sister-in-law and nemesis Yaru insists on raising him in what she considers the proper milieu of the Wang home. But she sacrifices most of all for the daughter she has not even borne of her own body, including the loss of the opportunity to become an intellectual, the loss of a steady job and income, and finally, the very loss of her physical abilities.

These exquisitely painful tragedies are captured in the crowning epi-sode of this middle portion of the melodrama. Huifang is pregnant. She is faced with a dilemma: should she have an abortion so that she can continue her intensive studies for the college entrance examination or should she give birth and abandon her dream of becoming an intellec-tual? This will be her only opportunity, for it is the late 1970s and the state has restored the national examination system but is giving the Cultural Revolution generation only a few opportunities to pass it be-fore barring them as being too old for college. Undecided after a visit to the doctor, Huifang returns home to study. But as soon as she enters, she finds her five-year-old daughter, whom she sheltered as an abandoned baby and has raised as her own, slumped over the table. Huifang anx-iously approaches Xiaofang, finds her overcome with a high fever, and sets everything aside to attend to her. We see Huifang grow more anx-ious, for she must find the proper medical care for her daughter before the illness grows more serious. We then witness a premonition of the impending tragedy when Huifang holds her stomach in pain, breathing jaggedly, as she offers medicine to her daughter. But her daughter con-tinues to moan with discomfort. The music swells, heightening the anxi-ety. With no transportation available, Huifang, a frail woman grown frailer through the various tribulations in her life, carries her daugh-ter on her back to the hospital. On their arrival, Huifang sinks to the ground in pain with an oncoming miscarriage that will force her to lose both the baby and her last opportunity to enter college.

We can begin to appreciate the storm of controversy that surrounded Huifang's character by examining how this domesticated woman becomes the grounds on which nation-ness and longing were rearticulated. Speak bitterness narratives are less relevant here than the iconization of a model socialist citizen named Lei Feng. Lei Feng was purportedly a young worker-soldier in the People's Liberation Army who, in the early 1960s, gave his life for his country. His posthumously discovered diary spoke of his undying love for the revolution and for his country and his unswerving devotion to Chairman Mao. Officially required study material during the Cultural Revolution, the figure of Lei Feng was dusted off by the party in the post-Mao period to counter, belatedly, their own promotion of material gain as the officially sanctioned "socialist" desire to accompany market reforms. He was also used to dampen the "counterrevolutionary" fires of democracy threatening the very foundations of the state.

In the 1990s, however, Lei Feng became a satirical figure in the eyes of most citizens. The invocation of Lei Feng's name at one point in the melodrama flirts provocatively with this border between parody and seriousness. Huifang's factory girlfriend teases Huifang's soon-to-be fiancé Dacheng about his services to the Liu family by calling him Lei Feng — not for his devotion to the state, but in his search for love.

If Lei Feng became the butt of much ironic reconfiguring, self-sacrifice remained an important sign of the Chinese nation. In this respect, Huifang embodied the quintessence of Chinese nation-ness. Feminist theory has convincingly argued that Woman is a sign whose signified incorporates more than the concept of woman. Lata Mani (1998), for example, demonstrated that debates about *sati*, or widow burning, in India under colonial rule were less about women's lives and more about Indian womanhood as the grounds for a rearticulation of tradition and by extension the Indian nation.

In extrapolating such a framework to *Yearnings*, I want to suggest that Huifang as a woman, or rather as Woman, represents the Chinese nation while rending that identity apart from socialist politics.[30] She is Lei Feng come home. The domestic sphere, as I have argued, represents that space in China in which people believe they can remove themselves from the "reach of the state" (Shue 1988). The national subject can thus maintain her integrity both within the country and in relation to other countries, unsullied by the historical degradation of state socialism. Moreover, this domesticated subject focused attention on keeping the domestic in order at a moment when the world outside China, especially international communism, had collapsed around it.[31] In this sense, *Yearnings* is above all a form of political allegory. It recalls Walter Benjamin's (1977 [1963]) definition of allegory as composed of a history that is a landscape of ruins. The story of Huifang's destiny is an allegory of China's embattled sense of itself as a nation, of what it stands for and whom it stands with.[32]

Perhaps the most vociferous debates about *Yearnings* revolved around the figure of Huifang. They were sparked by the intersection of feminine self-sacrifice as nation-ness with the constitution of Huifang as a gendered object of diverse gazes. In light of Teresa de Lauretis's (1984) emphasis on female spectatorship as a site of productive relations, one finds that, for women who followed this melodrama, Huifang and her nemesis Yaru compelled a controversial sense-making of the inchoate experiences of womanhood during the previous decade of economic reform.[33]

For if Huifang is a Lei Feng look-alike, she is also a character who reverberates with post-Mao reinscriptions of Confucian categories. She embodies the "virtuous wives, good mothers" homilies that were so worked over in the 1980s (see Honig and Hershatter 1988). Thus, a particular gendered form of self-sacrifice is here linked to nation-ness. Huifang embodies the ideal womanhood of Chinese masculine fantasies.[34] The fierce criticisms of Huifang were, in part, directed against this fantasy.

The post-Mao social landscape anchored this vision in a naturalized topography. The economic reform state's most pressing calls to legitimate its specific imaginary of the modern body politic revolved around the natures of women. It was on this terrain that the state could so convincingly claim that Maoist politics, especially the Cultural Revolution, overturned the "natural" order of things and that state cadres now in power were simply turning the world right-side up.[35]

These gender fantasies provided the social context in which *Yearnings* aired. Women's intense engagement with the melodrama stemmed from the ways in which the naturalization of womanhood imbricated in post-Mao politics has meant that women in China lead an uneasy and provisional existence as subjects of the nation. Their debates, in effect, raised questions about the basis on which women can claim themselves to be members of a national community whose image of itself as a community is so configured around *socially* engendered self-sacrifice. Mere personal self-sacrifice, for which essentialized, redesigned Confucian female models hold the championship, does not suffice. It may be viewed as a contribution to the nation, but not as the ground for playing its hero.

Yearnings captured the divergent stories women tell to insist on the worthiness of their self-sacrifices. The fiercest criticisms of Huifang came from those who have positioned themselves through the speak bitterness stories of intellectuals, women who have narratively fashioned themselves as ungendered (that is, male) intellectuals sacrificing for China's modernity through their labor. These women angrily disparaged Huifang as a model of feudal womanhood that should be left behind. One female journalist indignantly asked in her column how one was supposed to distinguish in *Yearnings* between feudal values of "virtuous wives and good mothers" and the communist spirit of service government cadres seemed to find in the program (Ren 1991). By invoking feudalism, a trope redolent with notions of backwardness in socialist historiography, she implied that the kind of woman Huifang represented was not natural but historically created. She certainly had no place in a modern socialist state.

On the morning I was to leave China, I said my goodbyes to a family of traditional Chinese medical doctors with whom I had become quite close when I first lived in Hangzhou. They had taught me how to be politically savvy in China and had offered the warmth of their home whenever I felt lonely. Sadly, on this trip I had learned of the grandmother's death the previous year. The grandmother had been highly educated at a time, in the 1930s, when few women had the opportunity to attend medical school. Her daughters, daughters-in-law, and granddaughters all had formal education. The second son, trained in Western biomedicine, had turned to traditional Chinese medicine to follow in his father's distinguished footsteps. He had married Luo Mingxian, whose specialty was medicinal herbs for women's illnesses.

Luo Mingxian accompanied me to the train station to help me board my train to Shanghai and thence to the airport. We happened to look up at the television monitor in the waiting room to find *Yearnings* being aired. Mingxian proceeded to spend her last moments with me offering her thoughts about Huifang and Yaru. Perhaps having more than a visceral identification with Yaru, Mingxian declared that she had decided Huifang was the selfish one while Yaru was right. First of all, she hurriedly exclaimed, it was not natural to take care of a child not one's own. Yaru was not acting in mean-spiritedness when she refused to have Xiaofang live in her home. Would you, she asked pointedly, take in a stray child and really devote your life to raising her? Quite the contrary, Huifang was the stubborn one. She was the one to cause the rift in her relationship with her husband by adamantly refusing to compromise about the child. The irony of invoking nature to support the strivings of female intellectuals was left unremarked by us both.

But other women I knew felt differently. These women, mainly factory workers or factory cadres who could but tenuously claim to be intellectuals, felt empathy for and defended Huifang. They interpreted her sacrifices as socially engendered and worthy of representing national heroism. For some, like Mo Ying, a silk prep worker who came of age at the end of the Cultural Revolution, the Lei Feng trope resonated most strongly. She explicitly applauded the return of workers as heroes. Others insisted on the strength of character in Huifang. If one could make the case that Huifang *chose* to sacrifice rather than embodied a feminine lack of will, that she was a product of social circumstance, then one could potentially argue that her tragedies were the result of historically rooted oppressions rather than the natural outcome of femininity. In this vein, it was pointed out to me more than once that Huifang stood up to her mother's old-fashioned attempts to arrange a marriage for her, insisting on a marriage built on mutual choice and love. And again, Huifang's initiation of a divorce from Husheng was an act of bravery in a social context in which divorced women were socially censured.

Those who disliked Huifang criticized those who defended her for advocating a return to feudal notions of womanhood. But those who took Huifang's side were not upholding her as a model of appropriate womanhood. Tania Modleski (1982) persuasively argued that women in the United States enjoy soap operas and romantic novels because they provide a subversive critique of the burdens of domesticity. This type of critique certainly appears to be an element among those who placed themselves in the position of Huifang. But more than this, they were attempting to establish the grounds on which she, and therefore they, could claim the worthiness of her/their sacrifices and thus the inclusion of women's activities as contributions to the construction of the nation. They took pleasure in the character of Huifang because, through her, they were not merely an audience but were addressed as "significant political beings" (Bobo 1988).[36]

THE HERO SAVES THE NATION

As an icon of the nation, Huifang is problematic in the end. Too much sacrifice on the part of China in the world of nations will lead to the kinds of crippling that Huifang finally experiences. China/Huifang must therefore be rescued by the intellectual hero, Luo Gang, the old boyfriend of her nemesis, Yaru. He embodies the hope that China will move forward out of suffering and will strive to succeed. In the final episodes, Luo Gang begins to care for the disabled child along with Huifang, "as if" he were the father. Continuing where Huifang's sacrifices left off, he refuses to claim the child for himself or Yaru after his realization of her "true" parentage, for fear of irreparable harm to Huifang's maternal sentiments. His most expansive rescue is his offer to marry Huifang after she becomes disabled, to ensure her lifelong care. (She refuses.)[37]

China needs its intellectuals in the end. Luo Gang has the right kind of intellectual qualities: his willingness to place himself at the service of China/Huifang and his conventional use of speaking bitterness, which leads him to accept the political resolution of his reinstatement as a professor and, by extension, to accept life under economic reform.[38]

Luo Gang is recognizable as heroic material not only by his intellectual qualities but also through the particular signs of masculinity he embodies. The mid-1980s in China witnessed an explosive search among male writers and filmmakers for something they discovered they had lost or, some feared, perhaps never had: masculinity (see Louie 1991, Wang 1989).[39] They attributed their newly found castration to the state.[40] Their desire for a hypermasculinity of forthright sexual feelings and a tough, indomitable spirit proved fertile ground on which to mount their opposition to the state.[41]

The politics of this masculinity gestured toward a devastating critique of the state, but it did so through a partial erasure of women's agency (Chow 1991b).[42] Thus, in Yearnings, Luo Gang takes over the elements of selflessness and reticence from Huifang. The torch of nationhood is passed on, as it were. Modleski (1982) maintained that in American soap operas and romance novels, the narrative progression is one of the feminization of the hero, signified by his increasing appreciation of domesticity. But Luo Gang is not the effeminate intellectual. Effeminate men, embodying the cultural qualities previously admired in intellectuals — aesthetic refinement and emotional delicacy — have been reconfigured as ineffectual political subjects. Husheng plays Luo Gang's foil on that end of the gender spectrum. He is a helpless dandy who breaks his ankle climbing a ladder to fix Huifang's roof, confirming the need for someone to "mother" him, whether it be Huifang, his sister Yaru, or his old college girlfriend.

If Luo Gang embodies the newfound masculinity of the 1980s, his character maintains a distance from the roughest versions of this type, which belong, in most of its representations, to the working class. Song Dacheng plays this version of manhood — the broad-shouldered, well-muscled, physically adept man who cannot express his feelings though they evidently tear him up inside. Luo Gang represents a softer echo of this masculinity that nonetheless shows us that it is in intellectual male subjectivity that the Chinese nation should find its future.[43]

WHO GETS TO YEARN? AND FOR WHAT?

The national controversy in China that erupted over *Yearnings* was produced through the manner in which this seemingly innocuous and apolitical dramatic miniseries narrativized political allegories of nationness. It did so by conjoining a historically specific use of the melodramatic form with speak bitterness narratives of national identity, which, in turn, became a site for divergent discourses of class, gender, and nation-ness. Further, these conjoined and divergent narratives produced intense longings. These yearnings, almost by definition, never get fulfilled. They are diverse but they all revolve around a "personal" life devoid of the most obvious signs of those passions that animated June 4th. *Yearnings* demonstrates the capacity of allegory to generate a range of distinct meanings simultaneously, as the allegorical tenor of nationness changes vehicles (Jameson 1986, 73). Whether Yaru and Husheng turned nasty because of their victimization as intellectuals in the Cultural Revolution, because of humanist notions of character and fate, or because intellectuals are, in the end, untrustworthy human beings made all the difference in a post–June 4th world in which intellectuals and the party-state grappled with one another over the effects of the violent repression of intellectuals' overt challenge to state power.

Can intellectuals still represent the nation? Are their longings legitimate? This question motivated the first explosive responses to *Yearnings* by intellectuals who read the answer as no. By the last episode, the answer seemed to be a qualified yes, but only if that intellectual is someone like Luo Gang, who still narrates his life through speak bitterness tropes that lead to political acceptance of the post-Mao state.

Can women garner the signs of nation-ness about them? What of their longings? The second moment of heated engagement with *Yearnings* revolved around this question. Is Huifang a heroine to be admired or a retrograde image of feudal womanhood? The answer depends on several deeper questions: Will the sacrifices involved in women's activities count as being socially configured so that they can be seen as heroic? Must those activities be gender neutral (that is, masculine) or can women *as* women still function as icons of the nation? An emphasis on sexual difference has replaced a Maoist vision of unmarked, nongendered bodies (at least within the same class). Depending on the answers to these questions, women could lead but a provisional existence as members of the national community because this community is predicated on socially construed measures of self-sacrifice that code sacrifice in the domestic sphere as unworthy. Those women who disparaged Huifang felt that such a heroine threatened to erase the sacrifices they had made for the nation through work in the public sphere. Those who spoke in her favor felt that she displayed and valorized the sacrifices involved in those activities conceived of as women's domestic responsibilities. Implicitly, they argued that Huifang's tragedies should make her eligible as an icon of the nation.

The controversy over *Yearnings* alerts us to the fact that nations are continuously re-imagined and contested through the creation of interpretive communities that have complex stakes in specific narratives of nation-ness. The radical ruptures in who counts as a national hero and which narrative form represents these figures open up the possibility of reading these texts as not only contextualized and reflective of a national space but constitutive of that entity called China. *Yearnings* produced a powerfully seductive knowledge of viewers' lives that led them, in part, to view themselves as the program portrayed them. In making cultural sense of this television text, viewers in China were also making sense of themselves. As with other forms of discourse, it would be impossible to distinguish the way they spoke about the program from the way the program "spoke" through them, that is, constructed their social identity.[44]

Though viewers in China experienced *Yearnings* as a realm separate from those themes most facilely associated with the state, meanings that official discourses circulated in the first decade of economic reform were laced throughout the narrative. The deep ambivalence about intellectuals, the use of gender in the creation of that which is called "personal life," and the assertion of a personal sphere that is felt to exist apart from the state have all been state projects. Indeed, one of the major visions of the state about itself since the Cultural Revolution is its claim to noninterference in that space that has come into existence as "the personal."[45] Moreover, the longings that threaded through the narrative were directed toward personal life and away from the explosive passions of June 4th. These narrativized longings captured citizens' frustrations with economic reform, even as they paved the way for an embrace of the neoliberal policies to come.

If people in China did not recline in a realm outside the state as they viewed *Yearnings*, they nonetheless seized on its narrative ambivalences to challenge the potential hegemony of meanings not only within this text but, by implicit extension, in the numerous social fields in which these debates had already taken hold. The social phenomenon of *Yearnings* did not, however, operate between two established poles of meaning and power, those of domination versus opposition. Accounting for the interpretive agency of people with conflicting views requires moving beyond a celebration of spectators' autonomy or resistance that relies on positivist assumptions about "choosing" meanings. But it also requires going beyond purely textual approaches with their assumptions of closed cultural worlds. The popularity — as well as the controversy — of *Yearnings* signaled an emergent process, a contested moment in the making of Chinese national public culture. It reflected a similarly contested historical moment regarding fantasies about the future of Chinese citizens.

2

Museum as Women's Space

Displays of Gender

*T*he nationwide controversy over the soap opera *Yearnings*, addressed in the previous chapter, marked a moment when public culture in China evinced an angst-ridden self-reflexivity about the nation's future in light of experiments with a market economy and the decline of socialism. "Actually existing" Maoism had surely come to an end but, as evident in *Yearnings*, traces of nostalgia for Maoist ideals—and kitsch for an idealistic youth lost in the Cultural Revolution—surreptitiously castigated the current regime even as it appeared to lend support. The women's museum I discuss in this chapter, founded by the well-known and controversial feminist scholar Li Xiaojiang, came into existence in 1992, just a year after *Yearnings* aired. That year marked a turning point for the production of "desiring China." Premier Deng Xiaoping took his famous Southern Excursion Tour. The Tour occurred after several years of uncertainty about China's direction in the aftermath of June 4th. Numerous Western nations had severed their initial economic endeavors in China to voice their displeasure with the government's actions. Deng toured the country to reassure the provinces that the central government supported expansion of market endeavors, further devolution of power to local governments, greater privatization, and a fast track for economic reform policies. In effect, the Southern Tour led to the legalization of the very socioeconomic arrangements that had galvanized the 1989 protests. The Southern Tour initiated a new period in which the central state and local governments together began to encourage foreign investment by establishing "special economic zones" along China's eastern coast that offered greater incentives for foreign entrepreneurs.

This moment also ushered in a discursive, political, and social shift in relation to desire. In public culture debates arose that the constitution of a post-Maoist humanity in China requires not merely the demolition of those politics portrayed as hindering human nature but a positive encouragement and elaboration of people's sexual, material, and affective self-interest in order to become (bourgeois) cosmopolitan citizens. *Yearnings* had taught viewers that postsocialist desire entails the art of longing. After the Southern Tour, the art of longing elaborated in such melodramatic fashion became wedded to the insistent fostering of desires in the name of postsocialist gender and sexual identities. At the broadest level, the explosive controversies surrounding *Yearnings*'s gender politics revolved around the recurrent anxiety that echoed everywhere: what constitutes the identity of China, now that the progressive, heroic story of socialism has slithered into the dust? This question pervaded both elite and popular culture, from controversial novels among Beijing intellectuals to internationally acclaimed films to mass media productions like *Yearnings*.

At the time *Yearnings* aired, feminist scholars of China were developing political positions not found in the soap opera. They challenged the project of women's liberation under Maoism. They went so far as to wonder aloud whether Chinese women had even had any female identity available to them after the socialist revolution. To anticipate my discussion, Li Xiaojiang founded the women's museum to visualize a female identity for women that, she argued, had not existed under Maoist socialism. In this regard, the museum project both furthered and challenged the commodification of gender that proved so productive for bringing "desiring China" into existence.

Attention to gender in China was not new. Throughout the twentieth century, gender served as one of the central modalities through which modernity in China was imagined.[1] In the early part of the century, Western missionaries, colonial administrators, foreign entrepreneurs, and the predominantly male Chinese educated elite made Chinese women the grounds for reinterpreting Chinese tradition and measuring China's ability to become modern. The socialist state's political imaginary continued to center on the question of women's liberation. Communist party leaders measured women's liberation under socialism as an indication of their own contribution to historical progress. In so doing, the socialist state crafted a discourse of women's liberation that reconfigured the meaning of labor and hence the subjectivity of women.

In the post-Mao era, debate opened once again on the nature of gender and sexuality. One can discern in these public debates what I have elsewhere called an allegory of postsocialism (Rofel 1999). This allegory tells a story of how Maoist socialism repressed human nature. Because such repression, like all repressions, produces the very obsessions, perversions, and fetishisms it hopes to forestall, socialism failed. Maoism deferred China's ability to reach modernity, so this allegory goes, by impeding Chinese people's ability to express their natural humanity that, all along, lay beneath the cultural politics of socialism. The "natural humanity" of this allegory is, of course, gendered. The allegory is an emancipatory story, holding out the promise that people can unshackle their innate human selves by embracing appropriate gender identities.

Li Xiaojiang's women's museum responds to this allegory. The museum, and Li Xiaojiang's feminist theoretical writings, question whether women in fact had been liberated by the socialist revolution. A number of feminists, along with Li Xiaojiang, argued that the overarching role of class difference in providing the foundation of subjectivity and power during the Maoist era obscured ongoing dynamics of gendered relations of dominance and inequality (Meng and Dai 1990, Gilmartin et al. 1994, Li Xiaojiang 1990, Liu 1991, Yang 1999). Protocols of official feminism, they argued, constructed a Maoist woman whose liberated femininity was put to the service of state interests (Barlow 2004a).

Owing to the centrality of gender in socialist politics and its aftermath, the allegory of postsocialism pervaded public culture in the 1980s and 1990s. Feminist cultural productions were thus quite visible but, paradoxically, to the extent that this allegory articulated with the increased commodification of social life in the 1990s, it also threatened to marginalize their political analysis. Li Xiaojiang created the women's museum in that moment, when neoliberal policies in China began to surpass the initial experiments with economic reform and the stakes for women seemed quite high. The museum was a strikingly creative effort to make gender identity visible. Perhaps it is indicative of the mobile grounds of neoliberal gender politics later in the decade that the museum had an ephemeral existence. It closed a few years after it opened, as Li Xiaojiang herself changed academic location and theoretical positions.

Li Xiaojiang is one of the most controversial feminists to emerge in post-Mao China. She is a prolific and outspoken author who has contributed to the formation of academic women's studies, made possible the publication of a series on feminism, and has written about women's issues for the commercial media (Li 1988a, 1988b, 1989, 1990, 1996, 1999). Li Xiaojiang's provocations have included public ridicule of the All-China Women's Federation (of which more below), who in turn made her a persona non grata at their national fora; an unwavering call to place gender at the center of any Marxist humanism; and a staunch refusal to make Chinese feminism appear to need Western feminism. Yet even as she theorizes gender identity in contradistinction to the official version of feminism, Li has not completely abandoned a Marxist analysis of the structural constraints women face. Her combination of Marxist structuralism coupled with her advocacy of a postsocialist desire to embrace sexual difference has led to her appearance as a paradoxical figure in China's public culture—a radical feminist who is "mainstream." Tani Barlow (2004a) has argued that Li Xiaojiang developed her feminism in the context of the market economy. Barlow emphasizes how Li's feminism fosters the idea of national development by enlisting women in self-betterment projects and by recovering women's feminine singularity. Li has also stirred debate among feminists who, like her, have moved away from state feminism. Her analyses of women as a social category in Chinese history lead her to reject Western feminism as a measure of Chinese women's progress—and, at times, to reject diasporic Chinese feminists who study and write about feminism in the United States.[2] Li has encouraged and fostered younger feminists under her direction while some have also accused her of failing to engage in a collective feminist dialogue.[3]

Li Xiaojiang opened the women's museum in Zhengzhou, Henan Province, where she was a professor of Western literature and women's studies.[4] Li Xiaojiang's ability to act as a lightning rod of controversy came unexpectedly from her location in Zhengzhou. Seventeen hours from Beijing by train, Zhengzhou is a dusty, polluted industrial city on the North China plain, where the dry winds sweep down and catch the loess sands in people's throats. In the early 1990s, virtually nothing in this city had been turned into a tourist attraction. Multinational capital from Hong Kong and Taiwan, however, had scented the cheap, desperate labor that exists here and moved in. But the women's museum stood in an indirect relation to these regimes of flexible accumulation. While Li Xiaojiang received Ford Foundation funds for a multi-provincial project on women's history, she never managed to attract funding for the women's museum. Zhengzhou is a seemingly marginal site from which to theorize feminism — the more prominent voices emerge from Beijing and Shanghai. This marginality paradoxically fostered Li's ability to challenge orthodoxy. Yet this ability in turn was supported by the fact that Li comes from a prominent local family — her father was the former president of Zhengzhou University.

Before my visit to the women's museum in the summer of 1993, rumor of its existence had already reached the United States. The commentary it generated among feminists in China indicated that it was one significant practice among many in the early 1990s that brought the burgeoning field of feminist studies into existence. Before the visit, however, I was wary. The promotional literature on the museum described one of its purposes to be the initiation of a "women's cultural anthropology" through the collection of cultural relics used by women. This statement resonated uncomfortably with anthropological critiques of museums as sites that fix otherness, imply the death of living colonial subjects, and recreate racist stereotypes (Clifford 1988, Haraway 1985). I anticipated a museum that would essentialize a folk culture of women, a museum that would be representational — that is, purport to provide images that merely reflected reality — rather than interpretive or deconstructive. The women's museum, however, displaced ethnographic critiques of the "museumizing" of culture. It did so by way of the materiality of its location and in the performativity of its displays of gender. As I eventually came to appreciate, the term "museum," though used in the Chinese designation as well, is somewhat of a misnomer. It produced a misrecognition of the museum's politics. The museum effected an activist construction of the social category of woman. It self-reflexively theorized gender by putting it on display. Such displays created gender identities by encouraging a visual performance of them. They resulted in a productive tension between the assumption that gender difference is natural and the idea that it is historically and culturally constructed. The women's museum thus at once reinforced and disrupted the postsocialist allegory of gendered human nature. Before delving into a description of the museum's displays, I first turn to Li Xiaojiang's feminist theories to contextualize the displays.

Li Xiaojiang's writings and her women's museum participated in a larger discursive field of women's studies in China both before and after June 4th and Deng's Southern Tour. In her writings, Li Xiaojiang joined other Chinese feminists in making a deceptively straightforward argument: she insisted that the past years of economic reform had turned back the tide of women's liberation in China (1988b, 1991). Li Xiaojiang asserted that the one inequality that served economic reform most crucially was that between men and women (1988b). She baldly stated that the road down which Chinese society was heading was in exactly the opposite direction from the road women should be traveling. Li Xiaojiang did not deny China's need for economic development. She embraced assumptions of progress and supported national development. But she did not think it was a coincidence that problems for women appeared at the same time that economic reform took off. These dilemmas, she concluded, were the means by which society resolved certain "social problems," such as labor surplus and the need to increase labor productivity. Women provided the cornerstone of China's economic development—so much so that their problems were no longer seen as socially significant. They had literally become *women's* problems. In the early 1990s, these included pressures to increase rural productivity that had led to the removal of women from production and their return to the home; the layoffs of women in urban industries disguised as overly long maternity leaves with lowered benefits; the fact that young women in cities composed the overwhelming majority of the surplus unemployed; the refusal to hire women college graduates in jobs that met their capabilities; and the decrease in women's participation in government.[5]

Li Xiaojiang readily admitted there was no necessary relation between economic development and women's liberation. Given China's desire for a high level of economic competitiveness and an increase in economic efficiency, coupled with women's double burdens, she agreed that women's experiences of reform not only did not constitute a social quandary but were an effective solution to social predicaments—from the standpoint of "society." But from the position of women themselves, economic reform ran directly counter to women's needs and to the ability of women to develop their full potential as contributors to the Chinese nation.

Women's liberation was a real moment in China's socialist past. When Li Xiaojiang made this assertion, she by no means assumed that "women's liberation" is an ontological state, something that, having once occurred, infuses the dialectic of history forevermore. Instead, she contended that at the present time, the old theory that socialism liberates women, parroted over and over again, had been exhausted: "We used to recognize that 'women's liberation is the entrance of women into society'. . . This certainly is a premise of women's liberation, but . . . women entering society is not the same as women's liberation . . . Class liberation is not the same as women's liberation . . . Men's and women's equality is not the same as women's liberation . . . The development of the productive forces is not the same as women's liberation . . . What is women's liberation? Simply, it is women's freedom and full development . . . It is the affirmation of every human being's social value and the value of their very existence" (1988b).

For women to reach this liberation, according to Li Xiaojiang, they had to come to consciousness of themselves as a social identity. As women. Women needed to recover their real, feminine singularity.

Deceptively simple. But within this project lay a subversion that unsettled conventional cultural politics in China. The museum, and other feminist cultural productions in post-Mao China, were multiply positioned across a number of intersecting political border zones from which they reconstructed the meaning and significance of Chinese women's gender identity. They placed this postsocialist gender identity for women alongside other subject-positions that dominated the social horizon in the early 1990s: the official "socialist with Chinese characteristics" subject, who sat comfortably if somewhat unstably in the interstices between capitalism and socialism; the Chinese cultural subject, popular among intellectuals but ignored by the state, who sought the reasons for China's imagined backwardness in cultural roots;[6] and the intellectual humanist subject, whose goal was to topple what he viewed as the state's constraints on his abilities to express his panhuman desires. The women's museum, as well as Li's writings, laced through and crossed over the boundaries of this post-Mao discursive landscape. It depended on but also destabilized critical cultural borders of difference that proliferated in the 1980s and early 1990s: the socialist state versus the oppositional humanist subject; the difference between women and men; and the constitution of China in terms of the West. The women's museum, as part of postsocialist feminism, did not construct social life in these stark oppositions. It did not choose one or the other of these binary terms. Rather, it spoke to the state but not as a male humanist; it challenged as well as supported the naturalization of gender difference; and finally, it replaced the China-West opposition with a concern about differences within China.

The most radical aspect of the museum project was the visual strategy to bring women into existence as a collective social category. The woman on display in the women's museum was in explicit contradistinction to the woman the All-China Women's Federation claimed to represent. As Tani Barlow has written, the Women's Federation, after its restoration following the Cultural Revolution, reasserted its claim to represent women as nationalist, revolutionary subjects whose lives were inextricably tied to the socialist state's past and future. The problem, as Barlow points out, is that the Women's Federation recapitulated their classic version of Chinese women's identity "at the very moment when the political consensus that had bound women to the state was collapsing" (2004a, 258). Moreover, their representation of women had to gloss over increasingly noticeable gaps between "the state's representational practices and the everyday life of citizens" (258). Li Xiaojiang stepped into this gap, accusing the Women's Federation of colonizing the category of woman in the name of the state, lacking a feminist theory based in gender identity and difference, and failing to find the courage to fight against new forms of subordination women faced as a result of economic reform (Li 1988b).

Li distinguished her feminist project from that of the Women's Federation. She took the position that the socialist state had bestowed and then imposed liberation on Chinese women. As a result, she and other women had never experienced their own struggles to define themselves as women. Indeed, Li insisted that for a long time she did not even know she was a woman. The most important step, then, to move beyond the statist Women's Federation's version of woman was to recognize sexual difference and identify with one's sexual identity as a woman. Li argued that women have failed, in part, because they have an underdeveloped gender consciousness (Barlow 2004a, 262). Li Xiaojiang's views thus resonated with the postsocialist allegory of repressed gendered natures even as her distinctive elaboration of sexual difference had the potential to unsettle the naturalization of gender subtending the state's neoliberal turn.

If Li Xiaojiang positioned herself in opposition to the statist version of feminism, she also moved unstably across the border of state power versus the oppositional intellectual. The latter configured himself as an unmarked humanist individual. He was someone who had had his fill of collective identities and social struggles over inequality. This post-Mao humanism included both Marxists and non-Marxists. The former emphasized development of a socialist market economy while the latter touted the need for talented individuals to run the government, as in the Confucian past. But the two converged in their valorization of individual agency and their idea that intellectuals deserved to succeed to state power in place of the communist party. Like the party, this humanist intellectual embraced inequality. These intellectuals' humanism, although poised in opposition to the state, inadvertently established some of the ideological framework for China's neoliberal policies. They paved the way with their embrace of the West, because they believed it to be the land of humanism and because Western humanism offered them a space of resistance to the state.

Li Xiaojiang moved across this political border zone by highlighting the masculinization of this humanist tale. Chinese humanism implicitly borrowed from the pervasive representations of an aggressive, if uncertain, masculinity that dominated public culture in light of the postsocialist allegory of repressed gendered natures. Popular stories represented explicit, assertive masculine desire as a more meaningful alternative to state politics but also as the means by which to challenge state power (Hershatter 1996, Zhong 2000). Women in these narratives were the objects and the ground for male agency or they represented the subject-position of victimization which the male author ultimately identified with and occupied (Dai 1995). This sexualized public culture provided a post-Mao masculinist discourse with which an emergent nonstatist feminism such as Li Xiaojiang's had to contend.

The masculinist version of the postsocialist allegory drew its strength, in part, from the explosion of China's public culture — especially film — into transnational networks of cultural production. A process of cultural accumulation was at work that wended its way through representations of Chineseness, national identity, and, most importantly, masculinity. The themes that sutured an exploration of masculine identity and national identity dominated those cultural productions that garnered the most transnational capital investment. They spoke in one direction to the desires of many in China to move beyond a socialist market economy, including its state-defined feminism, and in the other direction toward transnational publics that, as with the earlier history of nation-states, configured themselves on a division between the masculine public and the feminine private. Sasha Welland has argued that women artists from China, especially those addressing feminist issues, face difficulty in gaining recognition for their art *as* art and entering it in international exhibitions because the masculinized art in these exhibitions dominates the definition of contemporary Chinese art (2006). Welland concludes that even Western feminists have a difficult time recognizing the value of Chinese women artists. These women artists appear to be stuck in the "merely local." Writing about feminist projects in China can easily replicate this effect of localization unless one follows Welland's lead and highlights the intimate relationship between domestic and transnational art. The masculinization of transnational cultural space — fostered by approving audiences in the United States and Europe as well as in other Asian countries — allowed the allegory of postsocialism to appear as a natural description of reality rather than a just-so story. The allegory's masculinist heroics joined with other male backlashes against feminism elsewhere to construct the transnational gender politics to which Li Xiaojiang felt compelled to respond in her museum.

THE WOMEN'S MUSEUM

Let us begin then with the museum's location. The site of the women's museum was fraught with irony. It was installed on the grounds of the Henan Women's Federation school for training women cadres. I should add that the provincial women's federations do not always follow to the letter the positions of the national umbrella organization. Thus Li Xiaojiang was on good terms with the local women's federation. The Henan federation school had been on the verge of collapse for some time owing to lack of interest. Young women who came of age after the end of socialism did not see a future for themselves in becoming party cadres and representing the state. One can envision the school, then, as a site of the socialist state in decay. It recalls another kind of allegory, Walter Benjamin's notion of allegory as a tale of history in ruins. In his study of German baroque drama, Benjamin argued that with its allegorical qualities baroque drama addressed the immanence of history as torment (1977/1963). It did so through hieroglyphs, both linguistic and emblematic, that served as multilayered icons of human cruelty that leads to ruin. The women's museum literally wrote over socialist history by occupying a full wing of the school's central building. It wrote another allegory over this material history by reinscribing postsocialist feminist politics where state feminism once resided. Smadar Lavie, reinterpreting Benjamin in an ethnography about the Middle East, has taught us that allegory addresses the paradoxes of political domination (1990). The women's museum, far from offering fixity of representation, engaged an ironic politics of space. It built feminism from within the ashes of the socialist ruins, even as this palimpsest provided a visual statement that what exactly would arise out of those ruins would be a matter of persistent political struggle.

Li Xiaojiang led me on a tour of the museum. Its five large rooms held a dense variety of objects that Li wove into a story about women's culture. The first room we entered was filled with quilts that Li managed to gather from families in rural areas throughout Henan and neighboring provinces. Women's quilts. The quintessential icon of women's culture. The sort of icon that could be associated with a cultural feminism that celebrates and naturalizes femininity. But as one moved closer to the quilts, their historical detail belied this familiar critique. These quilts had a politically distinctive quality. Rather than displaying abstract designs, they were filled with large political slogans woven into them. A quilt made in the 1940s read: "Down with the Japanese devils." The one from the 1950s exhorted its user to "Resist U.S. Aggression and Aid Korea." The Cultural Revolution quilt instructed: "Follow the highest directive: Serve the people," while the late 1970s quilt directed us to "Become civilized, gain knowledge, study science." Finally, in the most recent quilt, made in the late 1980s, we contemplated love: "The spring has arrived with the peach blossoms." These slogan-laden quilts cannot be incorporated into an ahistorical narrative of feminine culture across the ages. They are rooted too firmly in a history of socialist politics. They move from the Anti-Japanese War and the anti-imperialism of the socialist state's early years to the mass politics of the Cultural Revolution and the subsequent rejection of Maoism. The invocation of science and love—the dual ideological frameworks of economic-reform China—succinctly captured the dramatic transformations of the previous decade. These quilts cannot be relegated to a "domestic" realm that is bounded and separate from a "public" one. Nor can they construct an essential femininity. A women's culture, perhaps, but one that is necessarily entangled with the state.

The next room furnished a sharp contrast with the first: it was filled with brightly colored paper-cuts highly stylized in the form of naive realism. Political slogans disappeared, replaced by what appeared to be unaffected portraits of women's daily life. Yet these were not the portraits of an Everywoman. Li Xiaojiang explained that these paper-cuts were the artwork of one Ku Shulan, who had gained national fame as the "scissor cutting lady." They told her life story, which Li Xiaojiang expanded into a story about women's oppression and women's creativity. "She ate much bitterness," Li said, echoing the narrative form of socialist stories about class oppression. But Ku's story as told by Li shoved class aside. "Her husband beat her constantly." In her pain and loneliness, and because she did not know how to write, Li continued, Ku Shulan poured out her bitter story in little cuttings. Little, indeed. Upon closer inspection, each figure revealed a pasted montage of myriad, infinitesimally tiny pieces the size of a teardrop: the figure of a woman alone, dragging a pail of water; a woman alone, with paper tears trailing down her face; a woman sending her child off to school.

The paper-cuttings exhibited "women's complaints." They artfully expressed women's lack of power, marginalized status, and silence. By reenacting daily scenes that follow in the wake of violent oppression, this art and its public display dislodged the constraints on women's speech. Such a public display made women's bodies, affect, and desire visible. Feminist discourse in the United States argues that women are always associated with their bodies and emotions and that this association makes women and racialized subjects visible in the public sphere, simultaneously obscuring the abstract invisibility of the white male body (Morrison 1992, Pateman 1989, Ryan 1990). In China, by contrast, Li Xiaojiang and other postsocialist feminists decry the invisibility of women's bodies, at least those bodily experiences that are distinct from socialized labor. They contend that this invisibility keeps women tied to an outmoded state feminism. It also makes it impossible for women to speak about new forms of devaluation they experience. This exhibit of a cutout life literally cut out the female body to highlight its presence and affect, to make it unmistakably visible. Displayed in a women's museum, it participated in constructing a femaleness that women would recognize but also interpret as distinctive from the Maoist political imaginary of woman — a femaleness developed on its own terms and in its own cultural representations.

The following room swerved from the pictorial to the textual. The artifacts were precious examples of "the women's script" (*nüshu*). The women's script garnered much lively intellectual interest from feminists and nonfeminists, linguists and social historians alike. It appears to be a unique example of a Chinese phonetically based writing system, written only by women to other women and only in one small rural area of Hunan province.[7] The women's script served before the socialist revolution as the means by which young women created non-kin social ties — girlhood couples and sworn sisterhoods. The conventionalized poems written in the women's script — often meant to be sung — express lasting attachments and lament the loss of one's coupled friend to marriage (Silber 1994). As a sociotextual phenomenon, the women's script was a language of communication the men did not share. Yet it was not clandestine; the girlhood couples and sworn sisterhoods could also be a conduit for arranging a woman's marriage. The antipathy toward marriage they often express was both culturally appropriate as well as an articulate depiction of unhappiness.

The museum room was filled with the striking black fans on which these poems were written, as well as the manuscript collections that managed to preserve the writings from their suppression under the socialist regime. Pictures of the two surviving script writers, elderly women in their nineties, also graced the walls. But this exhibit did not tell a strident story of resistance to patriarchy. Little in the exhibit hinted at laments about marriage; the writing itself was the focus. The display told rather a celebratory story of recovering the strands of women's creativity from underneath socialism.[8]

The last two rooms of the museum addressed women's reproduction and minority women. In one room, black figurines, in the shape of a uterus or penis and uterus together, lay chastely side by side in a glass casing. They were meant to serve as fertility symbols. Li Xiaojiang interpreted these figurines as deriving from early worship of the fertility goddess, Nüwa. The video that accompanied this display recaptured the early importance of female goddesses as well as the contemporary significance of Nüwa. We watched as multitudes of women and men entered the cave in the southwest where Nüwa's spirit is said to reside, praying to her for the gift of life.

The final room displayed so-called minority women's lives through their "typical" costumes. It held the various colorful costumes of women from the Miao and Dai groups of China. Wedding outfits, everyday costumes, waist belts, aprons, and multicolored caps with tassels adorned the walls. Their presence in the museum was meant to signal an inclusiveness among women in China that broke down the rigid binary dividing designated minority peoples from the Han majority. In the museum, they represented heterogeneity. Yet exhibiting minority women in this fashion separated them off from the general category of woman produced in the rest of the museum. Their use as a sign of heterogeneity inadvertently served to highlight their distinctiveness from the Han majority (see Schein 2000). Here, then, the women's museum jostled uneasily with differences within the category of Chinese women. The gaze structured in this last exhibit was that of Han women examining otherness. Minority women were made to stand for the difference that allows Han women to remain the unmarked norm.

GENDER PERFORMATIVITY

Mimesis and alterity characterized the women's museum. The exhibits did not merely reflect a reality of women's lives in Chinese society. They mimicked a fantasy of women that resides in the Chinese feminist imagination. Returning to the image of the ruins of socialism, one could argue that this mimicry was produced with the implicit alterity of state feminism as the unexhibited background. Postcolonial theories intimate the decentering potential of mimesis: the emulation of the colonizer by the colonized is never an exact replica, nor can it ever be an exact replica, for the dominated subject must also always stand for difference (Bhabha 1994, Taussig 1993).[9] Thus, mimesis unexpectedly throws the project of domination into a skewed trajectory. By turning these theories of mimesis slightly, one can discern that the mimesis involved in the women's museum did not, with the important exception of minority women, produce the alterity of the other but, rather, constructed the self: women making the category of women visible for other women.[10] Yet this self-mimicry also subverted the woman of state feminism. The politics of subjectivity at work here resembled the cultural productions of marginalized peoples in the United States rather than anthropological museums of natives. The numerous theatrical and artistic endeavors of lesbians and gay men come to mind, with their productions of self-images meant to support alternative lives, while also mocking dominant gender norms.[11]

Indeed, queer theory, rather than anthropological critiques of museums, might enable better insight into the radical potential in the women's museum. Queer theorists have effectively argued that gender is nothing more nor less than a contingent performance. Theories of gender performativity have arisen out of lesbian and gay communities in the United States because these communities have developed a remarkable self-reflexivity about transgressive behaviors that have marginalized them as abject or perverse but which simultaneously offer them enormous liberatory potential. Drag queen performances, transvestism, butch-femme relationships, and transsexuality have been extended in theory and practice to reveal the lack of ontological substance in sexual identities and therefore the contingent fabrication of gender. In an early ethnographic formulation, the anthropologist Esther Newton (1972) studied gay men who were theatrical drag performers. After following them in their lives both on and off stage, Newton concluded that it was not at all clear when these men were performing gender and when they were not. For they performed as "men" in public life off the stage with the same amount of artifice they used in their performances as "women" in the nightclubs. Therefore, Newton concluded, they implicitly subverted the belief that gender identity was "inside" the person while the "outside" was mere artifice. Instead they demonstrated that the "substance" of gender lay in the performance itself.

Later extensions of Newton, including most famously Judith Butler (1993), unsettled even further the cultural determinism and the naturalism that still resided in much gender theory. To appreciate the subversive qualities of the women's museum, it is worth rehearsing these arguments. Butler and other queer theorists have shown that gender is constituted not in a Durkheimian manner, by a static set of norms or by impersonal forces lodged in social institutions, but in reiterative practices in speech, writing, and bodily activities that "cite" powerful discursive norms that both produce and constrain gender identity. Far from a matter of free will, however, these performative practices are compelled by the compulsory nature of normative demands for identification. These demands include, but are not limited to, threats of exclusion and abjection. Gendered subjects find themselves compelled by a matrix of power relations to continuously produce their gender identities by assimilating to a heterosexual symbolic. Over time, this process produces the effect of a fixed boundary between the feminine and masculine while simultaneously, because of its very reiterativeness, opens up instabilities in the construction of gender. Such a notion of performativity also disrupts the sex/gender binary, in which "sex" is said to represent the natural basis upon which the cultural norms of gender are imprinted. In American culture, where gender and sexuality mirror one another (e.g., an "effeminate" man is assumed to be a homosexual), gender performativity produces both sexed body and gendered identity.

Through this lens, one might begin to appreciate that the women's museum in China fixed a category of woman, but only to hold it in place long enough to enable women who came to the museum to perform their gender in the mirror of its production. The category of woman proved to be elusive and wildly transitory in the post-Mao social imaginary. By fabricating it in a museum, Li Xiaojiang facilitated women's ability to hold onto the images even after leaving the museum. For these images did not have the ephemerality of a performance; their fixity in the museum created enough of a sense that the images might last for women to grasp them firmly. Li thus created a political tool for women to challenge state feminism as well as the new devaluations of women ushered in with economic reform.

The museum gathered meaning from but also challenged the allegory of postsocialism. The exhibits assumed a social category, "woman," has a relevant and expressive cultural existence, that quilts, paper-cut images, and fertility symbols meaningfully belong together as demonstrative of "women's" creativity. Yet the museum's performative aspect implicitly drew attention to the constructedness of gender and to the need for those who have experienced social life as women to transgress, through a display of gender, the norms of state feminism.

In the early 1990s, as Deng's Southern Tour began to fast-track what eventually could be called neoliberal policies, Li Xiaojiang's women's museum struggled for existence within multiple contexts: state feminism, nonstate gender politics dominated by the equation of a masculine self with a humanist self, and a transnational network of cultural communication that marginalizes postsocialist feminism. As an outspoken and controversial feminist scholar, Li Xiaojiang intervened into the naturalization of power by both the state and male intellectuals who placed themselves in opposition to the state. In both her museum and her writings, she called into question the imagined visions of post-Mao modernity that infused so much of the self-conscious sense of lack pervasive in China in the early 1990s. Her performative construction of gender in the women's museum also reflected her refusal of the West as a measure of Chinese women's progress. The East-West border and the orientalism that continues to sustain it have long occupied a key place in China. The West has represented the imperialist enemy, the source of wealth and technology, and the home of diasporic Chinese intellectuals. It is the space of resistance because the state has deemed it so. In the early 1990s, as Deng invited greater foreign investment into China, both conservative government cadres and cultural nationalists revived a colonial-era distinction between Western science and technology, on the one hand, and Western culture on the other. They welcomed the former while castigating the latter for its polluting effects. Both officials and citizens were nonetheless poised for China to recuperate its deferred reach of modernity and its world status as a formidable, nondependent player in the neoliberal game.

In the women's museum, Li Xiaojiang destabilized these overlapping politics. By moving across the state-oppositional intellectual boundary, she simultaneously displaced the East-West orientalism of this opposition. The displacement occurred through her construction of a third border: that of sexual difference. She created that border as much as it created her. She brought it into visibility. It was a powerful site from which she rejected incorporation into the unitary identities of the state, humanist man, and Western modern woman. Neither state cadres nor masculinist intellectuals could claim her while she stood on that border. Neither discourse they produced accepted women as social subjects. The political analysis that Li Xiaojiang developed in theorizing the position of women thus existed unstably within the Chinese body politic. For she refused the statist revolutionary nongendered woman. She rejected as well the state's version of economic reform with its embrace of all necessary inequalities. But she retained a collectivist, structural approach to social life. Li theorized women as a collective category. The experiences of this group, for Li, are defined by the economic structures of social life, not by individual uniqueness. She therefore refused the humanist embrace of unique desires and talents, for this was precisely the argument that left women in the space of nowhere, or "elsewhere." And humanists refused her, because any discussion of women's liberation smacked of the Maoist politics that had hounded intellectuals for thirty years.

Finally, she turned to Chinese history rather than the West for a sense of possibilities (not just negations). The masculinist politics that transnational capitalist and cultural productions brought to China operated counter to her desire to theorize women into existence. Western feminism was equally useless to her project. For Li Xiaojiang, Western feminism is a struggle for rights and equality. Since the socialist revolution, she pointed out, Chinese women have long had these rights. They have not led to liberation.

The destabilization of the East-West border zone in China might lead one to think of Li Xiaojiang as a postcolonial subject. But she certainly does not pursue the postcolonial politics of Achille Mbembe, with his descriptions of the postcolony as filled with banality, vulgarity, and self-consuming violence (2001). Nor does she follow the postcolonial arguments of Homi Bhabha, who has analyzed the ambivalent disarticulation (but never complete separation) of colonial representations through the mimicry of colonial subjects (1994). Nor, finally, is she a postcolonial critic like Gayatri Spivak (1999), for whom the history of the third world never stands outside colonial epistemic violence. Li Xiaojiang, I would argue, is not a postcolonial subject at all. Her struggle is an engagement not with Western colonialism but with the representational and practical powers of state socialism and postsocialism. In this struggle, she has highlighted the importance of subjectivity and identity for the construction of public spaces that might foster political discourse not wholly dominated by the state. She has reminded us that engendering this space could lead to liberation or oppression. Ignoring gender, on the other hand, can only pick up where state socialism has left off.

Perhaps it is fitting of Li Xiaojiang's constant border crossings that the women's museum did not remain in existence long enough to fix women into an empty, homogeneous past or an outdated future. Instead, its closure allowed women to remain in the "vanishing present" (Spivak 1999). Rather than create a unified vision of China, Li Xiaojiang has been committed to tracing its contentious boundaries, concerned about whether women will ever be full subjects of the nation.

3

Qualities of Desire

Imagining Gay Identities

B y the latter half of the 1990s, the public culture production of "desiring China" became more expansive and abundant than earlier in the decade and more self-consciously about encounters with multiple geopolitical others. The art of longing to which *Yearnings* had lent such force and the singular postsocialist gender identity that the women's museum had crafted both became attached to and subsumed by multiple desires and nonsingular, nonnormative gender identities. Government policies after Deng's Southern Tour had created dense nodes of transnational investments in China's major cities along the eastern and southern coasts. Emphasis on consumer and mass culture created new experiences of urban life, even as the gap between rich and poor widened significantly. Peasant migration to the cities increased as infrastructure projects to build urban cosmopolitan environments took off. An emergent bourgeoisie constructed gated communities, initiating new forms of postsocialist class segregation. The Chinese state increasingly embraced the neoliberal policies of international institutions such as the WTO to salvage a "desiring China" from the contradictions that had emerged so explosively in the June 4th movement. How did public culture join their stagings of sexual, material, and affective self-elaborations to these state and corporate policies? How did they make these various desires seem like they cohered with one another? Conversely, how did government reform packages and corporate strategies translate into popular desires? This chapter and the two following ones address these questions by tracing the overlapping public culture phenomena of emergent sexual identities, the constitution of "cosmopolitanism," and legal debates about the proper regulation among interest, desire, and passion. This chapter focuses on the emergence of gay identities. As I argued in the introduction, lesbians and gay men provide both a compelling and ambivalent challenge to postsocialist constructions of desire. Discussions among gay men about how to be properly gay signified a transnational dialogue that translated the terms of cosmopolitanism and quality (*suzhi*) into one another even as it divided gay men along urban/rural and class lines.[1] Aspirations to cultural citizenship in the new "desiring China" compelled gay men to domesticate the meaning of transcultural practices of sex, desire, and sexual identities. As with my other trackings of "desire" in China, my methods for interpreting the emergence of gay identities were part serendipity, part reflective of the implications of my own presence in China, and part the very means by which I came to understand the critical importance of public culture for life in post-Mao China.

In the mid-1990s, Chinese metropolises witnessed a veritable explosion of people who call themselves gay.[2] Semi-public spaces marked as gay proliferated. By the end of the decade, Beijing had at least five gay bars; weekly salon discussions; a national hotline; books, magazines, and videos from abroad; conferences; and more informal gatherings in people's homes. Not a few gay men conversed with other gay men from all over the world through the Internet. This emergent gay scene is decidedly transnational. Gay men and lesbians from every corner of the world reside in China's major cities, especially Beijing and Shanghai. The influx of foreign-born residents brought not so much gay tourism, which barely exists in China (in contrast to Thailand), as gay men who came to stay. At first blush, then, it appears to be a foregone conclusion that a global convergence of people now embraces a gay identity. Perhaps Michael Warner's queer planet (1993) has spun out its inexorable prophecy after all.

The Chinese women and men who call themselves gay in Beijing have both urban and rural origins; diverse occupations, ranging from factory workers to accountants and computer engineers; educational backgrounds from high school to Ph.D.; and class positions from those who use their elite cadre parents' power to acquire for themselves a nouveau riche status to those who see themselves as "ordinary folk." A few have traveled outside China, either as tourists to the sex mecca of Thailand (in their imagined sexual geography) or as students to North America and Europe in pursuit of advanced degrees. Yet one characteristic was shared by these women and men who described themselves as gay: they were predominantly young—thirty or under. Their narrow age range meant that most of them came of age after socialism had been dismantled in China.

Perhaps the following caveat is superfluous: the argument I present here does not eschew the fact that older women and men engage in homoerotic sex, nor does it promote the idea that only in the current era do people have a desire for or engage in sexual acts with someone of presumably the same gender.[3] What was strikingly different in the latter half of the 1990s was the construction of an identity based on these acts. Listen to these remarks by Ah Zhuang, a friend of mine in China, then forty years old, who around 1995 began to call himself gay:

> [Other gay men] don't have time to talk with you. They just want a *sex relation*.[4] 'Let's find a place, hurry up and fuck' . . . For many years this problem has made my head ache. To be a *gay* they [other gay men] are not capable of recognizing what, finally, this is all about. What should one need? This [question] gives other people an especially bad feeling: [*imitating a voice of disapproval*] 'You people, all you want is a *sex relation* with other people. You aren't able to think about anything else.' So I was like that, too. But after a period of time, I didn't especially want to go [to the park]. Also, I myself thought, as I was getting more mature and more cultured (*wenhua*), that *gay* should have a culture (*wenhua*), it is a kind of culture.

The emergence of gay identities and practices in China is tied, in certain critical respects, to transnational networks of lesbians and gay men. The initiation in China in 1994 of work on AIDS, with specific outreach to gay men, by one courageous individual who was subsequently sacked by the government led to networking both in and outside China. The arrival of hundreds of lesbians from around the world at the 1995 United Nations Fourth World Women's Conference, held in Beijing, also galvanized semi-public explorations of gay identities. The opening of the national gay hotline in China in the summer of 1997 by a diverse group of Chinese and Western gay men dramatically enabled conversations across China and the world. The presence of foreign gay men and lesbians in China who both create and participate in gay networks means that the transnational quality of gayness in China is both visible and visceral.

Not all Chinese women and men who identify as gay pass through these transnational spaces. Many deliberately stay away, either because they are wary of foreigners or because they believe that these spaces are themselves tainted with unrespectability. Some find it impossible to have equal or deep relationships with foreigners. Lou Wei, twenty-five years old when I met him, had trained in business economics. We met through an American friend in China and spent some time together informally before he agreed to be interviewed. Lou Wei emphasized in the interview that foreigners use Chinese people. "If the police were to surround the [café], you have a foreigner's passport. Who takes responsibility? If, for example, they find something written on human rights, who takes responsibility? It devolves onto everyone Chinese." Conversely, not all foreign gay men who live in Beijing want to be with Chinese men. Some rarely have erotic interchanges with Chinese men. Other gay foreigners lead lives reminiscent of colonialism, occasionally engaging with native Chinese men as sexual partners but having little interest in what the encounter means for these men. This transnational scene is not, in any case, simply about bodies marked by nation and race that mingle indiscriminately. Most important, these interactions are embodied ways of performing gayness, and they entail competing notions of what it means to be gay.

Still, the temptation to conclude that a singular "global gay identity" has come into existence and that China offers one more instantiation of it appears virtually irresistible. This essay is an effort to forestall the rush toward a discourse of homogeneous global identities, or at least to reconfigure our understanding of sex and neoliberalism. My concern is at once theoretical and political. The manner in which we imagine transcultural processes of identification shapes the kinds of alliances we create—or fail to create—to address the protean forms of homophobia around the world and, in related fashion, the culturally specific normalizations imposed through sex. I begin, then, with a deliberately provocative problematic: what kinds of investments lead to the assumption that such a subjectivity—a global gay identity—exists? To address that problematic, I examine one prominent assertion of this position. I then argue that the emergence of gay identities in China occurs in a complex cultural field representing neither a wholly global culture nor simply a radical difference from the West. Rather, Chinese gay identities materialize in the articulation of transcultural practices with intense desires for cultural belonging, or cultural citizenship, in China.[5] This articulation leads to doublings in which neoliberalism is haunted by reminders of cultural difference even as desires for cultural belonging face the spectral undoing of discourses launched in the name of globalization.

Chinese gay men index neither another exemplar of a global gay identity nor mere local particularity. Transcultural processes of gay identification shape the contours of cultural citizenship in China for gay men; conversely, desires for cultural belonging shape the way in which gay men in China construct the meaning of transcultural practices of sex, desire, and sexual identities. In developing this argument, I wed Foucault to anthropology, linking questions about the relationship of knowledge, sex, and truth and the historical contingencies of sexual identities to analyses that problematize culture and space.[6] Drawing one map of a sexual "geography of imagination," to paraphrase Jacqueline Nassy Brown (2005), I hope to invert the premises of sex and globalization that have so quickly colonized our imaginations.

GAY WESTERN ORIGIN STORIES

Before turning directly to China, I clear some conceptual space for future discussion by taking a somewhat lengthy detour through arguments that assume a global gay identity. One such argument is Dennis Altman's "Global Gaze/Global Gays" (1997).[7] I address Altman not because I find his essay the most exemplary but because his position in gay politics has enabled him to garner a large audience. Moreover, I believe that we share a concern with building alliances that do not quash diversity.

Altman addresses "the emergence of a western-style politicized homosexuality in Asia" (417). His essay purports to demonstrate that the ubiquity of Western rhetoric means that many Asian gay men describe their realities and their own feelings through this rhetoric. Altman alludes to the problem of Western gay theorists and activists positing the universality of an identity that developed out of certain historical specificities. Yet this initial recognition quickly recedes as he advances the claim that the universality of gay identities is emerging most significantly among groups in Asia. To make sense of his proposition, Altman places different sex/gender orders in Asia on a continuum from tradition to modernity. While acknowledging their coexistence, he denies their co-evalness, placing the forms that are culturally marked for him into the category of the traditional and the ones that approach what he conceives of as "western-style" into the category of the modern. Altman then concludes that in Asia "self-identified homosexuals" view themselves as part of a "global community" whose commonalities override cultural differences.

For the most part, Altman invokes "modern" and "western-style" as tropes whose content is self-evident. At various points, however, he alludes to the characteristics of what constitutes a presumably universal gay identity: it contests sexual rather than gender norms; replaces the idea of male homosexuals as would-be women with new self-concepts; leads to primary homosexual relationships rather than to marriage with homosex on the side; expresses sexual identity openly; develops a public gay political consciousness; and creates a sense of community based on sexuality (422–23).

Significantly, while Altman stresses the global, he never questions the fact of globalization or how to represent it. He merely reads globalization as the spread of Western models of homosexuality. This reading allows for a contradictory conclusion. Rejecting, on the one hand, the idea that "modern" homosexuality in Asia can be understood in terms of "cultural tradition" and allowing that new gay groups in Asia will "adapt" ideas of universal discourse and Western identity to create something new, Altman concludes, on the other, that the "claiming of lesbian/gay identities in Asia or Latin America is as much about being western as about sexuality" (430).

Altman's rhetorical strategy might be reduced to a mere problem of contradiction. Yet the predicament of his argument lies more pro-foundly in the ambivalence of his desire: to assert cultural diversity and the need to respect it while also recuperating identification in a monu-mentalist history of gay identity. Conversely, he wants to further gay rights yet, in pursuing this goal, elides diversity, articulation, and al-liance with radical cultural difference, thereby occluding the fault lines of power that emerge in global gay discourses and practices. Four prob-lematics suggest themselves: the dynamics of colonial discourse that structure Altman's argument; his concept of culture; his understanding of meaning and referentiality; and finally, his vision of globalization or universalisms.

First, Altman draws lines of radical cultural difference between the West and Asia. His occasional rhetorical gestures to the contrary fade away because he has no way to incorporate them into the main framework of his argument. Altman states, "On the one hand, Asian gay men, by stressing a universal gay identity, underline a similarity with westerners. Against this, on the other hand, the desire to assert an 'Asian' identity, not unlike the rhetoric of the 'Asian way' adopted by authoritarian regimes such as those of China, Indonesia, and Malaysia, may undermine this assumed solidarity" (418–19). Asianness, or a reputed claim to Asianness, can never be more than a distraction, a power move, or a distortion from the originary truths of gayness. Gay men in Asia can be either universal or Asian but not both, even as their Asianness continues to leave them in the place of otherness to global gayness. Altman's Western origin story of gay liberation places Asian gays forever in the place of deferred arrival. This universalization of particular stories of gay liberation establishes temporal hierarchies that, ironically, forget that the West is an imaginary location that can interpret its located concerns as a world-historical origin point. For Altman, invocations of universalism, whether by Westerners or by Asians, appear to be self-evident and self-referential rather than rhetorical strategy, double-voiced dialogism, the locational politics of representation, or strategic essentialism. Martin Manalansan IV (2003) brilliantly analyzes this story as a Western developmental narrative that begins with a "pre-political" homosexual practice — the "cultural traditions" — and culminates in a liberated "modern" gay subjectivity. His rich ethnography convincingly argues that Filipino diasporic gay men in the United States "are not passively assimilating into a mature or self-realized state of gay modernity, but rather are contesting the boundaries of gay identity and rearticulating its modern contours" (2003, x). Thus Manalansan eschews what he calls the "McDonald's" notion of a homogenizing global gay identity, with its redemptive narratives.[8]

Altman's concept of culture similarly derives from colonial anthropology. One might almost say that he offers a parody of the notion of culture as timeless, bounded, homogeneous, and unchanging. Only a radical imposition of modernity from the outside seems to change these

Asian cultures. Moreover, to paraphrase Renato Rosaldo (1989), there appears to be a "stepladder" version of culture and modernity here such that the more one looks like the West, the more one sheds any markers of culture. The critique of this notion is so well rehearsed in anthropology and cultural studies that I need point out only that Altman's conception of culture is undergirded by an imperial political economy of the sign that renders meaning stable and solidly referential. We all know what people mean when they call themselves gay or engage in gay practices because there can be only one, unified meaning. This aspect of Altman's argument is especially ironic because his list of stable signs of a gay identity and his examples of a public gay consciousness are at this moment in the United States fueling an intense debate among gay men and lesbians precisely over their appropriateness for gay people.

Certainly, I do not wish to deny the coming into existence in recent years of commitments to gay identifications or gay liberation that extend beyond national and cultural borders. On the contrary, I fear that the following discussion on cosmopolitan gay life in Beijing will disappoint some in queer studies who seek a cultural logic of absolute difference — and turn to anthropologists to provide it. Anthropological studies featured prominently in gay and lesbian anthologies have often been taken up as reassurances that "we" have always been everywhere or that a dream space of possibility exists where homophobia finally meets its limits. Or they have been allowed to stand in as gestures toward difference that, by resting on the exotica of sexual practices in other places, continue to allow Western gay identities to represent themselves as the teleological self of modern sexuality. Thus, they have not decentered the universalism of Euro-American notions of what it means to be gay. Nor have they addressed relations of power that link the latter with political and cultural hegemonies. Such a project would instead emphasize distinctions forged in unequal dialogues but not in archaic isolation and unequal subject positions produced in common fields of power and knowledge. Other problems with these studies have been spelled out elsewhere, such as their inattention to meanings of gender and relations of power.[9] To move toward a study of transcultural practices, we need to emphasize the complexity of cultural production in the interactions of the West and non-West — with attention, that is, to transcultural practices and representations.[10]

We might begin by following how postcolonial scholars, anthropologists, and those in cultural studies have reconfigured the concept of culture in the last two decades. These scholars approach culture not as a set of shared meanings found in a bounded space but rather as ongoing discursive practices with sedimented histories that mark relations of power. Thus, it becomes important to attend to how, by whom, and in what context "Chinese culture," for example, is invoked—that is, to the discursive effects of Chinese culture as an object of knowledge in (neo)orientalist geopolitics as well as in specific power-saturated contexts within China. Additionally, it becomes critical to examine how people live out these imagined invocations of culture—how they are pulled into normalizing practices that establish hegemonic cultural logics kept in place by ongoing iterations even as these logics reveal traces of displacements, instabilities, and engaged resistances.

The relationship between culture and space has also been reconfigured. Rather than assume that locality is an ahistorical given—that space exists outside meaning (or that we forget the meanings given by the nation-state)—or assume that the local and the global refer to transparent spatial arrangements, we might conceive of it, to quote Brown "as the power-laden symbolization process itself: the production of frameworks for defining and debating the edges and outer bounds of processes, practices and phenomena" (2000, 342). The local and the global are both acts of positioning, perspectives rather than merely locales, used as signifiers of difference. The local, rather than a synonym for particularity, is a spatial category given meaning through specific signifying practices.[11] Similarly, the global does not exist above and beyond the cultural processes of attaching meaning to places. Far from a deterritorialized phenomenon, it has been discursively produced in various contexts and has taken on specific imaginative appeal of which we might want to be wary (see Tsing 2005).

This approach to culture and space might help us move beyond invocations of similitude versus difference in our discussions of cosmopolitan gay identities outside the West. It also moves in tandem with approaches that view gayness not as autonomous but as an imaginary site that stabilizes heterosexual identity, a "flamboyant 'difference,'" in David M. Halperin's words, that "deflects attention from the contradictions inherent in the construction of heterosexuality" (1995, 43). To comprehend sexual identities in places outside the United States, then, entails examining how they articulate with discursive productions of culture and place.

In what follows, I propose to trace not a singular global gay identity but a social process of discrepant transcultural practices. My analysis emphasizes articulation, between Chinese gay men's desires for cultural belonging in China and transcultural gay identifications, in which these men nonetheless continuously discern and imagine differences compelled by China's colonial and socialist political histories with other nations.[12] Transcultural practices resist interpretation in terms of either global impact or self-explanatory indigenous evolution.[13] Instead, they open inquiry into contingent processes and performative evocations that do not presume equivalence but ask after confrontations charged with contentious claims to power. This uneven process of constructing Chinese gay identities illuminates how "desiring China" begins to appear as if it exists as a coherent project. It further reveals how neoliberal policies become wedded to subjectivity.

CULTURAL CITIZENSHIP

To be sure, what it meant to be gay in 1990s China was nothing if not about crossing cultural and national borders. Yet to understand the transcultural nature of gay life in China, we must begin with the simple question that Altman never asks: what motivates women and men in China to seek out, with some urgency, what it means to be gay in other places? What has allowed gayness to emerge visibly in China that cannot be reduced to the presumably inexorable power of global flows of images and ideas? And what do Chinese gay men do with the representations of gayness that they receive or seek from foreigners?

The answers lie in the realm of cultural citizenship. In postsocialist China cultural belonging, as connected to practices of desire, has replaced political struggles over class identity as the site on which citizenship is meaningfully defined, sought, and conferred or denied. Cultural citizenship creates "desiring China" as a coherent entity to which one must prove one's allegiance. By cultural citizenship, I mean to highlight how citizenship, or belonging, is not merely a political attribute but also a process in which culture becomes a relevant category of affinity. It is a process of self-making and being made, of active modes of affinity as well as techniques of normalization (Ong 1999). Cultural citizenship is a rubric or trope I use to convey novel processes of subjectification and new modes of inclusion and exclusion. Struggles over cultural citizenship are contests over new schemes of hierarchical difference, over who represents the cultural competence to carry China into the future and to create wealth and power for the nation under neoliberal capitalism. Cultural citizenship also signals blurred borders with Hong Kong and Taiwan, and with overseas Chinese in southeast Asia and the West. Sex is a critical site where the normalizations of cultural citizenship are being reformulated. If the passion to pursue the meaningfulness of sexual desire propels Chinese men into transnational networks, it also lies at the heart of cultural citizenship. Cultural citizenship, perhaps more so than legal subjectivity or theories of psychological personality, establishes proper and improper sex in postsocialist China.

Throughout the twentieth century the category of sex in China was the site of cultural production in discrepant dialogue with Western power. In postsocialist China of the 1990s, various Chinese cultural producers narrated alternative visions of the universal human as well as modes of cultural belonging through the category of sex. As I described in the previous chapter, the allegory of postsocialism told a story of how communism repressed human nature. Diverse public discourses put forth the view that the end of socialism meant that human nature — whether the human nature of the neoliberal free-market economy or of gender traditionalism — had emerged to find its freedom of expression. The allegory implied the overt and self-conscious expression of a range of sexual desires that, paradoxically, both subvert and uphold normalization. In the latter half of the 1990s China has witnessed the emergence of a bourgeoisie whose quest to mark its distinctiveness and justify its wealth involve the cultivation of bourgeois bodies, tastes, rights, freedoms, and desires. This emergence, tied to a desire for postsocialist humanity, has complicated the field of sex and its normalizations, for the bourgeoisie in China hopes to overcome the colonial division of particularity versus universalism that has haunted China since the early twentieth century.

Thus human nature is one trope through which many in China hope to move beyond the belatedness that socialism represents in the post–cold war era. At times, seemingly confirming Altman's observation, gay men in mainland China invoke an unmarked universalism of gay identity. For gay men, this terrain appears to hold out great promise, as well as potential danger. The promise lies in using the notion of a gay human nature in China to forestall the installation of homophobic normalizing techniques. The danger, of course, is that fixing an essential gay identity will not eliminate normalizing punishments but will merely install more insidious techniques for carrying them out. In either case, the universal humanness of homosexuality does not preclude a concern with Chineseness, for the very emphasis on universality makes sense only in a conversation about what Chineseness might mean.

The government has no law prohibiting homosexuality per se. Under socialism, homoerotic sex, together with a broad range of actions condemned as immoral and antisocial — as well as antisocialist — was swept under the rubric of "hooliganism," or activities that involved "roaming" beyond appropriate social borders or relations. The government has excised this category partly, I suspect, because of its associations with socialism but also because sweeping social activity out of public space no longer makes sense. Thus sex, once a political crime, has been redefined as a crime against social nature. The "sex criminal" has appeared as a figure in the law and psychology, but the label refers not at all to homoerotic activity. (This figure is most often arrested for rape, exhibitionism, and voyeurism.)[14]

This absence of criminalization does not mean that gay life in China follows a carefree course. Government officials have periodically invoked "public morality" to close bars, shut down publications, and arrest people. This form of repression should not be mistaken for a special type of communist repression but rather should be seen as quite similar to what continues to happen in the United States. Police harassment, for example, often slides into garden-variety corruption. Social disapprobation is keenly felt. Finally, cognizance of what the government might do — and power always works most effectively in its phantasmic presence-absence effect — makes people careful about how to organize. The state has provisions covering anything that might be construed to threaten its state interests, including public social organizations. Yet unlike gay men in the United States, gay men in China do not face random street violence.

Cultural affinity is as compelling a project for gay men in China as for everyone else. Their invocations of a global gayness articulate with the need to place themselves within Chinese culture in temporal, spatial, linguistic, and substantive terms. I turn to three moments in which these articulations have appeared: debates about family and kinship, appropriations of linguistic terminology, and the semiotic practices of the term "quality" that have led to divisions among gay men. Each of these moments displays specific and different kinds of transcultural articulations, none of which can be reduced to a global gay identity.

Gay Kinship   It was a Saturday afternoon and the weekly salon had begun. Men and women had been drifting into the discreet café on the west side of the city for two hours. Many were Beijing residents and regulars at the salon, but each week brought a few new faces, often men from out of town who traveled to Beijing on business for one of the proliferating number of capitalist companies seeking larger networks or government favors in the capital. They learned about the salon from the national gay hotline that operates out of Beijing. Somehow everyone packed into the one-room café and by the time the discussion began there were about twenty participants, most of them young men. The gay café owner, Mr. Wu, welcomes the salon and does not mind doing business besides. Groups of three and four pored over the latest cache of magazines and books that foreigners (including myself) had brought from the United States, England, or Hong Kong, as well as information downloaded from the Internet in China. Xiaolan, an economist who holds a high-level government post and knows how to run a meeting, called the group to order. She asked everyone to introduce themselves. The newcomers were nervous, for introducing oneself is a virtual admission that erotic interest in one's own gender has propelled one into the room. (It is also an astute way to assess who might be there for other reasons.) While everyone tried to decide the topic of discussion, those who had tired of the burden of political meetings over the years continued to chat with their neighbors or rustle papers and ignore the proceedings; they wanted socializing, not serious discussion.

We settled on the topic of family. Should you tell your parents that you are gay? Should you take care of your parents by marrying and having a child? It struck me that the focus was parents — there was no mention of siblings — and I wondered if these young men were eldest sons or only sons. The need for them to carry on the patrilineal family line seemed to be the implicit cultural common sense. Before this meeting many young men who identify as gay had told me that they felt a keen responsibility to get married, not because of what others in their social worlds might think but because they did not want to disappoint their parents. They felt an obligation to have a son. I rarely heard the same sentiments from women, who seem to feel freer to assert that they will never marry.

A few men jokingly asked if anyone there knew any lesbians they could marry. Then one young man bravely began. "We should all try to tell our parents that we are gay," he said, in something of a proclamatory tone. "If Chinese gays were more open with our parents in this way, then things would improve for gay people in China." In this way, he averred, he could find more personal freedom. Immediately Ah Zhuang interrupted. Ah Zhuang was one of the "elders" in the group, as a man in his forties. Many gay men turned to him for advice or to mediate conflicts with their parents. Ah Zhuang had spoken with me many times and I knew he advocated "harmony" with one's family, which he saw as the Chinese way of maintaining social relations. "Many of you know that I have worked for a long time on the hotline," he began. "I have talked with so many people through the hotline, and they like to talk to me for hours. And many of you know that I have been called on to deal with conflicts that some of us *gays* have had with our parents." Having reminded everyone of his authority to speak on the subject, he continued. "My whole family knows I am a *gay*. But we have never discussed it. In my experience, dealing with so many Chinese *gays*, it is wrong to tell your parents. This is not part of Chinese culture. We Chinese must look after our parents and not bring them so much grief. What can be the result of telling your parents? Only grief for them. It is selfish to think only of yourself. Perhaps that kind of thing works elsewhere, but not here in China."

Wang Tao, a young academic from Hong Kong, concurred. His position was well known through his books: Chinese people should not follow the "Western" individualist, confrontational mode of being gay. Like Ah Zhuang, Wang Tao advocates creating practices of gayness that conform to Chinese culture. He regaled the other participants with stories of Chinese men who live "harmoniously" with their parents without ever confronting them with their sexual lives. A fine storyteller, he humorously depicted (in a manner reminiscent of the movie *The Wedding Banquet*) how the parents finally revealed to their sons that they had known all along. One even encouraged the son to participate more in AIDS activism!

Wan Yanhai spoke vehemently against Wang Tao.[15] A rather infamous figure on the gay scene because of his run-ins with the government, Wan Yanhai was one of the first in China to work on AIDS. In the early 1990s he had begun discussion groups for gay men about safe sex. He had also taken it on himself to hand out safe-sex information in Dongdan Park and other cruising areas. The Central Ministry of Health — his boss — fired him and made it impossible for him to get a job in the health field for some years. Wanzi, as he is affectionately called, had become even more politicized. He feels that homosexuality in China is a human rights issue.[16] In previous discussions with me he had argued that those who frame sexual practices under the sign of Chinese culture are toeing the government line. For Wanzi, Chinese culture is an ideological phenomenon open to interpretation. "Society always changes and our ideas and practices should change with it," he once told me as we were driving through Beijing in a taxi. Wanzi was upset with Wang Tao over what he considers his apolitical position, motivated — as Wanzi sees it — by cultural nationalism. For his part, Wang Tao — like many others — has accused Wanzi of wanting to bring the human rights issue into gay life in China, thereby exposing everyone to a government crackdown. During the salon discussion, Wanzi once again sparred with Wang Tao. In the West, he said, people advocated telling one's parents as a way to improve life for gay people. The outcome, he averred, was not always negative.

Xiaolan decided to cut the argument short. If we want to know what happens in the West, she interjected, we should turn to our foreign friends. There were three of us "foreigners from the West" there that day: Jorge, a young man from Spain; Miriam, a lesbian activist from San Francisco; and I. Xiaolan turned to us expectantly. Jorge declined to speak, but I agreed to say something, fearing that it would be rude for all of us to decline. I quickly decided to direct my response toward destabilizing a monolithic view of the West and puncturing the fantasy that it stands for greater freedom, even though I sympathized with Wanzi's critique of cultural nationalism. Indeed, I felt caught in the delicate economy of transcultural politics. I briefly explained that I, too, had been wary of confronting my parents, though things turned out well, and I humorously suggested that perhaps the reason was that Jewish culture — which I marked to signal difference from within the West — and Chinese culture had certain things in common.

Miriam's response was to counter my approach. She presented what she viewed as the appropriate activist possibility. "I'm Jewish, too," she began. "When I came out to my family, they were wonderful. My father was very excited, because, he told me, a woman friend of his, who I thought of as an aunt, was a lesbian, and he was happy at the thought I would turn out to be like her. My mother didn't know how to deal with it. She said, 'I'm watching television right now. Tell me later.' I have always told my parents all about my girlfriends, and they never had any problems with it."

The discussion continued, with others sharing their stories of pain or confusion or harmony. No consensus was reached on the appropriate way to reconcile one's gay identity with respect for one's parents.

One can see how compelling the project of negotiating cultural citizenship is for gay men and how it articulates with transcultural discourses in the salon arguments about family. Family is the metonym for belonging, not simply to the nation-state but to Chinese culture writ large. In China ongoing discursive productions of family are indispensable sites for establishing one's humanness as well as one's social subjectivity. For gay men to establish their normality as men, they must marry, not to prove their virility but to produce heirs. Then, too, family still provides men with moral privilege and access to social power, which is not true for women and, I suspect, is the reason it has been easier for lesbians in China to renounce marriage.

Two complications persist in the meanings of family. One is that the Chinese culture that underlies the functions of family as metonym is itself under debate even as the rhetorical construction of a singular Chinese subject underlies the assertions by several prominent men in the group at Mr. Wu's café. The distinctiveness of this subject operates in the name of Chinese culture, which in turn hinges on repeated appeals to harmony and family. Yet the investments made in the discursive production of Chinese culture varied in the café. Wang Tao, from Hong Kong, produces a Chinese culture that erases the colonial history of division between Hong Kong and mainland China. In Hong Kong, a British colony until recently, gay white expatriates and Chinese gay men and lesbians have created distinct communities that mirror this colonial division (along lines of race, language, and culture). Chinese gay men from Hong Kong bring this split subjectivity with them to Beijing. More than many gay men in Beijing, gay men from Hong Kong tended to argue for separations between "Chinese" and "foreign" ways of doing things.

Ah Zhuang, by contrast, envisions a Chinese culture that creates a homology between family and nation and, while different from Western culture, does not stand in a mutually exclusive relationship to it. The transcultural conversation in the room betrayed tensions between diasporic and transnational identifications and avowals of difference. Are gay men from Hong Kong self-identical with mainland Chinese gay men, or do they bear the mark of some kind of difference? Are they diasporic or transnational? (Even though Hong Kong has been returned to China, residents of each still need visas to enter the other.) The (other) foreigners in the salon clearly reflect a difference of some kind, but for us, too, both identification and difference are not as stable as a global gay identity might lead one to assume. The undecidability and slippage in the term "Chinese culture" are dramatically evident. Contradictory normalizing forces—the need to assert culture, harmony, and family and the need to disavow the instabilities in such seemingly transparent assertions—enter into the fashioning of this figure.

The second complication is that a certain unintended political irony characterizes this subjectivity. Under socialism, the state had dedicated itself to a revolution that split the Chinese subject along agonistic class lines that overrode kinship obligations and, especially during the Cultural Revolution (1966–76), encouraged youth to denounce their parents. Under socialism, then, Chinese culture was not a relevant category of affinity. When invoked, it often served the purposes of repudiation. The family continued as a social force in constituting someone as a social being but it did so in a different form: the inheritance of one's family class label. Yet invocations of culture in the salon tended to be ahistorical—or, rather, as in China at large, to disavow that history and thus reveal its own historicity.

The salon discussion implicitly rests on an economy of sex and sociality that is distinct from an economy of the closet. Verbalizing one's gay identity to one's parents poses a dilemma less in a metaphysics of psychologized sexual subjectivity than in a social diacritics of face and status. This is not to support the assertion that in China the psyche is irrelevant and certainly not to affirm the colonial denial of depth in Chinese humanity. The discursive production of the psyche in China proceeded apace throughout the twentieth century, especially in urban areas in the 1990s. Nonetheless China does not have a history of Christian pastoral care or confessional therapy. The speak bitterness sessions of the socialist revolution and the self-confessions of political wrong-doing during the Cultural Revolution resembled Western modes of confession but did not indicate a separable, inner aspect of the self at the heart of these confessions. Rather, such confessions pointed to wrong-doing or perversity in social relationships or through a person's entire political life.

The relevance of "face" is not that it constructs an antinomy of surface and depth but that it marks the relevant boundary that articulates the self in social life (Zito 1994). There are two aspects of face: *lian*, referring to physiognomy, the fundamental layer that all human beings have, and *mianzi*, indexing the social layering on top of *lian*. Both *lian* and *mianzi* depend on interactions with others for their construction. But *lian* tends to be an all-or-nothing aspect of the self, while *mianzi* can expand or contract, depending on one's social status. Indeed, *mianzi* is indispensable to social status, and if others take the former away from someone, as they are able to do, they simultaneously unravel the latter. Thus, the economy of face and status means that gay men shy away from telling their parents that they are gay not because of an underlying antinomy of secrecy versus truth but because they fear that they will take away their family's *mianzi*, and with it their own humanity. In this regard, sexual identity is not about the existence within the self of a separate sexual domain that is a constitutive principle of the self.

Linguistic Appropriations of Affinity   If debates among gay men about Chinese culture and family highlight the importance of cultural citizenship that is at once transcultural, diasporic, and not so much local as located specifically in China, then the linguistic heterogeneity of terms for gayness equally exemplifies this complex terrain for an identity that refuses the opposition of global and local.

A compelling irony by which gay men offer up forms of identification to gay men and lesbians not simply in China but also in Hong Kong and Taiwan occurs through their appropriation of the term *tongzhi* (comrade). Indeed, the appropriation originated in Hong Kong. Chou Wah Shan, a Hong Kong sociologist, explains:

> The word [*tongzhi*] . . . has very positive historical references . . . After 1949 [when the socialist government came to power] *tongzhi* (comrade) became a friendly and politically correct term . . . as it

refers to the most sacred ideal of a classless society . . . Since the opening up of the market economy of China . . . the term has dropped its popularity . . . now giving way to a more capitalistic and individualistic way of using personal names . . . It is a telling point that as Hong Kong approached 1997, *tongzhi* adopted the most sacred term in Communist China as their identity, signifying both a desire to indigenize sexual politics and to re-claim their cultural identity. (1998)

Many gay men in Beijing have adopted this term since it was introduced by those from Hong Kong and Taiwan. They use it interchangeably with the English term *gay* and the Chinese medicalized term for homosexuality, *tongxinglian* (same-sex love). The interchangeability of these terms speaks of the fraught moments of identification and division that occur both diasporically among three political antagonists each of which sees itself as representing Chinese culture (Hong Kong, Taiwan, mainland China) and transnationally, across novel forms of sameness and difference produced out of neo-orientalisms in rhetorics of globalization. The term *tongzhi* can signal an emphasis on a characteristic Chineseness but can also slip into inclusion of Western foreigners and thus into universal applicability. *Gay* can begin as a gesture toward universal identification but can also pinpoint gay people in China. *Tongxinglian* indexes a conversation with people outside gay networks. Although the term "queer" was not used in mainland China in the late 1990s, it had become popular — transliterated as "qu er" — in Taiwan, where it does not evoke the history of abjection that it does in the West. Consequently, it has been taken up to refer to a broad range of transgressive possibilities, including the rearrangement of racial-ethnic hierarchies in Taiwan. In the last several years, however, Cui Zi'en, a prominent gay filmmaker and novelist in mainland China, has tried to displace the term *tongzhi* with the term "queer."[17] He explained to me his views one evening as we sat watching his films. *Tongzhi* normalizes gay desire as much as *tongxinglian*, he stated. It leads gay men to try to be good citizens of the state.

Qualities of Desire   The issue of *suzhi* (quality) is pervasive in discussions among gay men and the society at large. The term indicates a broad-ranging semiotic politics in China. It arises in discussions about population control and desired kinds of children (Anagnost 1995), about neoliberal capitalism and the kind of Chinese subject capable of making wealth, as a way to constitute proper bourgeois subjects, and to mark the divisions between urban and rural (Yan 2003a). Having heard the term at several salon discussions, I turned one day to Lou Wei to ask what it meant. He said:

> It's a sweeping idea. It means your level, for example, your family environment, ever since you were a little child growing up, your educational environment, the people you have come into contact with — these lead you to become a kind of person. [It means] how you interact with people, how you talk. Then people will have an evaluation of you. For example, there a lot of people from the countryside who come to the city to work. Perhaps one of them is gay. He goes to Dongdan Park because he needs to survive. He isn't willing to rely on his labor to earn money — he goes this way to ask for money. A lot of people have a hard time accepting this . . . because homosexuality is a kind of culture (*wenhua*). You meet people and you want to be able to communicate with them, to talk with them, including sexual communication. But once you bring money or materiality into it, you have polluted it.

When gay men use the term *suzhi*, they do so most often to express displeasure with or anxiety about male prostitution for men. Indeed, one heated debate among gay men in Beijing is what to do about males referred to (in English) as *money boys*. Gay men who have legal residency in Beijing assume that money boys come from the countryside and that they pollute city life with their transgressions of the social divisions between masculine wealth and masculine love, between urban propriety and rural excess, and between proper and improper expressions of gay identity. The passion focused on this issue draws its significance from the cosmopolitics of China. Money boys and the question of what "quality" will be ascribed to gay men if they are confused with money boys — or if homosexuality becomes symbolically associated with male prostitution in the popular imagination — connect an emergent bourgeois subjectivity, the proper expression of sexual desire, and a transnational capitalism that makes Beijing the object of transnational interest and the subject of a network of transnational bourgeois cultural life. *Suzhi* divides gay men even as it is used to exclude them from proper Chinese cultural citizenship. *Suzhi* means that the category "Chinese gay" is also based from its inception on exclusions. The primary exclusion of money boys signifies a rejection of the rural. Many urban-born gay men have anxieties, paradoxically, about exploitation by rural migrants and associate money boys with rurality (and also with effeminacy, since in their view acts of prostitution effeminize men). Thus, *suzhi*, like discourses of family and Chinese culture and like various linguistic terms of self-identification among gay men, imbricates desires for proper cultural citizenship and transcultural discourses, in this case those that constitute class subjectivity. The following scene is one example of this articulation.

Many had gathered for another weekly discussion at the salon. There was no particular topic but at some point the issue of *suzhi* arose. Several gay men declared it to be a serious problem that plagued gay life in Beijing, because it made it difficult to know where to hang out and how to meet the proper people. There should be *suzhi* requirements, one man stated, for letting people into these places. Xiaolan, the government economist, got fed up and responded: "Well, I'm not sure what you mean by *suzhi*. Take me. I'm someone of low quality. I think all of us low-quality people should form a group and talk about our problems being low-quality. Then all of you who are high-quality can form your own group. Then you can come and visit our group and learn about what it is like to be a low-quality person. Then we can have some mutual discussions." Xiaolan had left the meaning of "low quality" vague, perhaps to provoke a more pointed discussion of which people were meant to be excluded. The perplexity that Xiaolan's irony caused effectively ended that discussion.

Over several years during the late 1990s, I met men whom others designated as money boys. Several whom I met in Dongdan Park in downtown Beijing were clearly soliciting sex in the more conventional manner one might associate with prostitution. But others were more equivocal about the meaning of their sexual activities. Zhuang Zhuang and I met one afternoon in Starbucks. He was then twenty-six years old. I had been introduced to him through Zhang Yi, a gay friend then involved with a Chinese American lawyer living in Beijing. Zhuang Zhuang was more than happy to discuss his sexual prowess with me. He relished telling stories of the numerous men, especially foreigners, who had invited him back to their rooms. But when the conversation turned to the relationship between sex and money, Zhuang Zhuang was adamant that he was not a *money boy*. He insisted that he never demanded money for sex, instead allowing the other man to decide whether he was pleased enough with Zhuang Zhuang to give him a gift. Zhuang Zhuang appreciated receiving gifts. But he placed this relationship between sex and gifts in a heterosexual economy of exchange not unlike that of girlfriends and wives. Ironically, such a model had only recently been reintroduced in China after nearly forty years of socialism in which all women were taught to have public work lives.

Ah Mo held a similar interpretation of his sexual life. Ah Zhuang had introduced me to Ah Mo one evening after I said I was interested in meeting money boys. He brought Ah Mo to my room and said I should feel free to ask him anything. Ah Zhuang said he, too, would stay because Ah Mo's working-class Beijing dialect might be difficult for me to understand. Ah Zhuang, a highly educated doctor, also thought that Ah Mo might be rather inarticulate. But as I began interviewing Ah Mo, Ah Zhuang repeatedly interrupted, rolling his eyes and angrily accusing Ah Mo of lying. Ah Mo never contradicted Ah Zhuang, who managed to make Ah Mo fairly tongue-tied. It turned out that Ah Mo had lived with Ah Zhuang for several years until he had left him for a wealthy French man. To Ah Zhuang, this behavior clearly marked Ah Mo as a money boy, who only goes after men with the means to support him. But Ah Mo had a different explanation. One evening we ran into one another at a gay bar when Ah Zhuang was not around. Ah Mo approached me and began to describe how he saw his life. He explicitly compared himself to wives, those who need and deserve their husband's financial support. The French man was teaching him how to drive and helping him to better himself. Some years later, Ah Mo left with his lover for France, only confirming Ah Zhuang's view of him.

DISCREPANT TRANSNATIONALISMS

If the passion to pursue the meaningfulness of sexual desire lies at the heart of creating cultural citizenship, the same passion propels some Chinese gay men into transnational networks. Cultural citizenship, as I argued, is constructed by articulating desires for cultural belonging, including invocations of universality, with transcultural ideas and practices. We can now return to the more self-conscious moments in which the transnational terrain of gay networks comes into existence in Beijing and view it not as an exemplar of a global gay identity but as a rich, contested field of diverse ways of imagining gayness. The foreign men who move in and out of gay networks in Beijing are from the United States, Canada, England, France, the Netherlands, Mexico, the Dominican Republic, the Philippines, Malaysia, Ethiopia, and Russia, as well as Hong Kong and, occasionally, Taiwan. They come on business, as students, or as representatives of international nongovernmental organizations. These spaces both reflect and exceed the hegemony of Euro-American sexual identities. They are both contingent and overdetermined, both discrepant and invoked as if gayness were universal.

One might describe Chinese lesbians and gay men as doing anthropological work in Beijing on what it means to be gay in other places, not so much to construct a singular global identity as to place Chinese gayness within transnational networks. This work of locating sexual identity means forming historical divisions at one moment and revoking them in another. Thus the importance of transnational networks in China lies in their production of spaces of identifications, rather than of identity, in the sense that Diana Fuss (1995) distinguishes those terms.[18] Chinese gay men trace the unequal contours of various self-fashionings of gay identities that offer them the occasion to engage in debate about the best way to fashion their own identities. While "Western" modes of gay identity might predominate, the mode that Westerners bring with them is by no means homogeneous. Moreover, as I have indicated above, "Western" models of gay identification mingle with diasporic identifications and divisions among Hong Kong, Taiwan, and mainland Chinese gay men. Finally, men from elsewhere — Latin America, Africa, Southeast Asia — are viewed neither as exemplary of their cultural locations nor as models to follow. This fact, too, is tied to China's colonial and socialist histories, which have occasioned the force wielded by certain global identifications over others.

For example, several gay men and lesbians from the United States and England who live in Beijing have been prominent in advancing an activist agenda. Jamie, a twenty-eight-year-old from England, originally came to China to conduct his Ph.D. research on sexually transmitted diseases and the semi-underground private health system in China. In England he had been active in queer street actions and had taken up the study of Chinese serendipitously. Jamie remained in Beijing to research AIDS for a foreign development agency and was a central figure in maintaining the gay hotline. Sally, a twenty-seven-year-old also from England, had studied Chinese since she was thirteen and worked for the

United Nations in China. One of the first to organize bar gatherings, she was willing to be outrageously and publicly a lesbian. Sam, a Chinese-American who was active in the United States fighting the ban on gays in the military, lent his home for parties and meetings. He moved to China to help his father's business. Others, such as Miriam and myself, consistently brought videos, such as *The Life and Times of Harvey Milk*, which describes gay life in San Francisco.

These foreigners have brought with them a certain imagined way of enacting a gay identity. It presumes that gay men ideally have relationships with other gay men, even as sexual desire for a variety of men is seen as natural; that gay identity therefore refers to all forms of homoeroticism; that sex lies at the crux of one's identity; that for this identity to signify, others must know about it and recognize it in public space; that one builds community around sexual identity; and that this community supersedes other forms of community. Yet Jaimie and a few other Western gay men also playfully displayed drag queen behavior, deliberately and self-consciously destabilizing gender dichotomies. Moreover, Jaimie felt it was inappropriate to hold public demonstrations demanding gay rights. China, he explained, changed him, not the other way around. Sally argued forcefully for acceptance of bisexuality. Sam felt strongly that his desire to become more Chinese made it impossible for him to represent one side of an East-West divide. Thus those from the West by no means presented a homogeneous version of gay identity.

Nonetheless, both the activism of these foreigners and the prestige and cultural hegemony already accorded to the United States in China make the interest in some form of identification compelling. But Western gay identity did not enter China simply as an unimpeded flow. Whether or not we want to argue about the extent to which these individuals might embody discursive formations, the fact remains that gay men in China view them as at once idiosyncratic and representative of Western culture. Where the dividing line between these categories is drawn depends, again, on the matter of cultural citizenship. Jaimie's drag queen behavior was regarded as idiosyncratic, since it transgressed respectable performances of gayness in China. But his desire to further people's sense of normality about being gay was completely accepted.

Several activists from Hong Kong who come for short visits and longer stays work in the same circles. Chinese-language books and magazines from Hong Kong have circulated in Beijing for some time. Those in

China who write about sexuality and gender, such as Cui Zi'en, also have their books published in Hong Kong. Identification with gay men from Hong Kong, as I argued above, slips between sameness and difference. The bifurcated gay identity of Hong Kong leads mainland Chinese gay men, in line with public discourse, to view Hong Kong simultaneously as a very foreign place and as connected to China — but as never simply having a self-identical relationship with China. One day a young gay man who calls himself Edward spoke to me passionately of his need to get out of China to lead a freer gay life. He recounted for me a recent gay tourist trip he had taken — to Thailand and Hong Kong. For him, this exotic imagined geography represented alluring sexual freedom.

Gay men from other places who participate in this transnational scene are not elevated to exemplars of distinctive sexual systems, even if at times they portray themselves that way. Owing to the histories of colonialism as well as current world hegemonies, these places have had scant ties to China and have not sparked the imaginations of people in China who hope for a transnational gay future. Allen, a thirty-four-year-old from the Philippines, presented himself as someone with a preference for straight men and for taking care of them, even if they were married. He explained that in the Philippines those who call themselves gay tend to find partners in married men, although these men always break their hearts. But most Chinese gay men who knew Allen did not think he represented a distinct cultural system, certainly not one that should be considered a model. On the contrary, they felt he had an individual problem. Allen had gotten involved with a Chinese male lover, whom he agonized over but felt committed to. He wanted to take care of him. Ah Zhuang cautioned Allen repeatedly that getting involved with straight men was the wrong thing to do; he should get involved only with other gay men. But Allen told me this type of orientation — gay men getting involved with other gay men — was new in the Philippines and that while the idea of it made him more proud to be gay, it was not easy for him to change his erotic desires.[19]

"Global gayness," with its assumptions about the similitude of identity, the homogeneity of values, and a sliding scale of identity development, fails to capture the intricate complexity — what Donald Donham (1997) has called "the conjugated transitions" — of gay life in Beijing. The insistence on identities that do not break down and on categories that are self-contained ignores the discursive processes of exclusion and differentiation. While the visions of many Chinese gay men in China about what it means to be gay are certainly connected to the knowledge that gay people exist all over the world, these men do not simply imagine a global community of horizontal comradeship. If the models of what it means to be gay emanate from outside China, they nonetheless construct a transcultural space by opening up a process of working them out in China. This process involves unexpected outcomes as people who bring different imaginations to their transcultural encounters contend with the way in which they will connect to one another. These transcultural encounters illuminate the construction of a "desiring China" through which gayness resonates with both Chineseness and a cosmopolitan life. They highlight how economic policies introduced into China in the 1990s did not automatically produce a linear alignment of subjectivities.

By looking beyond discourses of identity, we can consider how these categories are necessarily incomplete, how they cannot mark their own limits and thus, paradoxically, create a measure of indeterminacy. This indeterminancy haunts claims of neoliberal coherences. Moving from the global to the transcultural means moving from identity to identifications, which means toward a politics of contingent alliances rather than toward simple essences or self-identical recognition. There are more fruitful ways to understand gay identifications that decenter the universalisms of the global gay identity; namely, transcultural gay identities are crafted in ongoing processes of historical and cultural contingency. Such processes remind us that the idea that neoliberalism fully encompasses all aspects of social and economic life, that it exists as a neat package, is a fantasy that needs a lot of work to make it seem plausible, exciting, or worth pursuit. We might want to heed the words of Emmanuel Levinas (1996/1951) who urged us, in reference to other formations of identity and difference, to replace our attempts to reduce alterity to sameness with engagement in a nonsubsumptive relation to alterity, forgoing the mediation of a universal category of identity.[20] This way of imagining the emergence of gay identities in China might serve us better than the invocation of an always already global gay world.

From Sacrifice to Desire

Cosmopolitanism with Chinese

Characteristics

Cosmopolitanism" is central to the constitution of "desiring China." It serves as one of the key nodes through which sexual, material, and affective desires bind citizen-subjects to state and transnational neoliberal policies. In the previous chapter, I argued that gay men learn how to be gay by wedding cosmopolitanism with cultural citizenship. This chapter turns to the cosmopolitanism that young heterosexual women embody. This cosmopolitanism consists in two aspects in tension with one another: a self-conscious transcendence of locality, posited as a universal transcendence, accomplished through the formation of a consumer identity; and a domestication of cosmopolitanism by way of renegotiating China's place in the world.

Cosmopolitanism has been constructed in relation to what the government calls "socialism with Chinese characteristics." "Socialism with Chinese characteristics" is how the Chinese government comes to grips with tethering economic reform to neoliberal capitalism. It is the official portrait of these transformations as a coherent whole. Although the content of "socialism with Chinese characteristics" is quite distinct from Maoist socialism, its manner of attempting to fasten together economic policies, moral evaluations of social life, and the emergence of new kinds of persons closely resembles the earlier socialist articulations of power, knowledge, and subjectivity.

Within China, "socialism with Chinese characteristics" normalizes new forms of inequality, new ways to value human activity, and new ways of "worlding" China, of placing China in a re-imagined world.[1] The cosmopolitanism it produces is intimately tied to the emergence of a bourgeoisie. The dizzying economic growth of the late 1990s produced contradictory affective energies. A belief that anything was possible mingled with anxiety about the meanings of such rapid transformations, even as the material environment reflecting the rapid transition transformed the senses as it folded past and future into one another. Cosmopolitanism, then, is a site for the production of knowledge about what it means to be human in this reconfigured world, knowledge that is being embraced, digested, reworked, contested, and resisted in China. These struggles over knowledge of the world and the ability to embody this knowledge are what I refer to, playfully, as "cosmopolitanism with Chinese characteristics."

Young heterosexual women provide a site distinctive from gay men for grappling with the tension between transcending the local and re-negotiating China's place in the world. For young women embody the tension between transcendent desire and protective Chineseness. They are normalized as the mediators of cosmopolitan desire, in contrast to gay men, whose cultural negotiations continuously struggle with marginalization. Young women are pulled into negotiating the meaning of Chineseness because they are posed as the ultimate—and proper—consumers.[2] Although cosmopolitanism is often presented as an entirely new historical conjuncture, in fact "cosmopolitanism with Chinese characteristics" is similar to worldings of China that occurred throughout the twentieth century, including the Maoist world of international socialism. When people in China domesticate cosmopolitanism they also pull from this heritage. At the same time, the way they domesticate cosmopolitanism is through a series of structural dichotomies and structured forgettings that reinvent the past.[3]

These new mappings and subjectivities seem to share the major characteristics highlighted in recent discussions of cosmopolitanism (Breckenridge et al. 2002, Held and Koenig-Archibugi 2003, Nussbaum 2002, Cheah and Robbins 1998). While the range of these scholars' political vantage points on cosmopolitanism varies widely, with few exceptions they all share a tendency to take a substantive and formal approach to the question of what constitutes cosmopolitanism. "Citizen of the world" would perhaps be the most basic definition on which they might all agree, but even as some of these scholars qualify and pluralize which worlds, they are nonetheless convinced that a substantive content for cosmopolitanism can be found. Moreover, this content provides them with the possibility of being for or against cosmopolitanism. The most prolific of the recent scholars hold out progressive hope in cosmopolitanism, especially as they see it poised against the nationalisms and patriotisms that have brought so much devastation since the breakup of the Soviet Union and the end of the Cold War. While I am sympathetic with critiques of nationalism—and never more so than now—my approach to cosmopolitanism is, by contrast, a genealogical one that traces the political struggles to be counted as human in the context of neoliberal capitalism. Cosmopolitanism is constituted differentially, and thus through exclusions that return to haunt its politics. It shares the contradictions of neoliberal capitalism, both opening up and shutting down conceptual horizons. While posing as a universal category, it fundamentally depends on its concrete manifestations. Hence, the ever proliferating lists of cosmopolitanisms: vernacular, rooted, plural, religious, and so on. A genealogy of cosmopolitanism, by contrast, necessarily reveals its spatial and temporal articulations. Thus, I digress for a moment to discuss the spatial and temporal modes of that which has come to be called globalization, for I see them as providing the staging, as it were, for contemporary enactments of cosmopolitanism and, by extension, neoliberalism.

Many scholars have been swept up in the fervor of pronouncements about globalization and have drawn the conclusion that changes in China are just another instance of a deterritorialized globalization that is out there already fully formed. I would like to step back from those heady pronouncements and take another look at this thing that everyone is calling "globalization."[4]

Questions about the cultural constitution of place and locality have long been at the heart of cultural anthropology. They bear repeating because troubling assumptions about place continue to dominate recent scholarly discussions within and beyond anthropology about contemporary transformations. These discussions often assume a radical disintegration of temporal and spatial distances and a reconfiguration of localities and local subjects. These debates, reflected as well in writings on cosmopolitanism, often circle around questions of homogenization and hybridity. Formulations of this type rely on binary metaphors between the local and the global that are increasingly obfuscatory.

In their place, we might reconsider questions of locality and, by extension, cosmopolitanism, by refusing to assume we already know the content of the local and the global. Instead, what is called for is close examination of globalization as heterogeneous cultural and political process, and similarly of locality as created by the politics of placemaking. By locality, I mean not a narrow site but rather a location from which one views and experiences a world that one participates in crafting imaginatively. In contemporary theory, local versus cosmopolitan frameworks refer us to the scale and spread of social phenomena. Rather than disparaging locality as only a site for grasping the effects of neoliberal capitalism and thus as something cosmopolitanism takes us beyond, we might examine the making and remaking of geographical and historical places as that which produces cosmopolitanism and attend to the forms of agency of those who make these places. Anna Tsing (2005), for example, draws our attention to shifting, competing claims about scale (i.e., local, regional, national, global) while Jacqueline Nassy Brown (2005) describes multiple interpretations of movement. She argues that we should not take movement for granted but should ask after its meaningful construction. Cosmopolitanism today is not newly marked by "movement," only the latest version of a particular kind of movement.

Only from specific social and geographical locations can the remaking of place be apprehended and the significance of transformations in locality and thus of cosmopolitanism be effectively analyzed. The very same term, for example, "Chineseness," can denote the local in one context and the cosmopolitan in another. To carry out such a genealogy will require grappling with a paradox: to view what we might call cosmopolitanization as an overarching, universal force versus attending to the politics of representation in that portrayal. Cosmopolitanization sometimes appears as a *sui generis* social actor that makes things happen in other places. Just saying "other places" already points to the paradox. For as soon as the implication arises that cosmopolitanism is a deterritorialized force, or an unfixed force, or an overpowering force, or even a totalizing force — the place of no place — the next move should be to interrupt that image by (1) locating the specificities of placemaking and identities and politics formed through attachments to place, and (2) decentering these representations of the "cosmopolitan" and the "local" by reversing their assumed hierarchies, telling histories of unexpected locations, and capturing the ironic and compelling commentary of those people assumed to be the most "local" — treating them, in short, as representations. The paradox, then, between cosmopolitanization as force versus as representation is that it seems impossible not to hold onto both sides of the "versus." Each is wrong, or perhaps incomplete, in some fundamental way, but it is a wrongness we cannot give up at the moment. That which is invoked as "cosmopolitanism" clearly is far from being a force acting over the rest of social life. Yet we seem pulled into treating it, at times, as if it were. On the other hand, we know that placemaking — as the seeming obverse of cosmopolitanism — is a representational practice only in the strongest sense — that narratives have real potency in the world and the imaginations they suggest get institutionalized and acted on. Theorizations concerning the intersection of the local and the cosmopolitan have neglected attention to the ways social actors distinguish and mark phenomena as local and/or cosmopolitan through, for example, representations of gender, nation, race, class, and sexuality — representations which themselves have origins and dimensions (see Brown 2005). These approaches to the construction of placemaking inform my analysis of "cosmopolitanism with Chinese characteristics."

CONSUMPTION AS COSMOPOLITAN IDENTITY

I begin with a story one woman told me, Ding Yingquan. Ding Yingquan was twenty-six years old when I met her in the summer of 1999. She is a journalist for the Xinhua News Agency, China's equivalent of the Associated Press. Her job is to put out news about China for the English-language foreign press. Given the pressures of her job, Ding Yingquan had been difficult to pin down for an interview. As I have often experienced in China, she called me just a few moments before she felt she had the time to chat. That happened to be very early on a Sunday morning. I quickly dressed and met her at a place she had chosen — an American fast-food restaurant, A&W. I first explained to her that I was interested in the lives of young women in China today, especially those young women doing work that had not existed or was rare for women under socialism. I described my earlier research tracing the distinctiveness of different generations of women under socialism. I said that in recent years I had had long conversations with women who were her mother's generation about their concerns for their daughters, but that I wanted to speak with the daughters themselves. I then proceeded to my usual first question: "Do you see any differences between your mother's generation and your own?" Ding Yingquan offered me a wonderful allegory in response, striking not only for its content but its narrative genre, which is classical Chinese morality tales based on historical fables.

"I'd like to tell you an ancient story that illustrates this. May I?" she began. "There was a prominent statesman (*dachen*). He decided that he wanted to go into business and became a wealthy man. He had two sons. One son grew up with him while he was still an official and did not have a lot of money. The other was born after the statesman became wealthy. One day, the leader of a foreign country captured his good friend and sentenced him to death. The statesman was going to send his youngest son with a bundle of money to give to one of the officials there so that he would let his friend go. The oldest son objected, 'Why do you send him and not me? I am the oldest and I should go.' So the father gave his oldest son the money and sent him off. The oldest son got there and gave the money to one of the country's officials. But then he heard that the king had granted a special pardon to everyone and was going to let them out of jail. So the son quickly went and retrieved the money. But then the king changed his mind and so the statesman's friend was beheaded. He came back and the father said, 'I knew you were going to fail in this matter. You grew up poor and for you, this money is very precious. My youngest grew up after this household was already wealthy, and he wouldn't think twice about letting go of that amount of money.' "

This fable and its telling capture succinctly the kinds of transnational encounters that lie at the heart of cosmopolitanism in China. The moral of the tale is that wealth and, by association, consumption make a better cosmopolitan person. In telling the fable, Ding Yingquan traces a transition from a socialist world in which prestige rested on political power to a postsocialist world in which prestige rests on the wealth one accumulates in the market through jobs and commodities. The father knew the younger son would succeed in the delicate political matter of saving his friend because the son did not think wealth was precious. This son, by implication, was accustomed to consuming large quantities of wealth without giving any thought to waste or sacrifice, let alone issues like poverty. Another implicit moral of the tale is that the son, as a carefree consumer, embodies the perfect cosmopolitan subject, for he would have been able to handle international politics much better than his older brother, who obviously grew up under circumstances similar to those portrayed for the socialist period: extreme want, extreme privation, extreme hardship. This point is driven home by the unprecedented move on the father's part to skip over the elder son in favor of the younger one. In Chinese kinship relations, this move is tantamount to shaming the eldest son, and perhaps even disinheriting him. Intriguingly, the tale is told in a cross-gendered manner, for I had asked about mother-daughter differences and Ding Yingquan offered me a tale about fathers and sons. Implicitly, Ding Yingquan captures here a dilemma for women: in post-Mao China, it is imperative to make radical distinctions between femininity and masculinity and yet the cosmopolitan self one should embody is both implicitly nongendered and easier for men to achieve.

Ding Yingquan herself went on to explicate this classical-sounding fable for me: "For my mother, they look first at the price of everything and decide whether it's too expensive. I buy things according to my interests and my tastes. My mother often criticizes me and says that I am wasteful." Under socialism, urban women and men were required to work at a job designated by the state, though gendered divisions of labor often skewed women toward lower-paying, less-skilled jobs; women were given rights to marry whom they wanted, rather than someone their parents chose for them; and with communal landholding, the preference for sons was not as absolute as before the revolution. For both women and men, the major preoccupation was the state's class status labeling system. Just after the revolution the state assigned everyone a class label. Although not the original intention of the new socialist government, these labels became inherited. They determined individuals' access to education and prestigious jobs, and formed the basis of assessing political consciousness, a difficult thing to measure. The post-Mao transformations instigated by the state have abolished class labels, abolished state distribution of jobs and commodities, and witnessed a popular denunciation of Maoist feminism, which, as I argued in the first two chapters, is said to have emasculated men, masculinized women, and mistakenly equated the genders.

The younger women I spoke with, like Ding Yingquan, retrospectively imagine this period to have been nothing but a life of sacrifice and constraints for their mothers. Strikingly, these daughters are often unclear about the details of their parents' lives during the Cultural Revolution. The daughters' narratives of sacrifice come out of the literature known as "scar literature" and films such as *Sacrificed Youth* that captured the imagination of the immediate post-Mao years and lent a great deal of weight to the legitimacy of economic reform (see chapter 1). Indeed, the post-Mao government gave broad support to these narratives that saturated the popular landscape. This corpus of literature and film always portrayed the protagonist as a passive victim of larger forces. Perhaps not surprisingly, almost never do we find in scar literature a description of someone who actively participated in the Cultural Revolution. In this genre of literature and film, those who came of age in the Cultural Revolution are portrayed as a ruined generation, who sacrificed their lives for meaningless power games. This genre accomplished a sentimental move from one destiny to another. It generated an affective investment in what might come next.[5]

The daughters, then, imagine themselves as having within their grasp the possibility of becoming free of all constraints. But consumption, one of their measures of freedom, is not just about pleasure. It is a postsocialist technology of the self by which Chinese young women and, by metonymic association, the Chinese nation, enable themselves to transcend the specificities of place and identity and be part of the "world." Of course, in many respects, this worlding is specifically about an ideology of the American middle class and the domination of American consumer goods in the networks of globalization. Consumption is about embodiment, embodying a new self. At the heart of this embodiment is *desire*. A properly cosmopolitan self is supposed to be desirous and this desire is supposed to be open and unconstrained. What struck me most in my fieldwork was the absolute insistence on the part of everyone I spoke with that they were a desiring subject, whether that desire was for sex, consumption of various sorts, or a desire to be a subject who just has multiple desires. As with all cultural productions of desire, these desires, too, are historically and culturally specific and have specific modes of normalization and transgression at the heart of them.

As I lay out in more detail in chapter 5, "Legislating Desire," the desiring subject in China is evaluated according to two axes: one is whether the desire expressed can reduce the dangerous passions of politics to the seemingly benign interests of either possessive individualism or acquisitive consumption. This process, perhaps we could call it reification of the subject, enables the assignment of very specific value to discrete desires. It also subsumes desires under interests, defined in the narrow terms of possession or acquisition. An embrace of variegated desires in postsocialist China has been accompanied by a rejection of what have become portrayed as the dangerous political passions of socialism. This view of socialist passions as dangerous has further slid into an evaluation of all political passions as dangerous. By contrast, desires interpreted as nonpolitical are viewed as benign interests. While this opposition targets socialist passions of the past, it also can address itself to the more recent political passions reflected in the democracy movement of 1979, the June 4th movement of 1989, and the ambiguous political passions of the Falun Gong movement. For that reason, the state is itself both implicated and interested in fostering this opposition.

The benign interests have the added attraction of making China appear cosmopolitan. In revisionist history, China is portrayed as isolated and closed during the socialist period, thus accomplishing the historical forgetting of a world that no longer exists — the world of international socialism. This historical forgetting produces the felt need for China to become cosmopolitan. But there is also a felt need to find that which is distinctively Chinese. Thus, the second axis for measuring the desiring subject in China is according to whether that subject can be simultaneously a universal, cosmopolitan person but one with Chinese characteristics. How to be both cosmopolitan and Chinese at the same time? This axis of cosmopolitanism with Chinese characteristics articulates with class-inflected definitions of desire and abilities to display them.

Young women repeatedly described to me the need to cultivate a self that lacked constraints in order to express itself properly. Tao Ming, a woman then in her early thirties, who works for the *Workers Daily*, explained, as we sat in another American fast-food restaurant, Roaster's: "My mother is very frugal (*jiejian, jiesun*). That whole generation was. Very diligent (*qinlao*). They didn't treat themselves very well. They would sacrifice for others before doing something for themselves. Our generation is more selfish." By selfish, she meant literally centering on a self that is allowed to desire.

Luo Min is a woman also then in her thirties who holds a prestigious position at the Shanghai Stock Exchange. Luo Min thought women should be free, sexually as well as intellectually. She, too, placed a great deal of emphasis on the "self" (*ziwo*). She spoke about the importance of "self-realization," "self-development," "self-actualization," how the "self" needs "freedom" and reflexivity. She spoke about how the self's need for self-realization is in conflict with commitments to marriage and also to children. She said that the mother-child relationship is unequal, because the mother loves, selflessly, but the child only acts out of duty and not love. She used her own relationship with her parents as an example, how she did many things for them out of *xiaoxun* (filial piety) but did not love them as a dutiful daughter should. She would not stay by their side when it came time for her to decide where to live.

There were several aspects to these women's everyday practices that were supposed to lead to the embodiment of this desirous, consuming self who could live without restraints and thus remake the body and the social self: food, sex, fashion, and language. While in China, it did not strike me at first as an ethnographic insight that the vast majority of the young professional women I spoke with wanted to meet me in American or American-style fast-food restaurants: A&W, McDonald's, and others.[6] Only afterward did I think about the significance of our meeting places as I began to realize that the creation of a consumer identity domesticates cosmopolitanism even as the goal of such a creation is to transcend place. These spaces do not simply reify consciousness. We must move beyond Lukács (1972) to understand how these fast-food restaurants are the new Paris Arcades, the new dreamworlds of cosmopolitan consumption (see Benjamin 1999 [1972], Buck-Morss 1989). They embody the paradoxes of neoliberalism: they appear as an overarching, universal force that folds people into its dreams of a world beyond that evokes America but only viscerally. At the same time there is ready commentary in China on the politics of representation in that portrayal. This commentary only reinforces the material, sensuous folds of the environment. Paradoxically, the absence of a shared content with others in this space constitutes the promise of its universal cosmopolitanism. This fast-food environment is a world in miniature. These spaces mark a break with other identities. They are not in the least bit recognizable as something Chinese. They do not attempt to signify their presence either in architecture or the kind of food they serve. Their interior design signifies cleanliness, impersonality, and a world that can be carried anywhere. They foster the idea that you are what you eat. But the food is actually not the attraction. It's the mise-en-scène that beckons, an enclosed space of temporality where one can distance oneself from what appears antiquated, including the recent past, and where one can embrace a utopia in which political morality and its attendant dangers become superfluous. While these fast-food restaurants signify middle-class consumption in China, in part because of the cost of the food, they beckon toward the everyman figure, the flaneur. Like the flaneur, Chinese citizens seek refuge here in the crowd. But unlike the flaneur, who witnesses a scene that opens out as if onto a landscape or panorama, this mise-en-scène is protectively enclosed, a place not to see or be seen but to display one's ability to maneuver in such a space. It is a cross between an airport waiting room and a street fair. The dialectical image of the fast-food restaurant contains within its mesmerizing cosmopolitan consumption the signs of hope that the pleasures and self-modifications it promises will truly liberate China from its place in history. Thus, these sites carry one set of the sacred bundle of characteristics that make people believe they can be cosmopolitan.

Other bodily practices that try to capture the paradoxical desire to transcend locality and domesticate cosmopolitanism include sex and fashion. In the 1980s, virtually no one ever discussed sex with me. Married women told me they did not want to discuss that sort of thing with me until after I was married. In the 1990s, by contrast, the whole point for young, urban women was to be savvy about sex. Discussions of sex were everywhere in China: sexology had burst onto the scene alongside increasing attention among psychologists to novel genres of sexual abnormalities. Sex crimes became a more refined category; people searched for their sexual identities, and, as I discussed in the previous chapter, certain people began to embrace a gay identity.[7]

To be sure, sex is often about sheer pleasure. But it is also a national discourse about normality, about which kinds of citizens will represent China to the world. Many of the women I spoke with explained to me that sex is the measure of humanity, that site where we can see what is natural or unnatural for all human beings and then measure China's progress toward that humanity. Again, this discourse is not new in China; it began most vociferously in urban areas in the earlier part of the twentieth century.[8] I leave to the following chapter a discussion of the ambivalence surrounding homo-erotic desire.

Luo Min bemoaned the fact that she learned about sex so late in life and had been, in her view, too conservative in the past. "Women do not get the education they need. My classmates from Guizhou, they are all ignorant. In college, one of my classmates thought you could get pregnant from just holding hands! So you see the problem! . . . Really, the teachers themselves were not well educated in this regard, so they couldn't really teach us students anything. I had a classmate, she got pregnant and had to have an abortion. She was benighted (*yumei*). Her education back at home was like the Puritans. My parents were very strict, they wouldn't let us have anything to do with boys. That wasn't good because then we never learned how to interact with boys. We were completely ignorant. My parents never considered the issue of how there is a certain repression around sex, that it's not good to repress sex. Women then don't understand anything. Boys, at a certain age, have to express themselves sexually. At the university, I wanted to study psychology. Many women are afraid of being exposed because they are not married. They are afraid people will think they are eccentric."

It is important to avoid the conclusion that in China a simple dichotomy exists between a repressive past and a liberated present. It would be dangerously facile to accept the idea that Chinese people were actually more repressed in the past while people today are more open.

If we have learned nothing else from Foucault, as well as countless other theorists of sexuality, it is to realize that discourses of sex contain their specific forms of power. A lot of work, worry, and effort must be put into figuring out how to express the proper sexual self. The opposition between repression and liberation functions to make cosmopolitanism both make sense, by domesticating it within China's recent history, and appear desirable.

I continued the discussion with Luo Min by asking how she finally learned about sex. She offered me a striking answer: "In Beijing, the girls studying foreign languages are more open-minded. They know a lot more; they have a reputation for being casual with the boys. So I learned from my classmates who were studying foreign languages. I was studying Chinese literature, which is a much more conservative discipline. One of the girls studying foreign languages encouraged me to read about sex, to read Freud."

This response is most striking for its equation between the consumption of knowledge about sex, rather than its mere enactment, and the cosmopolitan. Luo Min naturalizes the idea that those who learn foreign languages are more open about sex. Finally, Luo Min made liberal use of stock-market metaphors to explain relationships. She spoke about "investing" in the emotions and personal relationships and the "profit" one derives from it. She compared "investment" in relationships versus in one's career and how the latter brings a bigger "harvest" or "results." She spoke of how people's lives are "mobile" and "unstable." You never know what might happen in the relationship, it could go up or down.

Fashion, too, literally signifies cosmopolitanism with Chinese characteristics. Most of these young professional urban women sported clothing with noticeable company labels on them. Ding Yingquan, for example, was wearing a shirt with "Boleno" written on it when I first met her. Boleno is a Chinese company, using an English logo. And while the Armani and Commes de Garçon choices displayed in upscale boutiques lie beyond most Chinese people's incomes, plenty of street markets exist that are stuffed with clothing made fashionable, in part, by sporting English-language labels. The fashion and its English writing are signifiers of the transcendent global consumer. Women wrap transparency around their bodies when they don this clothing. It paradoxically marks and unmarks them.

STRUCTURED FORGETTINGS

Consumption, then, is one of the key means by which urban young women, as well as other urban residents, bring cosmopolitanism into the heart of the self. By embracing consumerism as an identity, they can make claims about transcendence of place, about moving into a seemingly universal, unmarked globe, at the same time they domesticate cosmopolitanism in China. This consumer identity in China, as I stated earlier, revolves around a key tension between transcendence and domestication. This tension, in turn, is put into play by a series of structural dichotomies and structural forgettings that reinvent the past of socialism and, by so doing, allow these women to culturally construct a locality which they can leave. These structural dichotomies between past and present are central to what it means to be cosmopolitan in China today. The three main structural dichotomies and their attendant forgettings that I heard most often were between (1) consumerism and the search for wealth versus politics; (2) consumerism and the search for happiness versus kinship; and (3) consumerism and the search for freedom versus communalism.

Every single one of the young women I spoke with began our conversations with a striking, and unsolicited, statement that, at first, I thought had nothing to do with the questions I asked. Usually I began our conversations asking them to compare themselves with their mothers' generation. They all began their answers with this declaration: "I am completely uninterested in politics." Then they proceeded with what I thought was the answer to my question. As I repeatedly heard that declaration, I began to ponder its significance. This moment was an ethnographic epiphany. I realized that this declaration was not a simple means of warning me off of dangerous topics. Everyone volubly, vociferously, and satirically condemned the government's treatment of Falun Gong, for example. Rather, this assertion stressed that the passions of the self were not in the least bit directed toward the state. I eventually realized that these young women were declaring that they were completely unencumbered by the government. Recall the historical fable with which I opened this essay. The son who grew up while the father was a statesman, in a political household, knew nothing about how to handle the world, whereas the son who grew up in a household dedicated to the pursuit of wealth, after the father had left service in the imperium to become a businessman, was unencumbered by the constraints of a political self. Indeed, the main criticism of life in China that these women offered was that the self is still too burdened, that it needs greater freedom in order to pursue its meaningfulness.

When I asked Ding Yingquan a very open-ended question about the main problems in China today, she responded immediately: "First, I think they need to give people more latitude, more freedom of choice. Both in work and in marriage. My brother, he has changed his job a lot, at least ten times. He is now a legal consultant for a company. But still there is not enough latitude. If you go to college, the government pays for your education. Then after you graduate, you have to work in a government workplace, otherwise you have to pay them back for your education. And you have to sign a contract for five to eight years." Recall Tao Ming's statement that her mother's generation "would sacrifice for others before doing something for themselves. This generation [meaning her own] is more selfish." Both Ding Yingquan and Tao Ming have created an opposition between a self who desires to be flexible, to consume things, to treat jobs as if they were items for consumption and also as a means to wealth, versus a past they reimagine as one filled with constraint, sacrifice, and deprivation.

This lack of openness resulting from political interventions by the government, it seems, has also shaped people's very consciousness. Ding Yingquan expressed a common sentiment when she said: "Another problem is that people's thinking is not sufficiently open (*kaifang*). Take the people who are unemployed. Actually, they could look for other jobs that might even be better jobs, but they are used to relying on the government and they would rather do that and live on that little bit of money than look for another job." In expressing this view, Ding Yingquan marked herself as simultaneously cosmopolitan and middle class, distinguishing herself from the urban workers who have been laid off and, obliquely, the peasant migrants who form the new urban underclass.

This opposition between a past where politics equals constraint versus a future in which consumption and the pursuit of wealth means freedom is, as I said, a structural dichotomy that depends on structured forgettings. It forgets that politics once inspired many in China with a passion that gave meaning to their whole lives as well as the most menial or trivial tasks in which they might be engaged. It forgets that in their youth, many of their parents thought of politics not as constraint but as the ultimate moment in taking control of their lives and giving them more freedom, as least for a brief time. Finally, it forgets that many young women who came of age under Maoism felt empowered by the transgression of gender boundaries enabled by calls for women to participate fully in socialist construction (Wang 2001). The term "liberation" was not a cynical cover for an oppressive revolution but had its actual liberatory meaning, for some though not all.

If this generation of young women poses consumer freedom and the pursuit of wealth over and against politics, they also structure an opposition between consumerism and the search for happiness versus kinship. When Tao Ming said that her generation is more selfish—she used the term *zisi*, meaning literally "self privacy" or "unto the self"—I was not sure whether selfishness, a focus on the self, was a good thing or a bad thing for her. I asked her. Her answer implicitly acknowledged that both were true: "Yes, but there have been good changes, too. My friend and all her sisters don't want to have any children. Their mother says they are selfish." Tao Ming, in other words, thought the decision not to have children was a positive sign that women, too, can have a free self of desire as opposed to a kinship-oriented self that seemingly characterizes her mother's generation.

In story after story these women told me about their lives, their desire to be global produced a split gender subjectivity: the single, free woman versus the respectable, married woman. Women spoke of the impossibility of inhabiting this split subjectivity. In grappling with the tension between the two, they engender globalization and, by extension, neoliberalism. Luo Min, for example, explained this dilemma when she described the troubles her friends have in their marriages. "Nowadays," she stated, "women want to go back into the home. They want to find a rich husband and rely on him. Nowadays, people have a broader education, they are 'diverse' (*duoyuanhua*). With my parents, they have the traditional Chinese thinking about family, that you should form a family. But if both the woman and the man are too capable then it won't work. I have a friend. She wanted to find a husband she could lean on. So she found a husband who was a big official. But she's a very capable woman. So eventually they got divorced."

Like many other young women, Luo Min participates in a broader discourse about Chinese culture and its "traditions" that has come to the fore in post-Mao China. As I argued in the previous chapter, in postsocialist China, "culture" has replaced "politics" as the site where Chinese subjectivity is meaningfully defined, sought, and conferred or denied. "Culture" of course is a highly politicized category, but it signals something other than the politics of the Maoist period. The category of culture, rather than politics, confers affinity, signals novel modes of inclusion and exclusion, and contests over hierarchical difference. A paradoxical process takes place in the construction of this category. On the one hand, it is naturalized, as if the category had no history. This naturalization allows people to treat the socialist period as an aberration in a seemingly five-thousand-year-old "tradition" of Chinese culture. On the other hand, people continuously and sometimes vociferously debate which kinds of behaviors should be deemed appropriately Chinese.

Young women placed their mother's generation in the category of "traditional culture." Their goal, as they constructed it, was to transcend this tradition in order to become desirable, globalized subjects. Listen carefully to the explanation that Tao Ming gave me in discussing why she isn't married: "Women I have seen who are married and have a child don't lead a very good life. I think it's important to develop oneself and one's abilities. The women I know who are married have given up that possibility. They are very capable but they have abandoned (*fangqi*) their abilities. I have been very influenced by psychology, and I believe in the theory of personality (*renge lilun*). I believe that people should first develop themselves. They must have ability and then second, a healthy personality. I believe people should keep developing themselves. With my classmates who've married, I really can't talk with them anymore, we don't have much in common to talk about. They really envy my life."

But women worry, nonetheless, about how to be a sexually open woman and maintain respectability. They feel they should experience romantic love, and they construct an opposition in which they believe that their mothers married in order to have sons, carrying on the cultural practice of patrilineal succession, and that the husband was secondary in her affections. They, on the contrary, should have modern, affectionate marriages. Ding Yingquan stated unequivocally: "I think people should be able to live together before they are married. This could resolve a lot of problems, both physical and psychological. You get to know each other before marriage and you get to know what each other needs." But when I asked her if she were planning to do so, she averred that her parents did not approve and that her boyfriend did not have the courage to do so.

Young women's views of their parents' "traditional Chineseness" has been confirmed in the explosive national debate in urban areas about "the third one" (*disanzhe*). The third one refers to extramarital affairs. Older cadres in the Women's Federation made this issue one of their primary targets. They contemplated support for new legislation being discussed that would make it a crime to have an affair outside a marriage. The kind of affair imagined as deserving of punishment is that of a married man with a younger, unmarried woman. The new law poses as a protection for married women; the object of potential punishment is the young, unmarried woman, "the third one."[9]

Young women's imagined opposition between their open desires for sex, love, and happiness, which makes them properly cosmopolitan, and their mothers' experiences when they presumably married only out of kinship obligations once again reflects a structured forgetting. After all, their parents, and even their grandparents, grew up with ideologies of companionate marriage that were written into the first constitution of the People's Republic of China. The kind of revolution they fought for based itself on an ideology of gender equality that posed class identification over and against kinship identity. During the Cultural Revolution, moreover, their parents participated in movements in which many of them denounced their parents for having the wrong politics. Far from being mere subjects of a traditional Chinese culture, their parents also thought they were fighting the four "olds" of feudalism in China.[10]

The final structural opposition, with its structured forgettings, that I encountered was consumerism and the search for freedom versus communalism. These young urban women refuse the space and time of nation building and imagine themselves as transcending city, country, class, and, ultimately, China. For the young women I met, as well as for others in China, excitement about the possibilities of a cosmopolitan future includes a search for the freedom to move through space and time that their parents, they imagine, did not have. They imagine that the socialist state fixed people in place in order to regulate and stabilize social relations. Of course, there were attempts to fix people in place, such as the household registration system that drew a strict line between the countryside and the city. People in the cities were organized into work units, often though not always including housing organized by work unit. This arrangement was meant to stabilize full employment and social welfare benefits. David Harvey (2000) has argued that utopias are usually spatialized, that spatial form controls temporality, and that an imagined geography controls the possibility of social change and history. Unlike the utopias Harvey addresses which, he claims, repress the dialectic of social process, the stabilized spatial arrangement under Maoism produced the opposite. Part of the structured forgetting entailed in the imaginations of these young women is the history of the social struggles under Maoism that addressed the issue of space and place: should certain young people remain in the city or be sent to the countryside? Should urban residents remain in their work units or transfer out to other work units? It also forgets the experience of *chuanlian*: during the Cultural Revolution urban youth enthusiastically traveled everywhere to experience revolution as Mao urged them to do and to learn from the peasants and each other.

Many today have emphasized the apparatus of control and surveillance also involved in the Cultural Revolution, forgetting the other kinds of movement. Not a few of the young women I spoke with had migrated to Beijing from small towns across China. For them, one of the key ways to embody the global self is to travel across space — not, as they frame it, for the purposes of desperately seeking work or trying to move up in social status but for the purposes of pleasure.[11] The emergent bourgeoisie in China has enabled a thriving business in tourism. Cultural tourism consists in travel both within and across national borders. Domestic travel for pleasure, in contrast to travel for political goals, is supposed to indicate the truly free self, reflected not in the travel location but in the sensibility embodied in the act of traveling. These women regaled me with stories about travels to the south or the southwest of China, and also travels within the tourist circuit most accessible to Chinese people — Southeast Asia, specifically Thailand, Malaysia, and Hong Kong.

These young women have also acquired a distinctive approach to time that marks them as having bourgeois cosmopolitan aspirations resonant within the dominant imaginary of global capitalism. This temporal sensibility is no longer premised on modernist notions of linear progress. While these young women assume their lives will improve continuously and China will become more developed, they do not measure the movement of their lives across time in these terms. Just the opposite. Several of them expressed the view that they could only live from moment to moment because they had no sense of certainty about historical progress. Time under socialism had a contradictory effect: on the one hand, it was marked by a political-philosophical commitment to the idea and practice of dialectical revolution as a way to move beyond the continuities of exploitation. But the very campaigns that marked Maoist socialism, what Gail Hershatter calls "campaign time" (2002), had the effect of disrupting temporal progress, leading to a temporal effect of discontinuity. These disjunctures of campaign time taught Chinese citizens that the future is uncertain and unknowable. Linked to an imaginary of "flexibility" emanating from American versions of global capitalism, such an experiential effect of disjuncture has produced a generation whose bourgeois cosmopolitan aspirations are post-progressive. They no longer view time as that empty homogeneity that Benjamin so eloquently described as underwriting modern bourgeois notions of progress. Instead, they experience a temporal sensibility of radically discontinuous movement.

WORLDING CHINA

How is China's position reconfigured in this newly imagined world? The contradiction of transcending China to become a cosmopolitan self and domesticating cosmopolitanism within China rests, as I have been arguing, in the bodies of young women. Gay men, by contrast, cannot fully domesticate cosmopolitanism because of the ambivalence with which non-gay citizens view the extent to which gay men themselves can be domesticated. Young women literally embody Chineseness, both reproductively and as objects of desire. They thus provide the site for figuring out how to domesticate cosmopolitanism. But Chinese women, as consumers and subjects of desire, also represent the potential to transcend Chineseness. I turn to three different moments that highlight this contradiction in the bodies of young women. These moments are prescient; they are veritable histories of the present. They speak back to contemporary barbarisms and provide a warning to those who might envision cosmopolitanism as a universalism uncontaminated by alterity.

The first moment is a 1995 Chinese television movie, *Sunset at Long Chao Li*. The film tells the story of a young Chinese man who returns from studying architecture in America. He brings with him his new Caucasian American wife and her son from a previous marriage. The movie focuses on his attempts to negotiate between remaining a filial son to his father, an architect renowned in the past, and becoming accomplished in ways that the West (embodied by his wife's father, who owns a construction company) will recognize and acknowledge. Kathleen Erwin, an American anthropologist who happened to star in the movie and argued with the producers along the way about the story, concludes that *Sunset* constitutes an effort by elite men to contest images of China in the international arena. The film's producers highlighted an alternative representation that emphasizes China's global dominance, one that Erwin concludes "depends in part on reimagining the nation as masculine and (sexually) desirable" (1999, 238). This reimagining entails representing white women rather than Chinese women as the object of Chinese male desire. Erwin argues that such a representation "eclipses Chinese women . . . as symbols of the Chinese family/nation, as agents in the pursuit . . . of a transnational Chinese modernity, and as legitimate subjects in the constitution of their own sexuality and desire" (238).

The masculine cosmopolitanism Irwin emphasizes and that seems to prevail in China today provides a countervailing allegory to the ones that served as warning tales in women's engendering of cosmopolitanism. These warning tales provide the second moment. In the midst of my discussion with Tao Ming, for example, I asked her if she had spent time with foreigners. She replied very firmly, "No, I haven't had any contact with foreigners. Chinese children are really tragic (*beican)*. Because poverty chills ambition [she used an ancient scholarly phrase: *renqiong-zhiduan*]. I have another friend who found a *laowai* husband [*laowai* is a derogatory term for "foreigner"]. These are friends who study foreign languages. They are tragic (*bei'ai*); maybe because they are poor they want to marry *laowai*. I think they are like prostitutes. At Liberation, they had some very high-class prostitutes, who were well educated. They are like them . . . I have another friend who met a French man at a nuclear power factory where she was working. She was very unhappy; now she's gone to the United States — with her Chinese husband."

I asked if she would be willing to have a foreign boyfriend. She answered: "No. Maybe it's cultural prejudice. I think foreigners have a curiosity about Chinese women, but I think they look down on Chinese people. I have a lot of relatives in other countries. They don't look for foreign boyfriends. They have experienced prejudice there. They have a background experience. Middle-class foreigners [in foreign countries] look down on Chinese as working class [here she reverts to using Cultural Revolution terms for class, such as *chengfen*, which have virtually disappeared from people's vocabularies]. They see Chinese as foreigners, not as French. Chinese lovers of foreigners, when they go back with them to foreigners' apartments, are not allowed inside the gate. They will take you as a lover but they won't marry you."

These two moments reflect a dual strategy in worlding China. One is to erase the woman in order to make the nation cosmopolitan. The second strategy is recoup the woman as a defensive maneuver, thus recouping civilization. From the perspective of these tales, it becomes clear that the reason China needs to become such a prominent figure in the globalized world is to continue to offer civilization over and against barbarism. I end with another ethnographic moment, an allegory about cosmopolitanism that Ding Yingquan offered. Her comments, made in 1999, are prescient. I had asked her which kinds of foreign influences were having the most effect in China. I carefully did not specify Western or Japanese or other meanings of "foreign." She replied: "It's everywhere, all these American fast-food stores. But this American culture is superficial; it is *laji wenhua*." "Excuse me?" I asked. For I thought I had heard the term "rubbish culture." Ding Yingquan spoke the phrase in English, "*Rubbish culture*. Like the movies — the ones that are pirated — they are all rubbish culture."

ME: So you think foreign influence is bad?

DYM: No, because without the superficial contact, you can't have any deeper conversation. I have read many books about the United States and learned about the United States. But I wouldn't be able to do that without having the superficial contact first.

ME: What is your impression of American culture?

DYM: It's declining (*shuailuo*).

ME: What makes you say that?

DYM: From the language. I read books, and *Time* and *Newsweek*. They all use jargon. They use all the same jargon. The language is declining. Language is not just a tool; it is reflective of a culture. I see the language in decline and I take this to mean American culture is declining.

I wish I could leave Ding Yingquan with the last word. But I must insist here that the vision of cosmopolitanism she shares with other young urban women is itself haunted by the specter of that which it excludes: the rural migrant workers who populate their urban worlds but whom they appear not to see. These migrant workers come from the interior, poorer provinces to the large coastal cities to be domestic servants and do other menial labor (Gaetano and Jacka 2004, Huang 1999, Song 1999, West and Zhao 2000, Yan 2003a,b). Migrant men do most of the construction work, of which there is a great deal as Chinese cities rebuild new dream worlds into the landscape.[12] Migrant women and men are often blamed by urban residents for urban crime and social instability; migrant women are portrayed as conducting extramarital affairs that destabilize urban marriages (Zhang 2001, Sun 2004).

The women migrant workers I came to know also have visions of cosmopolitanism, but their affective energies bespeak a desire to become cosmopolitan by transcending the divisions within China. Ma Xiaoduo is an activist member of the Rural Women's Association in Beijing. Like these urban, middle-class women, she, too, tells a colorful tale of her travels around China that transcend her rootedness in the countryside. While her travels were caused by her need to find work, she highlights less the hardships than the adventures. She, too, signals the remaking of herself through consumption. Her first act when she arrived in the Shenzhen special economic zone bordering Hong Kong was to tear off her country clothing and buy a new set of clothes. She wants to live in the city because she refuses to do agricultural labor. Her cosmopolitanism includes an ability to avoid domestic service, especially the care of children, that most migrant women end up doing when they first migrate. But, she says, "The city is not ours." Migrant workers from the countryside live illegally in the cities and, reminiscent of undocumented workers in the United States, are periodically swept out whenever there is a need to make the urban environment look pristine (see Zhang 2001). Ma Xiaoduo narrates her cosmopolitanism through a tale of overcoming her prior view of what it means to be a migrant worker in relation to urban-born residents.[13] Her cosmopolitanism lies in the way she grasps the incommensurability of her life in relation to theirs: "I can't enter their circles and I don't care what happens to them . . . with their going abroad, getting into Beijing University, or their unemployment problems." For Ma Xiaoduo, to be cosmopolitan with Chinese characteristics means to begin from this point of incommensurability within China. Her story, and those of other migrant women in China, leaves a trace of alterity, of the unassimilable remainder, which renders the cosmopolitanism of urban women ghostly to itself, even as their cosmopolitanism in turn haunts American universalist cosmopolitanism.

In the face of complex changes in capitalist dynamics around the world, academics in different disciplines have turned to narratives of cosmopolitanism, which they often accompany with images of a newly global capitalism. Such images and narratives are used in both celebratory accounts that stress the triumph of the marketplace and capitalist democracy and in critical analyses that highlight the apparent eradication of platforms or possibilities for concerted opposition. Yet both celebratory and critical emphases on cosmopolitanism and neoliberal capitalism manifest assumptions that, too frequently, are accepted as unquestioned truths. The broadest of these assumptions is the idea that neoliberal capitalism and cosmopolitanism exist together as a coherent package, that the one determines the other. In this essay, I have offered an alternative route. Rather than assume coherence, I have traced the makings of that coherence in the historical encounters of a postsocialist generation. "Cosmopolitanism" does not have a stable meaning, nor is it merely the opposite of "the local." To understand how "desiring China" comes into existence, we need to follow the instabilities of categorizing peoples and views as either cosmopolitan or local. To pursue the politics of claims made in the name of cosmopolitanism means accounting for how those claims are acted upon by subjects differentially able to make their imaginations stick. We might fruitfully recast much current theorizing if we thought of "cosmopolitan" and "local" not as transparent subjectivities-cum-spatial arrangements but as analytic categories given meaning through specific representational practices. Locating activity, rather than "local" activity, might help us to position the "cosmopolitan" in determinate cultural practices rather than treating it as a deterritorialized phenomenon or wholly a penetration from the West. Precisely these kinds of specificities offer insight into the heterogeneous and uneven practices that create what, only after we have traced their motivated interconnections, we might call neoliberalism.

5

Legislating Desire

Homosexuality, Intellectual Property

Rights, and Consumer Fraud

*I*n March of 1999, a Mr. Xu brought a legal complaint of defamation against one Fang Gang, a journalist of social reportage, and his publisher, the Jilin People's Press, who had published Fang Gang's book *Homosexuality in China* (1995). Mr. Xu claimed that Fang Gang had brought him irreparable harm, of an emotional and professional sort, by writing about him in his book. Fang Gang had written a passage describing the first-ever Valentine's Day gathering of gay men in Beijing, at a café whose bar manager Fang Gang described as a "homosexual." The exact passage reads:

> Valentine's Day, a term that Chinese people have gradually become familiar with, that day in 1993, when many young men buy roses for their girlfriends . . . in Beijing's Xidan district, in a small bar, an event of very special significance was taking place. This was the fifth event of the "Men's World' "s cultural salon. The manager of this bar is a thirty-something homosexual, a volunteer on the hotline. The afternoon of Valentine's Day, the bar turned away customers and tightly closed its windows and doors. From 2:00–5:00, it became the world of male homosexuals. The two experts Qiu Renzong and Chen Bingzhong came, Wan Yanhai and other organizers of course were not absent, five newspapers, *China Daily, Beijing Youth, People's Daily,* the China News Agency, and the German *Daily Mirror*

each had a reporter there, two of whom were women. There were over 50 homosexuals, the most ever at a salon event.

The event did not have any special content, mainly singing and dancing. Wan Yanhai remembers: "When male couple after male couple went to the floor to slow dance, those who looked on had a very solemn feeling. Those dancing were very dignified." Probably only those who understand the predicament of homosexuals can feel that kind of solemn feeling . . . When the gathering came to an end, many shed tears. For each person who participated in the activity, that afternoon left them with an unforgettable impression. (1995, 50–51)

Perhaps Fang Gang should have been sued for maudlin voyeurism. This passage, as the reader will note, does not name the bar manager by name. It does name Wan Yanhai, then working in the Ministry of Health on HIV-AIDS prevention and subsequently fired from his job for organizing gay men to prevent the spread of AIDS. I have come to know Wan Yanhai quite well; he is one of the most outspoken advocates of treating gay rights as an issue of human rights in China. In 2002 Wan Yanhai spent several months in jail because he exposed the government's lack of response to the spread of AIDS among poor farmers who donate blood in exchange for money at clinics that repeatedly use unsterilized needles. However, the said Mr. Xu, not named, claimed that the bar manager referred to was indeed he. In court, he had to prove the reference was to himself by specifying six pieces of information. He enumerated his age and occupation, the place of the event, the organizers of the event, the content of the event, and the participants. Mr. Xu claimed that after the publication of this book, he lost his job, his fiancée, and his friends and had found it impossible to proceed in a "normal" way with his life. Mr. Xu brought this case four years after the book had been published.

This case was the first legal case to be adjudicated about homosexuality in China since the end of socialism. As I argued in chapter 3, a gay identity only became widespread in the 1990s; such a legal case would not have made sense before then. China's socialist legal system would not have entertained such a libel case, for there was no such provision for civil suits of this nature under socialism. China's legal system does not work on precedent; each case is distinct.[1] Nonetheless, the case generated much anger and debate among gay men out of concern for its normative power. Whenever I pondered with gay men and lesbians the sources of homophobia in China but also the seeming ambivalence toward homosexuality, they repeatedly pointed out to me that there are no sodomy laws or any other laws that specifically outlaw homosexuality in China. Thus this case acquired added significance.

Another case—or actually series of events that did not turn into a legal case—occurred prior to this one. Two women living in a small rural town in the interior, rather poor province of Anhui met because their places of work were located near one another. One of the women had been given her father's old job in the town's government-run business office. The other had moved to the town to take up an apprenticeship in a tailor shop. The two women gradually developed a friendship, which turned into a sexual relationship. Eventually they decided to live together. In August of 1991, the father of the woman apprenticing in the tailor shop brought a complaint to the county public security bureau, charging the other woman with "hooliganism." "Hooliganism" is a catch-all socialist criminal category that has to do with, paraphrasing Mary Douglas (1992 [1966]), movement out of place. The father did not connect these women's behavior with any category of identity such as "homosexuality." He condemned their actions as morally reprehensible activity and as damaging to public morals since their relationship was carried out in view of other townspeople. The county public security bureau was unsure what to do with the father's complaint, as there is no law against two women living together or having sex. But since they wanted to honor patriarchal sentiment, the local public security officials sent the case up to the district public security bureau, who, also unsure of what to do, passed it up to the provincial public security bureau, who, again unsure of what to do, forwarded it finally to the national public security bureau.

This case was also famous among gay men and lesbians in China; it has served as a banner case for those desirous of gay rights in China. I searched for the details of these two cases because so many Chinese gay men and lesbians had mentioned them to me. In the interest of heightening suspense, I leave discussion of their resolution until later. These controversial cases raise questions about how to understand the meanings, representations, and place of homoerotic desire in China at the turn of the millennium. How did these cases and the public discussion of them among gay men and lesbians participate in the constitution of "desiring China"? How does nonnormative sexual desire get valued in a world that fosters the proliferation of desires? Finally, how does nonnormative desire become entangled with neoliberalism?

Answers to these questions require discussion of other desires that provide the social field in which to understand nonnormative sexual desires. Rather than approach sex as a separable domain, I believe queer ethnography must examine the articulations of "sex" with broad and varied cultural practices. As chapter 3 demonstrated, to treat sex as its own domain leads to the privileging of a certain normative gay identity —the Euro-American white male. To decenter this version of a gay identity necessitates taking seriously the articulations that have historically made sex more than a statement of sexual identity. The previous chapters addressed the connections between identity, sex, and cosmopolitanism in the making of "desiring China." In this chapter, I bring the two public debates about nonnormative sexual desires into conversation with two other legalistic debates. One is about copyright and intellectual property and the other about consumer fraud and proper consumption. These three types of cases triangulate the legal arena's adjudications between licit and illicit desires. These judgments, in turn, operate to fasten these desires to neoliberalism.

REPRESSION, PASSION, INTEREST, DESIRE

To elaborate this terrain further, I would like to detour momentarily to quite a different time and place: seventeenth- and eighteenth-century Europe. The historian Albert O. Hirschman wrote a provocative argument some time ago about the earliest ideas that arose in support of liberal capitalism in Europe in a slim work entitled *The Passions and the Interests: Political Arguments for Capitalism before Its Triumph* (1996 [1977]). Hirschman argued that these ideas first arose not out of a new class, the bourgeoisie, though they certainly played a central role later, nor from a Weberian search for divine providence, but within the old order out of concern to block the excessive passions of the aristocracy with their effects on statecraft. Prior to the seventeenth century, the pursuit of wealth as an end in itself was viewed in a negative light, as avarice that, along with the lust for power and sexual lust, provided the three main passions that medieval Christianity and society condemned. In the seventeenth century, political philosophers sought new ideas about how to restrain the destructive passions of aristocratic rulers, exemplified in their overweening love of glory, power, and pleasure. They turned to something they called "the interests." At that time, "interest" had a rather broad meaning; it signified the totality of human aspirations and desires but denoted an element of reflection and calculation with respect to the manner in which desires were pursued. Political theorists argued that the interests comprised a set of benign passions that could serve as a countervailing force to destructive passions. As the concept of "interest" focused increasingly on the production of wealth through commerce, "interest" came to be seen as having a number of additional assets: predictability, which would make human actions transparent and thus more easily subject to rule; balance, which would create a web of interdependent relationships difficult for the excessive passions of rulers to upset; and finally, harmlessness, for compared to the nobility's wild and dangerous passions, the commerce of commoners was seen as harmless and was thought incapable of creating evil on a grand scale. "Interest" as a benign set of passions thus began to bestow upon the pursuit of wealth a positive connotation. Eventually, Adam Smith and other ideologues of capitalism reduced this opposition of interests and passions by subsuming all desires into interests.[2]

I find Hirschman's philosophical genealogy of liberal capitalism quite suggestive of the transformations in China. As I have conveyed, many in China would like to move beyond what they view as the destructive passions of politics. To displace them, they have embraced profit-making activity, also previously cast in a negative light, to counterbalance those destructive passions.[3] But the postsocialist dilemma is distinct. First, because Maoist socialism, of course, is not the same as Europe's feudal aristocratic order. And second, because socialism is portrayed, paradoxically, as having repressed human nature in addition to having fostered excessive passions. To encourage the formation of postsocialist subjects in China, then, requires not just the restraint of passion but the development of desires. Thus, Hirschman's model must be refashioned. My argument, which I illuminate through the legal debates, is that a triangular relationship has been constructed in China among repression, which signifies the inhibition of human nature; interests, which signify self-regulation; and passion, which signifies excess. Between repression and passion lies socialism, while between passion and interests lies capitalism. The dilemma for China is to find the proper balance between interests and passions. To do so means letting desire erupt out of "human nature." One of psychoanalytic theory's basic insights is that desire is unpredictable. Nevertheless, it is essential for the creation of postsocialist subjects. Yet desire is not utterly self-regulating like interests nor predictable with rational choice models. It travels the whole continuum. Desire results from negating repression, but the problem is that it can go toward either excess or self-regulation. Try as one might to subsume desires under interests — the goal of postsocialist governance — full control over where desire might end up is impossible.

Interestingly enough, sexual desire drops out of Hirschman's story. As we will see these legal cases reveal, homosexual desire plays a critical role in that it generates a decided ambivalence. This ambivalence simultaneously serves to create the sense of a neoliberal formation and betrays it as an unfinished project. I elaborate on that ambivalence in the discussion that follows. The legal arena is critical to the project of ridding Chinese citizens of historically induced "repression," and balancing interests, passions, and desire. For law establishes the frame of neoliberalism. It encourages desire while curbing excess to create the proper kinds of neoliberal subjects. I include within this legal arena debates about public policy and public culture in China that have increasingly been developed within a culture of law.[4] At the risk of deferring the reader's desires a bit longer, I turn first to the other legal cases that adjudicate the proper balance between passionate excess and self-regulating interest.

POSSESSIVE INDIVIDUALISM

China's intellectual property rights law was galvanized by the government's desire to become a member of the WTO and by large American corporations like Microsoft suing over copyright.[5] The intellectual property rights case I focus on here is a case about opera singing stylization.[6] The case began in the spring of 1998, when the northern Shenyang Opera House decided to stage an award-winning southern opera, *Tale of a Demoted Official*. They hired Mr. Xuan Bo, who did not work at the Opera House but at an opera research institute, to change the southern singing style into a northern Peking opera style. (This would be comparable, for example, to taking a country-and-western song and turning it into hip-hop.) The opera was so successful that it was chosen to be aired on one of the national stations during the Chinese New Year.

Xuan Bo informed all his friends and relatives. But when he watched the airing, he saw that the opera's name had been changed to *Tale of an Official*, that some of his design had been rearranged, and that his name and those of the other two colleagues he had worked with had been entirely removed from the credits. Their work had been credited as the work of one person, Liu Minggao, a cadre in the municipal culture bureau.

Feeling that his reputation and his self-respect had been injured, Xuan Bo lodged a legal complaint, accusing the Shenyang Opera House and Liu Minggao of infringement of authors' rights, of his reputation [indemnification], and rights of honor. In court, Xuan Bo and the Opera House cadres argued over several issues. First, they disagreed about whether singing stylization is covered under intellectual property rights laws. They then disputed the role of the cadre whose name appeared on the opera. Liu Minggao stated that his version may have displayed unintentional coincidences with Xuan Bo's work but that he did not mean to give offense. Moreover, both he and Xuan Bo had taken their material from the traditional style of opera. " 'Could it really be," he asked, "that this Beijing opera singing style, that has developed through several hundreds of years and several generations' of people's labor, that only you Xuan Bo are allowed to use it?' " (Ding 2002, 3). Xuan Bo countered that opera stylization includes original, creative work. Too many parts of the opera stylization that appeared on television were the same and could therefore not have been independently designed.

China's Copyright Protection Authentication Committee concluded that certain scenes were entirely different but that several scenes were similar or exactly the same. Their findings supported Xuan Bo's case. The Shenyang Opera House then proceeded to argue that the work belonged to the work unit. Vice-Director Yan stated, " 'You cannot take people who were given the responsibility to design certain pieces of the opera and masquerade them as individual authors. It would be like taking a statue created by a work unit and recklessly cutting off an arm' " (Ding 3). But Xuan Bo's lawyer argued that authors enjoy full rights in their works. " 'It's like a painting," he said. "After I have finished the painting, I sell the painting to you. As the buyer, you enjoy full rights of ownership, but the rights of creation are still in my hands as the painter' " (Ding 3).

On August 16, 2001, the Wenji District Court of Liaoyang municipality reached a decision. Shenyang Opera House lost the case. They did not accept the decision and appealed. Just as the appeals court was about to announce the decision, Shenyang Opera House abandoned its position and offered to settle with Xuan Bo. Xuan Bo won Y30,000 in compensation and also an agreement that in the future, whether the opera was acted in the theater or shown on television, Xuan Bo's name must appear in the acknowledgments.

This well-known and controversial case is a wonderful microcosm of creative negotiations in the legal arena to replace the dangerous passions of socialist politics with the seemingly benign desires and interests of, in this case, possessive individualism.[7] The case never openly discussed socialism's excesses. It did not need to. Their signs were embedded in the case and clear for all to see. To begin, one must understand — as everyone in this case did — that the Shenyang Opera House is a government-run institution. It has all the trappings of the old socialist system: it is a "work unit" rather than a "company," with "comrades" rather than "employees." It is run by "cadres" rather than "CEOs." In the past, these socialist institutions made resources available to the arts without regard for profit but with great regard for their political effects. Hence, the opera's name change indirectly signals the state's unwillingness to accept political criticism. Under socialism, the labor in such art institutions was collectively organized but also hierarchical; the results of the labor belonged to the work unit and, ultimately, to the state. Artists and writers were paid a monthly wage. During the Cultural Revolution, none but the eight operas Jiang Qing, the wife of Mao, had designated as politically acceptable could be performed.

In the postsocialist world, these socialist institutions and the government-appointed officials who run them have been represented in public discourse as negatively signifying, first, the searing political struggles of the Cultural Revolution; second, the desire to subsume art under politics; and, finally, the corruption of political power, especially the corruption that links political power with preferential abilities to seek wealth. Of course, one system's corruption is another's normal way of doing business. Thus, discourses of corruption in China also tend to normalize and naturalize capitalist practices as noncorrupt.[8]

These negative significations of political passion are embodied in the figure of the municipal culture bureau cadre, Liu Minggao, whose name ends up as the sole author of the singing stylization. One could call him the villain of the case. To have his name appear as sole author on the production signifies everything that both official and popular discourse rejects about Maoist socialism. He represents socialist political passions at their worst. As the villain, he recalls the degradations of Maoist socialism in which hierarchies of political prestige warred with socialist ideologies of egalitarianism. The case offers the figure of Xuan Bo as Liu Minggao's replacement. Xuan Bo appears to be a benign figure who is merely the originary creator of a work, an idea reflected in legal form in the copyright. Xuan Bo eventually turns into the hero of the story. To forestall his heroism and the naturalization of intellectual property rights on which that heroism depends, Shenyang Opera House and Liu Minggao attempt to cast Xuan Bo's desires in the realm of excess. Isn't his claim to proprietary authorship rather a mark of hubris? Hasn't he stretched authorship beyond the bounds of appropriate desire?

In tracing the history of copyright in England, Mark Rose (1993) argues that the peculiar notion of the singular individual as the originary creator of a literary work arose out of the articulation of Locke's political theory of the possessive individual — the person who owns himself as his own property — with the novel idea of the creative genius and the vastly increased spread in the publishing and marketing of books. Rose reminds us that authors do not create in any literal sense and that it is almost impossible to distinguish the origins of literary ideas when the work in question deals with a conventional form such as Peking opera. He highlights the contradiction that exists between this romantic conception of authorship found in copyright law and recent cultural theory's insistence that literary works are always social and collective, just as the Shenyang Opera House argued with its example of the statue and its claim that the work belongs to the work unit.[9]

Yet individual authorship and possessive individualism provide critical imaginary resources for producing neoliberal subjects of a market economy.[10] In its quest to fold economic reform into neoliberal institutions such as the WTO, the Chinese state actively sought to put into place legalistic practices such as copyright. As I have argued throughout, numerous public discourses, both those encouraged by the state but also those either ignored or condemned by the state, play a central role in binding subjectivities to neoliberal policies. The court enacted such an articulation in this case. Thus, the court, in its interpretation of recent copyright and intellectual property rights laws, concluded that Xuan

Bo's desire reflects benign interest. He wished not merely to have his authorship recognized. More importantly, he aspired to an honorable reputation in his authored work — what Mark Rose calls "propriety" rather than just "property." This "harmless" desire subsumes and reduces the passions to an interest in the possession of one's self and the works and name associated with that self — in a word, possessive individualism. One could call this type of desire for propriety, as linked to valuation of ownership in one's intellectual labor, the self-regulation of the subject.

ACQUISITIVE CONSUMPTION

The second set of legalistic debates addresses consumer fraud. Over the last several years, the Wang Hai phenomenon has caused quite a bit of controversy. Wang Hai is a young man who became famous in China as a professional consumer of fraud. A new law in China, Consumer Protection Law #49, states that any consumer who is sold fraudulent goods may return the product to the store and demand compensation at double the original price. Wang Hai began making his living by buying what he already knew were fraudulent products and then returning them to collect the double compensation. After six years of a successful practice, Wang Hai formed his own consulting company. Wang Hai had invented a new genre of creating surplus value. Indeed, the "phenomenon" of Wang Hai refers to the numerous other citizens said to be copying him. His Web site WangHai.com is instructive, for it playfully justifies turning the consumption of fraud into a profession. I quote it at length:

> "Wang Hai — A Vanguard (*xianfeng*) in Protecting Rights"
> Wang Hai, born in 1973 in Qingdao, Shandong Province, is currently the executive director of the Beijing DaHai Business Consulting Limited Liability Company, and CEO of WangHai.com Information Limited. He has written *I'm a Rascal, Wang Hai's Sincere Advice* and *Sharp Warnings*.
> Wang Hai's diligent efforts in the past six years to expose fraud has meant not only the recovery of losses on behalf of the country and consumers from fraudulent manufacturers and sellers but also the awakening of many consumers' and businesses' consciousness about the protection of their rights . . .

Wang Hai and his DaHai Limited have helped companies investigate and attack manufacturers and sellers of fraudulent goods. At the same time, he has launched an attack on fraud in the interest of social responsibility. Whether it is a matter of "smuggled handsets," "travelling clinics for venereal disease," or a twenty-cent "toilet company," Wang Hai always displays a Shandong real man's heroic character (*bense*) of defending injustice. He frequently creates "losses" in the tens and hundreds of thousands for the manufacturers and sellers of fraudulent products. This makes Wang Hai's business full of danger. Wang Hai's work is like dancing on the edge of a knife . . . In his determined pursuit of justice, fairness and equality, Wang Hai is becoming a moral leader. Wang Hai recognizes that the most basic morality should include: 1. Each person should pursue the maximization of his interest by living by the sweat of his own brow; 2. To be a proper person one cannot harm other people's or the public's interest; 3. Each person must bear some social responsibility by protecting the public interest.

The publication of *Sharp Warnings* inevitably attracted a conflict between old and new views. However, no matter what others say or what danger exists, Wang Hai . . . continues as before with his article of faith based in honesty, conscientiousness and sense of responsibility as he goes about the practice of making a business out of attacking fraud.

In light of his claims to the high moral road, Wang Hai's endeavors prompted a wide debate. Do his activities signify benign, legitimate, and clever interest — exactly right for a neoliberal subject — or does this type of entrepreneurship come closer to greed and therefore represent not self-regulating interest but excessive passion? It is important to understand that consumers in China have been turned into subjects with rights. Indeed, one could hardly exaggerate in saying they are the subjects with the most elaborate rights. The consumer protection movement exists as China's only legitimate social movement; it has spawned numerous organizations and offices throughout the country. Consumer protection law affirms the sovereignty of the consumer and the consumer's "inviolable rights" (*shenjing buke qinfande*). Wang Hai legitimates his activity by transposing the old socialist rhetoric "to serve the people" (*wei renmin fuwu*) into consumer protection. But he takes the conceit further. Wang Hai's intimation that he leads a life worthy of crime thrillers — he sports reflective sunglasses and refuses to have his photo taken — makes consumption appear more thrilling than politics.

The reduction here of the dangerous passions of politics to the harmless desires of consumption nearly serves to subvert its aim. To some, Wang Hai is an "everyman's hero." He does not simply replace the socialist party vanguard; he walks a fine line between mockery and mimicry. Wang Hai's elaboration of the government's emphasis on the consumer as the ultimate bearer of rights echoes hilariously if also uncomfortably, at least for the state. The semi-official Consumer Organization, prompted by the explosion of interest in Wang Hai, decided that perhaps they needed to amend the law. Consumption, they stated categorically, is for the purpose of life's necessities. Someone who consumes for profit is not seeking life's necessities. They implicitly concluded that Wang Hai had veered beyond the self-regulating subject of interest.

One of the legal experts who had drafted the original compensation law disagreed. He asserted that the law was meant to encourage exactly Wang Hai's type of behavior. "Consumption for life's necessities includes material and cultural life," he argued. "If a consumer makes a profit out of this behavior, it is a type of spiritual enjoyment, like people watching the World Soccer Cup games."[11] Wang Hai, as of yet, has never been taken to court or charged with any crime.

THE AMBIVALENCE OF HOMOSEXUAL DESIRE

The Wang Hai controversy and the opera singing stylization court case adjudicate the creation of neoliberal subjects by attempting to reduce the destructive passions of politics to the seemingly benign interests of, respectively, acquisitive consumption and possessive individualism. These legalistic debates provide the essential context for comprehending the ambivalence toward homosexual desire expressed in the cases to which I now turn. The first case, against the journalist Fang Gang, like the opera case, addressed the issue of reputation. Yet the two cases differed in the aspect of reputation they disputed. Xuan Bo argued that he was an author of the singing stylization and that his reputation for originality and creativity had been violated, while Mr. Xu, the bar manager, claimed defamation rather than originality or authorship. Libel not copyright occupied center stage. In his defense, Fang Gang argued seemingly paradoxical positions. First, he asserted that homosexuality is not wrong or disgraceful (*bumingyu* — literally, "not reputable"). In other words, it reflects a benign interest. Thus, to describe someone as a homosexual does not mean an attack on that person's reputation. Fang Gang then followed that argument with another: since the plaintiff states that he is not a homosexual, he cannot claim invasion of privacy. Mr. Xu, the plaintiff, countered that since the publication of *Homosexuality in China*, he had suffered suspicion and censure. His family and friends had distanced themselves from him; his girlfriend of one year, whom he was planning to marry, left him; his business had dropped off considerably; and he faced severe obstacles to finding normal employment.

Unlike the infamous Oscar Wilde case, Mr. Xu never had to prove whether or not he actually was a homosexual. Thus, the case was never tried on errors of fact but merely on the matter of reputation. Presumably, Mr. Xu could have brought charges of defamation even if he were a homosexual but did not want it revealed in public.

In his decision, the judge rejected Fang Gang's arguments. He stated: "The people's right to their reputation is protected by law. At present in China, homosexuality is seen as an abnormal sexual behavior; it is not accepted by the public (*gongzhong*). On page 50 of his book, *Homosexuality in China*, Fang Gang described the plaintiff as a homosexual, without actual proof (*shishi yiju*), which has brought emotional hardship to the plaintiff. It has also influenced his work and life. It is an invasion of his rights to reputation. The Jilin Publishing House did not investigate conscientiously but published and distributed this invasion of rights; they also bear a certain responsibility, and also invaded the plaintiff's rights of reputation. They should bear a certain civic responsibility."[12]

The judge's opinion that "homosexuality is seen as an abnormal sexual behavior" generated enormous debate among gay men and lesbians about this case. Note that he did not state that homosexuality is unnatural. His was not a Christian-inflected decision nor a psycho-biological one. By "abnormal," the judge meant that homosexuality goes against Chinese social and cultural norms. In his view, then, homosexual desire leads to excessive passion and not benign self-regulating interest.

Fang Gang decided to appeal the case in order to persuade the judge to delete this statement from the decision. In his appeal, Fang Gang argued that no basis exists for the court decision that the public does not accept homosexuality nor is there a proper means for establishing such a basis. Moreover, he argued, this case is historically unprecedented; it is the first time that a court in China has decided on the quality of homosexuality. " 'Abnormality' (*xingbiantai*) is a medical judgment, a specialized term; its demarcation is from the world of science. But scientific circles have long rejected this outworn, backwards thinking . . . The court should embrace progressive not regressive moral views. We assert that homosexuality is not an abnormality, nor a crime. Nor is it immoral. Homosexuals have the same equal rights as heterosexuals."[13] Fang Gang did not have much hope of winning his case. He merely sought to remove the statement "homosexuality is abnormal." Implicitly, he thought the court should treat homosexuality as a benign interest.

In the interval between Fang Gang's filing the appeal and the second decision, many people weighed in on the case. Numerous sociologists and psychologists stepped forward with written opinions to the court; gay activists set up Web sites to discuss the case.[14] Many of them echoed Fang Gang's contention that homosexual desire is natural. The ability of sexual desire in post-Mao China to occupy the terrain of the natural, reinforcing the appearance of "desiring China" as commonsensical and inevitable, lays the ground for the ambivalence manifested in this case. Sexual desire has come to represent naturalness par excellence and thus potentially provides the strongest foundation for "desiring China." As one self-identified gay critic of this case argued, "protecting biology's diversity is common ecological knowledge; having only one sexuality is what's frightening. Darwin said, 'Heredity and change are common conditions of the biological world. Without change, there would not exist the rich diversity of today's natural world and human culture.' " This critic implicitly suggests a view of homosexuality as a benign, self-regulating interest.

Zong Zhong, a psychologist who weighed in on this case, disputed point for point the arguments in public discourse that supported the judge's decision. In response to the idea that homosexuals are abnormal because they are in the minority, he countered that left-handed people are also the minority in China but are not considered abnormal (though actually until recently they were thought to have something odd about them). As against the view that homosexuals' sexual behavior is not the norm, he referred to the obvious diversity of sexual behavior among heterosexuals. He rejected the belief that homosexuality is a diseased behavior that flouts morality. Conceding that traditional Chinese morality does not approve of homosexuality, Zong Zhong detailed the heterosexual behavior likewise condemned, such as extramarital sex, prostitution, and so forth. Yet they are not considered to be mental disorders. Zong Zhong also engaged a point he insisted was part of popular discourse: that to diagnose homosexuality as an illness is China's special characteristic (*tese*). He asserted: "Unlike *qigong*, homosexuality is not one of China's cultural products, nor was it brought in on a foreign ship. Homosexuality has existed from ancient times, in China and in foreign countries, because it is a natural phenomenon; it is not one of China's special characteristics. Foreigners medicalized homosexuality, not China. When the Chinese historical records mention homosexuality, they never call it an 'abnormality.' In foreign countries, it took one hundred years to solidify the idea that homosexuality is a mental disorder. But that has changed in the last several decades. If China insists on maintaining the idea that homosexuality is a mental disorder, then it will be behind foreign countries by several decades."

In the final appeal decision, the judge deleted the offensive phrase "homosexuality is seen as an abnormal sexual behavior," but he still found Fang Gang guilty of defamation. Gay men and lesbians in China celebrated this decision as a victory. How could the conclusion to this case produce such a paradoxical state of affairs? The case expresses deep ambivalence about how to weigh nonnormative sexual desires in relation to the triangulated concerns with socialist repression, self-regulating interest, and excessive passions. Desire is central to adjudicating among this assemblage but is unpredictable. Advocates for free trade capitalism have claimed that the reason for neoliberal capitalism's ability to spread globally is its naturalness. Thus homoerotic desire would seem to be the perfect poster child for the ability of postsocialist pleasures to reject Maoist politics and embrace neoliberalism. Yet a great deal of ambivalence exists among non-gay-identified Chinese citizens and also among some gay men and lesbians. As a type of desire, even if natural, how far does homosexuality go toward the end of excess? How should the natural be weighed against the moral? Does Chinese morality in fact have something to say about homosexuality? While all sexual desire in post-Mao China might claim the ground of the natural, not all of it is seen as healthy for the nation. Thus, collectivity creeps back in as it propels homoerotic desire into public debate about its legitimacy for the reproductive life of the nation and the metonymic and literal families on which the nation is said to be built. Yet, it cannot be outlawed entirely, because the whole point of creating "desiring China" is to encourage the development of myriad desires.

Debates among gay men and lesbians in China about the case further reflect this ambivalence. Some gay men pressed the harmless nature of their desires. They argued that the case was "too political," that it should have remained a civil matter between Fang Gang and Xu, rather than turn into a confrontation between the courts and gay comrades. Others contended that homosexuality should be private and therefore Fang Gang was wrong to discuss anyone's private life in a published text. This reduction of homosexuality to a benign interest located in the private lives of individuals suggests a resonance with possessive individualism. But it does not transform the subject into an object that one desires to own. Nor does this view lead to the practice of marking one's ownership in public for all to see and recognize. To the contrary. I called Ah Zhuang, a Chinese gay activist who had moved to San Francisco from Beijing (we met him in chapter 3), to hear his thoughts on the case. He dismissed the case with annoyance, saying that Xu was just greedy and out to make money. My friend had turned on their head the positions of excessive passions and benign interests.

Fang Gang himself encourages the reduction of homosexuality to a benign interest in a self-criticism he wrote of his original book after having received scathing criticism from Hong Kong gay activists for his condescension toward gay people:

> Today I have to admit, when I chose that topic to write about, it was not without an attitude of curiosity. But this year's work has thoroughly changed me. I saw for myself too much suffering of homosexuals, felt the pressures of mainstream culture toward them, the stifling nature of traditional beliefs toward them. Many homosexuals are very good people, some among them glimmer exceedingly fascinating character and charm, many are the cream of human intelligence. Their only difference lies in their minority sexual orientation. This difference does no harm to others. To the contrary, our mainstream views are harming them. Thus . . . I wrote in the book:

"Homosexuals are not criminals, they are not sick people, we should treat them with equality and tolerance" . . . But the insufficiency of what I wrote is easy to see. It has an excess of emotion and insufficient theory . . . I even pronounced in the media that I am not a homosexual; today thinking about it, it was a very immature, silly gesture. Since homosexuality is not a crime or illness, what was the sense of my making this kind of proclamation? Didn't it reveal that, deep in my inner heart, I did not see homosexuals as equal? Doesn't it prove that I was worried that others would misrecognize me as a homosexual and I would "lose face"?[15]

Fang Gang's normalization of gay people in this self-criticism underlies an anxious desire to make homosexuality appear benign and to meld seamlessly with a middle-class–inflected vision of propriety. His reflections betray the belief that homosexuality has the potential to express passions that disrupt as much as they fulfill the role assigned for benign desires. Does homosexuality participate in a turn away from the dangers of politics? Does its seeming claim to the terrain of the natural forestall or rather create a displacement in the naturalization of postsocialism?

The case of the two women in Anhui Province addresses this question. Recall that the father of one of the women filed a complaint of hooliganism against the woman involved with his daughter. The father's complaint was as follows, excerpted from his letter:

> I am a person from Jiangbei township Number 5 Village. There has occurred in my family a strange thing that since ancient times has never happened in our area. Otherwise common citizens such as myself would never dare casually disturb our leaders with a petition.
>
> This is how it happened: In the spring of 1989, my oldest daughter Lin Yongxia studied tailoring in Jiangbei township, but Pan Yuzhen (an employee at the Jiangbei government business department) took a liking to her. This Pan has a woman's body, dresses like a man, lives a man's habits, being a hooligan became her second nature. Before this, she had fooled around with a few other girls. From the moment she had numerous encounters with my Lin, she reeled her in and wouldn't let her go. From that moment, my daughter Lin Yongxia, stepped into an abyss.
>
> In 1990, Lin was at Jiangbei Cotton Ginning factory, and even lived temporarily at her boyfriend's home. But Pan many times stirred

up trouble, sending letters at night, climbing up the window, inticing Lin to go out and fool around. The marriage arrangement was broken up by this. Afterwards, Lin went to Nanjing to work, Pan kept writing to her to come back. From that moment, the two of them set up house. To prevent their same-sex love affair, we tried everything, delaying [agricultural] production for over a year. We asked our relatives and friends to exhort her, to educate her, and we used coercive means to separate them. Many times we asked government officials to intercede and resolve it, but to no effect. Things went from bad to worse. Lin wrote a letter saying she wanted to live with Pan the rest of her life. Pan publicly proclaimed: "In ancient times the emperor's son-in-law committed the crime of deceiving the emperor, in order to take a beautiful woman as his bride. But no one can do anything to me."

The head of the business office scolded Pan and ordered her not to spend the night with Lin on the office desktop. And he ordered all the employees not to give the key to Pan at night. But Pan ignored her boss and treated the law as a plaything. She secretly copied the key and entered the office at night and slept with Lin. What's more, Pan smokes and chews tobacco. Renting an apartment cost them 5 yuan a night, add in two people's living expenses and it goes over their wages several times. She doesn't have any other sources of income. I'm sure she was using public funds, please go check for yourself.

Recently, the two of them rented an apartment right across from the police department at Wuwei County's southern city gate. Now they have rented another apartment in Jiangbei.

It's clear and easy to see that in this situation, this same-sex love is hooliganism. It's a repulsive thing that a socialist system cannot abide. And it brings social instability. What's more, our country is glorious [literally "the mountains and rivers are strong and beautiful"] and the net of justice vast. How can it let these two criminals get off scot-free, insulting the country and harming the people? If the law isn't brought down on them soon, disaster will be infinite.

Under the influence of public opinion and the destruction day and night of family relations, I am forced to ignore what might come and fight with these two hooligans to the bitter end. This little person [referring to himself] cannot bear the responsibility for what happens then. For this reason I have prepared this letter, to beg you not to treat it lightly. I urgently request that you deal with it severely, to release people's indignation.

Your petitioner, Head of Household Lin (Fang 1995, 306–07)

The township police took the complaint seriously. They initiated a long investigation of Pan, including a physical exam. The results of the physical exam were: "outwardly male; not married, a virgin, membrane whole, no abnormality discovered." The physical exam did not help them resolve the case. They could not discover any criminal behavior that the two women were committing. Since everyone knew about their living together, however, the town police recommended that Pan Yuzhen be given a sentence of fifteen days' detention to calm public opinion. After the affair, the two township police who handled it said to reporters in interviews: "We thought only of handling this affair through moral principles (*daoyi*), we didn't look at it from the legal standpoint. There doesn't exist an actual 'homosexual crime.' Besides, the two of them are women, how can you define their crime? Because their parents were resolute in wanting it dealt with, we had no choice but to make this report" (308).

After the case passed up to the highest national levels, the public security bureau responded as follows:

> What defines homosexuality, and where the blame for the problem of homosexuality lies is not clearly defined at present in our country's laws. In this situation, the case you have handed up in principle cannot be accepted and heard [in court]. Nor is it appropriate to administer punishment under the rubric of "hooligan behavior." To decide how to resolve this case, you could turn to the inspection bureau, the courts and other relevant government agencies. (Fang 1995, 309)

Gay men and lesbians in China also cite this case as a great victory. This case once again highlights the ambivalence that same-sex love generates. Is it hooliganism? If so, then it reflects the dangerous passions of excess reminiscent of socialism. If not, can it be seen as benign? This case reminds everyone that desires are unpredictable. This instability leads some to hold onto remnants of socialist public morality, even as they find it impossible to make the charge of hooliganism stick within that morality. Public morality is the name for subjectification processes under socialism. In the postsocialist view of socialism, public morality ranged from puritanism to excess. Public morality is the opposite of self-interest and therefore cannot be embraced wholeheartedly if neoliberal subjects are to thrive. As if in acknowledgment of this new truth, the crime of hooliganism was removed from the law several years after this case. To abandon public morality entirely, however, is just not feasible, because it also contributes to keeping desires away from unpredictable and excessive passions.

The legal case addressing intellectual property rights and legalistic debates about consumer fraud, together with the cases about homoerotic identity and desire, demonstrate the historical triangulation of interest, passion, and desire essential to the constitution of "desiring China." In the context of the other cases, those about homosexuality reveal the ambivalent status of homoerotic desire in China. As such, homoerotic desire lies at the center of constructing a neoliberal formation. It is not outlawed or fully condemned nor is it encouraged or fully accepted. Neither those who speak in the name of the state nor a broad array of public discourses has produced a definitive judgment on whether homosexuality is benign interest or excessive passion.

Homoerotic desire is not condemned outright, either by the state or by a wide range of citizens, for the production of sexually desirous subjects provides coherence to "desiring China." Yet homoerotic desire lies between the interests and the passions. Thus, it is not fully accepted, for it might not operate to subsume excessive passions under benign interests. Such desire exposes the instabilities in the creation of self-regulating desiring subjects. It exposes the operation of desire as not quite as predictable as a governmentality approach to neoliberalism might imply. Homoerotic desire could just as easily be seen as excess, because it does not appear to embody family values that would tie it to public morality. To fully rid society of all public morality, then, is impossible. It would be ideal for neoliberalism to get rid of public morality, but both state and society need to maintain it, at least a little, to produce self-regulating desires rather than allow desire to veer toward passionate excesses.

I would like to end with some musings for activism. I believe that understanding the transformations in China can help gay men and lesbians not only in China but elsewhere think about the politics of sex. Context shapes which battles we think relevant or germane. China's construction of neoliberalism occurs in a context in which the American empire has never been more hegemonic. Let us not reproduce that hegemony within transnational queer politics. To construe gay identity as a benign interest leaves out the marginalized "others" of queer life: those who are poor, those from rural areas who migrate to the metropolises, those who enjoy public sex or nonmonogamy, or who identify as perverts. I hope that we become more attentive to our pursuit of acceptance so that we ally ourselves not with those who support neoliberalism but with those who still find the need to criticize its destructive inequalities.

6

Desiring China

China's Entry into the WTO

In the international imagination China has seesawed dramatically in the short time from the late 1990s to the middle of the new millennium's first decade. In the late 1990s one still heard complaints that China did not desire financial gain sufficiently or properly. Nor, it was said, did China know how to or perhaps did not care to present itself as desirous to (Western) others for their gain. Members of the United States Congress, for example, avowed that China needed to "open" itself further to the longings of American businesses, including among others those who wished to sell religion (i.e., the Christian Bible) in China (U.S. Government 1999). A mere six years later, one hears ambivalent complaints that China's desires for profit are too precipitous and voracious and that China has seduced others too well. In August of 2005, U.S. Secretary of State Condoleezza Rice made a frustrated acknowledgment that perhaps China had become too adept at embracing capitalist desires. She warned that China still needed to undertake significant changes in its economic policies, lest it remain "a problem for the international economy" (Brinkley 2005, A9).[1] Rice went back and forth in the interview between threats and appeasement. Her palpable anxiety was the immediate result of Chinese state corporations' bids to buy an American oil company and a major appliance corporation, the mounting issue of textile "dumping," and the dawning realization that China is second to Japan in holding the U.S. government's debt. That same month, rumors also flew that China might step into the breach of providing military aid and training for those countries the United States has punished for noncompliance with key U.S. policies.[2]

The swervings in these images in such a short period of time raise important questions about how "desiring China" has come into existence in relation to transnational neoliberal institutions. The previous chapters took us through other routes to a desiring China: public culture routes of soap operas, museums, and gay bars; cosmopolitan fantasies of consumption; and legal adjudications of the proper balance between interests and passions. These phenomena produced "desiring China" through diverse narratives and practices: by crafting the art of longing, asserting the need for a postsocialist gender identity, modeling the proper way to be gay, fashioning the meanings of consumption by revisioning movement through time and space, creating cosmopolitanism by inventing a past one can leave behind and finally, by establishing legal guidelines for homosexual propriety, intellectual property, and consumer rights that together triangulated the lines of licit and illicit desires. Each of these routes highlighted a distinctive historical moment in China's postsocialist experiments. They also established exclusionary boundaries that marked certain kinds of people as either incapable of embodying these desires properly (e.g., rural migrants) or as displaying passions that marked them as being of "low quality" (e.g., money boys). Finally, these resolute yet nondeterministic practices provided a series of worldly encounters that encouraged experiments with how to become a cosmopolitan citizen.

"Desiring China" has continuously come into being in dialogue with multiple geopolitical others. In this chapter, I turn to the production of "desiring China" through the tense and contested process of China's entry into the World Trade Organization (WTO) and the ongoing disputes in the aftermath of that process. The WTO is an extension of the General Agreement on Tariffs and Trade (GATT) signed after World War II as part of the Bretton Woods Agreements to stabilize the world economy.[3] After numerous rounds of negotiations on tariffs in the intervening years, the WTO was formed in 1995 at the end of what is known as the Uruguay Round and after the first member countries signed the Marrakesh Agreements. Dedicated to the idea that trade between countries should be freed from governmental intervention (i.e., free trade liberalization), the WTO extends GATT's coverage of trade in goods to trade in services, intellectual property rights, and financial investments.

China's relationship to transnational capitalism clearly delineates the contours for the longings, needs, and interests people seek to embody in China. But neither structural determination nor logical principles will get us very far in understanding how this relationship works. A close examination of the debates addressing China's entry into the WTO reveals several surprising aspects of how the organization works: first, contrary to the popular assumption that the WTO presents a unified package of neoliberal agreements to each of its members, the WTO actually holds together a welter of "special cases" and specific exemptions, quotas, and tariff levels for hundreds of different goods, industries, and services. The details of the separate agreements for each country are based on whether a country can get itself labeled "underdeveloped" or "developing." Most importantly, these details implicitly reveal the central role of culture and history in a country's entry into the WTO, even as the WTO presents its neoliberal principles as universal and timeless. Thus, rather than assume that China was confronted with a uniform bundle of neoliberalism, it is more fruitful to turn the proposition around: that the WTO's neoliberalism only emerges through the negotiations that produce "desiring China." The analytical goal then becomes tracking the work it takes to hold the WTO's neoliberal policies together rather than begin with the a priori assumption that they exist as a seamless whole. The process of China's entry into the WTO became wedded to an implicit transnational dialogue about how to make neoliberalism appear as a coherent set of principles. But we should examine the efforts to make that appearance real, rather than assume its existence in advance. The goal of the negotiations over China's entry into the WTO was to craft a "desiring China" that would not only cultivate an internal desiring machine yielding endlessly proliferating desires for foreign goods and services but also turn China into an object which others could desire freely, without obstruction. How did the WTO negotiations attempt to produce such a thing?

To answer this question, it might be best to adopt a heretical perspective in order not to naturalize the beliefs that underlie the WTO. One problem that has plagued critical approaches to the neoliberal version of globalization is their acceptance of the descriptive veracity of its proponents. To condemn the exploitative effects of neoliberalism is surely a pressing matter. But we would get further in that project by following more closely the spirit of Marx and turning neoliberal ideas inside out rather than merely upside down. Selling Bibles suggests another lens. What would happen to our understanding of the WTO's neoliberal principles if we playfully decided to regard the WTO as if it were a church and its documents as if they were a bible? Then we could adopt the analytical strategies of those who have interpreted literalist approaches to the Christian Bible. Susan Harding (2000), for example, treats evangelical exegeses of the Christian Bible as complex, creative, and agile. She views Bible-based language as a social force more alive and less fixed than a scholarly acceptance of literalness would otherwise presume. Rather than unveil the falseness of literalist commitments, Harding traces their import in the everyday lives of church members as they borrow and customize the Bible-based speech of their preachers. Similarly, we might track the language of the WTO debates as a social power that produces the reality it purports to describe. This strategy illuminates the second surprising aspect of the WTO and its neoliberal principles: the WTO debates to induce a country like China to sign on to its churchlike doctrines reveal neoliberalism's ongoing paradoxes and inherent instability. The "orthodoxies" of the WTO's principles are constantly at war with the "heterodoxies" revealed by the specific histories of capitalist encounters.

"Predictability," for example, is a key principle of the WTO. It means that capitalist investors and entrepreneurs should be able to operate in predictable market conditions, without having governments suddenly change the rules. But the wildly proliferating accusations of dumping since the growth of the WTO highlight not so much the ideological falseness of this principle as contestations over its polyvalent meanings as member countries put WTO rules into practice. Accusations of dumping, as I elaborate below, have become a lightning rod for adjudicating licit and illicit capitalist desires. Dumping, after all, from another perspective could be viewed as ingenious capitalist practice rather than unfair competition. As witchcraft accusations have historically blurred the line between orthodox and heterodox, dumping accusations displace the boundary between legitimate and illegitimate capitalism. These accusations remind us that the heart of capitalism rests in unfair competition.[4]

China has become a particularly compelling target of dumping accusations. Thus, the negotiations over China's entry into the WTO reveal an unstable process of conflict over what counts as beneficial and proper or, conversely, adverse, unacceptable, and even immoral capitalist practices. To switch metaphors from the Christian church to scientific experiments for a moment, I borrow from Bruno Latour (1993) to think of the neoliberalism that informs the WTO as discursive practices that reach for the pure forms of capitalism but in the very act of doing so create strange hybrids. The WTO makes weighty claims for economic purification but must engage with the messy cultural practices of specific geopolitical histories. The seemingly pure economic forms and actions that WTO rules and regulations specify — efficiency, transparency, liberalization, predictability, national treatment (i.e., no discrimination against foreigners in favor of domestic industries and companies), avoidance of unnecessary barriers to trade — cannot contain some of the unruliness of historically and geopolitically informed economic action.[5]

In what follows I begin by asking why China bothered to join the WTO. I then move among various documents, texts, and disputes to trace the production of desiring China. These include the documents of the Working Party to China's accession to the WTO, debates in U.S. Congress to set the terms of China's accession, the writings of Chinese government officials, economists, and philosophers who hold quite different perspectives on the implications of the WTO for the life of Chinese citizens, and, finally, international disputes over dumping and "unfair" trade.

One final impetus for writing this essay should be noted. As the dominant force behind the WTO, the United States arrogated for itself the right to set the main terms for China's entry. I was not at all surprised at this turn of events. But the anti-China position taken by U.S. Americans who identify themselves as progressive and who, from varied vantage points, are critical of globalization did come as a surprise. I refer to the coalition of labor, environmentalist, and human rights groups who opposed having the United States grant permanent normal trade relations (PNTR) to China (a necessary precursor, as I explain below, to China's entry into the WTO). This coalition voiced its opposition to China at the Seattle demonstrations against the WTO. I had difficulty fathoming why progressives singled out China, as if preventing its entry into the WTO would solve the enormous problems posed by the enactment of global neoliberal policies. I thought their position was not only wrongheaded but racist. I also worried that one of the unintended consequences of their position was to strengthen U.S. government demands in the negotiations. Although this essay is not a direct critique of those progressive positions (see Bello 2001 and Cockburn 1999), I hope it makes a contribution to transnational progressive politics that does not inadvertently privilege the United States' imperial longings.

WHY BOTHER TO JOIN?

China formally joined the WTO in December 2001. The years prior to its accession witnessed the rapid expansion of China's economy, including an explosion in foreign trade. China quickly became one of the fastest growing economies in the world. By 2000, it was the world's seventh largest trading country (Lardy 2002). One could argue that China was already well integrated into the global economy prior to its entry into the WTO. Why, then, bother to join? Jiang Zemin and other central government leaders never felt compelled to explain to Chinese citizens why they pursued China's accession to the WTO as vigorously as they did. But a simple answer might be that government leaders saw they had little choice. Indeed, the consequences of being left out of the WTO seem dismal, since the WTO privileges members with those trade advantages that it, along with the World Bank and the International Monetary Fund (IMF), claim are the sine qua non of economic growth for all.

The 1997 "Asian" financial crisis brought home this dilemma to China. The crisis made an indelible mark on the thinking of those in China in favor of "opening" to the West but who did not want to repeat China's semi-colonial history that the socialist revolution had so tenaciously overcome. The crisis did not affect China directly, mainly because China's financial system was not open to foreign speculation at the time. But it had an impact on China's economic relations with those countries most affected. As importantly, it served as a moment of "economic terror." In China it was read as a warning, a threat, and a possible premonition. It led to the realization that the neoliberal version of globalization was no longer external to China but internal to it.

This interpretation of the Asian financial crisis as economic terror perpetrated by the West struck me forcibly in a reunion I had several years after the crisis with old friends in Hangzhou, where I had conducted field research for my first book. The Lius are a family with a complex political history. The grandparents were famous traditional Chinese medical doctors. Severely persecuted during several political campaigns, including the Cultural Revolution, they regained their previous stature under economic reform. Although their five children were considered to be descendants of intellectuals and therefore suspect, one of the older ones managed to get through medical school prior to the Cultural Revolution. The others, however, were sent down to the countryside and had their education disrupted. One became a truck driver; several worked in factories. The various family members expressed the sardonic view of those who had never believed in the party-state. Talking with them about politics was thus always illuminating and often a pleasure.

When I visited Hangzhou in September of 2000, nearly ten years had passed since we had last seen one another. The whole family had gathered in honor of my visit: the five brothers and sisters and their children. We reminisced about the grandparents who had passed away, and then they launched into a discussion of politics. I remembered that this generation, who had come of age during the Cultural Revolution, felt that politics, particularly what I have elsewhere called the "politics of authority," was the most important defining feature of their lives (Rofel 1999). I felt a keen pleasure in our conversation. I had spent a great deal of time in the intervening years with those who had come of age after the end of socialism and who had come to believe that politics, at least of the state-level variety, was meaningless. The Lius brought me back to that earlier moment. The youngest son, Liu Xinghuang, the truck driver, opened the conversation by remarking on the Asian financial crisis. Although the crisis had occurred three years previously, for my friends its import was still worth reflection. "How one man, like Soros, can pull his money in and out like that is impressive," Xinghuang began, somewhat neutrally. He waited to see how I would respond. I condemned the action without hesitation, commenting that this kind of globalization was not a good thing in my view. Then Xinghuang and the others felt free to give vent to their feelings. They continued to dissect the details of the crisis, concluding that it certainly showed how the West can throw its weight around. They were the first ones I heard use the term "terror" to label the crisis, remarking humorously that there are all kinds of "terror" in the world.

This perception of the Asian financial crisis as economic terror also informs a key essay by one of China's main negotiators with the WTO, Long Yongtu. His essay, "Some Thoughts on Questions Pertaining to Economic Globalization" (1999), enumerates the reasons for China's aspiration to join the WTO. Tellingly, he opens with the Asian financial crisis: "Last July Thailand's financial crisis began and quickly spread to the other Southeast Asian countries. It continued its assault on Korea and Japan, causing tremors throughout the globe. It led everyone to become more deeply conscious that all countries' economies are increasingly interconnected, that they permeate one another, influence one another, and depend on one another for their existence. Economic globalization has become an unavoidable reality" (1999, 42). One cannot underestimate this interpretation of the Asian financial crisis in pressing China to join the WTO.

In addition to terror, one should also consider the desire to join. As I noted in chapters 4 and 5, the constitution of "desiring China" rests in part on the emergence of a vast world of consumption, especially after Deng Xiaoping's 1992 Southern Tour. The arena of consumption is positioned not merely as that which will fulfill a hunger distilled from the Maoist era for a non-ascetic life but as that which will respond to all longings and aspirations. For that reason, I call this conviction "consumer fundamentalism."

Consumer fundamentalism incorporates the pleasures of consumption into a belief that the deep answers to life's dilemmas lie in consumption. More like religion than economics, it is founded on eschatological anxieties about hopes and dreams for the future. Like religious fundamentalisms, consumer fundamentalism offers a literalist interpretation of consumer practices and, most importantly, renders dangerous thoughts of turning elsewhere or raising other questions subsumed under consumption, such as questions of social inequality, social justice, or the appropriate role of the state. My concept of consumer fundamentalism is not meant to belittle the true pleasures citizens have gained in China in the comforts of their everyday lives. Rather, it is meant to highlight the beliefs that surround these pursuits. Joining the WTO fosters this consumer fundamentalism. The two main benefits the WTO cites for itself are a change in the scale of economic activity and an increase in consumption choices. "Desiring China" rests on this consumer fundamentalism. Accession to the WTO thus enables further pursuit of this belief.

Nicholas Lardy, a research scholar at the Washington, D.C.–based Brookings Institution, has offered other answers to China's desire to enter the WTO, returning us to a narrower comprehension of the economic. Lardy's *Integrating China into the Global Economy* (2002) was written for those who might wish to invest in China, especially those in the United States. In its liberal vein, it cautions readers to understand China's dilemmas. Far from condemnatory or condescending, Lardy lauds China's economic achievements. Still, the arguments are contained within a neoliberal framework of free trade liberalization. Lardy argues that the central government turned to the WTO because economic growth in China had been much slower than stated in official reports. Increased inventories of unsalable goods and slow productivity compounded this overstatement. Moreover, despite the fact that the state-owned industrial sector appears to be an increasingly small part of the economy, it still controls a majority of fixed assets and working capital (15). Lardy asserts that central government leaders believed that entry into the WTO would push the state-run sector to become more efficient (i.e., be willing to lay off more workers).

Han Deqiang (2000), in his widely read book *Peng Zhuang* (*Collision*), disagrees with an economistic explanation for the central government's desire to belong to the WTO. Han argues that "market romanticism" (5) propelled China into the WTO. For Han, the WTO's essence lies in an ideology of complete market freedom, a theory that the market itself can create the greatest good for society. "Market romanticism" is thus the belief that so-called free competition will automatically lead to progress. Market romanticism, Han argues, is the means by which countries with strong economies demolish countries with weak economies, not allowing them any self-protection. This idea of market omnipotence has become pervasive in China, according to Han. Market romanticism, Han concludes, has allowed foreign investment to overwhelm domestic competition. "According to the logic of 'weed out the backwards elements,'" he writes, "those who were able to survive were only the labor intensive industries and Chinese subcontracting factories of multinational corporations that produce local products and market locally. China has been weeded out" (1).[6] While sharing the central government's goal to develop a strong China, Han believes the Chinese government's efforts to join were based on a misguided faith in the possibilities for greater economic growth that the WTO represents.

Another progressive intellectual in China, Wang Hui, a historian and philosopher of science, holds a different perspective. In his dense historical meditation "The Year 1989 and the Historical Roots of Neo-liberalism in China" (2004), Wang subtly eschews the nationalism of *Peng Zhuang*. Rather than treat "China" as a unified subject, he emphasizes the social inequalities resulting from what he terms the government's "radical marketization." In implicit agreement with Lardy, Wang argues that China has already become one of the most enthusiastic participants in the global economy. But contrary to Lardy, Wang asserts that this participation, and China's broadening market economy, depend not merely on the state's close involvement in economistic measures like the transformation of state property into private property and price reform. It also relies on ideological articulations such as the utopian myth of development and the idea that China is in a "transitional period" toward "socialism with Chinese characteristics." Wang concludes that the ongoing legitimacy crisis of the state together with a globalization that had already become internal to China led to the Chinese government's desire to enter the WTO. In Wang's view, this ongoing legitimacy crisis stems not from simply instituting a market economy but from the nondemocratic manner in which the state did so. The result has been the marketization of power, official corruption, inequalities in the redistribution of state resources through privatization, and increased social polarization, including the widening gap between urban and rural life.

Economic terror, consumer fundamentalism, the perceived need for certain types of economic growth, market romanticism, and state legitimacy together provide the historical context for the Chinese government's dialogue with the WTO about the appropriate way to become a member. The neoliberalism evident in this process emerged together with the "desiring China" it was meant to produce. Signing on to the WTO's beliefs, however, did not obviate the political and historical encounters that entailed anything but a smooth process of articulation. Instead, differences and similarities were constituted, power was produced in unexpected maneuvers, and gaps and misapprehensions abounded that led to an unstable social field of neoliberal interaction.

THE LONG DURÉE OF CHINA'S ACCESSION

"In China's economic world, we have only the disciples of a market economy. The United States, on the other hand, is the pope of the market economy. To enter heaven, the disciples take their last pennies and give them to the pope. But the pope seeks pleasure and laughs derisively at these simpleminded disciples" (Han Deqiang 2000, 1).

Han Deqiang's satirical description of the market economy leads us back to the playful metaphor of joining the church. The central government's keen desire to join the "universal economics" of neoliberalism despite its terrors provided the necessary precondition for the WTO negotiations. Yet this desire and these terrors set the terms of the negotiations in a manner analogous to religious obligation and hierarchy. To join the imagined universal world of neoliberalism is similar to joining the universal religion of Christianity. One must agree to believe in these truths, even as they might contradict everyday experience and established habits, and even as church members continuously disagree with one another's interpretations of them.[7] Otherwise, the consequences of purgatory loom large.

The idea that free-trade liberalization represents and enacts a universal truth actually belies a long history of alternations among protection, regulation, and different modes of free trade (Arrighi 1994). Following nineteenth-century British mercantilism and prior to the end of World War II, for example, the United States government was opposed to the idea of free trade. Arguments that imports ruined the domestic economy and increased unemployment predominated (Peet 2003). When the United States emerged as the world's most powerful economy after World War II, it was able to shape the GATT to further its hegemony but it was still opposed to unilateral free trade, refusing to adopt the model the British colonial government had once instituted. GATT was merely a forum for negotiations on tariffs between countries. Only in the 1960s and 70s, after the United States firmly dominated world trade (as signaled by its ability to replace the gold standard with the dollar) and had attracted the majority of foreign financial investment yet faced decreasing profit margins due in part to competitive pressures from Japan and Germany, did U.S. capitalists push for the liberalization of trade.

It should not be surprising that when China began negotiations to enter the WTO, it had to contend above all with the United States. This despite the fact that the main investments in China continued to be from Hong Kong, Taiwan, and Japan. Nonetheless, the Chinese and U.S. economies had become more thoroughly enmeshed in one another. China had grown into the fourth largest supplier of U.S. imports and the second largest source of the U.S. trade deficit (Wong et al. 2000, 24).[8] The United States serves as a contradictory site of identification and competition for China. In the initial years of economic reform, it provided a source of critique for those in China opposed to the communist party and a source of dreams about democracy. But as the years wore on, key events exposed deep contradictions in what America signifies to Chinese citizens: the U.S. government involvement in the rejection of China's first bid for the Olympics; the translation into Chinese of Samuel Huntington's *Clash of Civilizations*; the U.S. bombing of the Chinese embassy in Belgrade during the Kosovo War; the invasion of Chinese air space by a U.S. spy plane; the Wen Ho Lee case; and finally, the appearance of U.S. military bases in former Soviet countries, which means that China is now completely surrounded by the U.S. military.

These tensions set the stage for the kinds of debates held over the bilateral trade agreement between China and the United States, which the latter made the condition for China's accession to the WTO. These negotiations further depict the historically contingent production of both "desiring China" and neoliberalism. They illuminate the strange hybridity of neoliberal encounters and the difficulties of drawing the line between licit and illicit capitalist desires. The negotiations were long-term and acrimonious. They began even before the formation of the WTO, when China petitioned in 1986 to have its GATT status restored. For thirteen years, the United States raised objections and conditions, as these negotiations turned toward the issue of China's accession. In 1999, after many years of fraught political maneuvering, China and the United States were close to an agreement.

To get a sense of the negotiations at this stage, I turn to one of the final hearings held before the bilateral agreement was signed, the June 8, 1999, hearing at the U.S. House of Representatives before the Subcommittee on Trade of the Committee on Ways and Means. This hearing entertained testimony from committee members, other members of Congress who wished to express an opinion, and various invited speakers, including government officials, business executives, trade association representatives, and one labor representative.

The hearing occurred after a significant agreement had nearly been reached in April between China and the United States in which China had acceded to many of the latter's demands. But that agreement got derailed. As the chair of the committee, Congressman Philip Crane, put it: "With the recent revelations of our lax defense against Chinese espionage activities [referring to the Wen Ho Lee case] and the bitter reaction in China to the accidental bombing of the Chinese Embassy in

Belgrade, United States-China relations continue down a rocky road" (U.S. Government 1999, 5).[9] This rocky road, however, was worth traversing, even for a Republican. As Representative Jennifer Dunn put it, "The open exchange of goods and services has been a critical component of fostering understanding between nations for centuries. It permits Ned Graham, the son of Reverend Billy Graham and strong proponent of trade with China, to distribute millions of bibles in mainland China" (9). Chair Crane's contextualizing remarks helped to fan the missionizing fantasy: "In exchange for steep tariff reductions and wholesale reforms of the Chinese trading system, the United States gives up nothing" (5). Indeed, nearly the only concession the United States had to make was to give up its annual review of China's trade status and grant China permanent Normal Trade Relations. In previous years, the United States had arrogated the right to hold an annual ritual to review China's behavior and decide whether to continue granting it what was then called Most Favored Nation Status. The heart of the hearings in fact centered on whether to grant China permanent Normal Trade Relations (NTR). Tellingly, some of those present kept slipping between this agenda and the idea that the hearings were to grant China accession to the WTO.

The hearings reflected a surprising field of political tactics. Liberal Congress members felt obliged to denounce China and painted a picture of a draconian, authoritarian state with no market economy, while corporate CEOs lauded China's openness. The way in which various speakers linked economic activity to political and social activity created strange hybrids that belie the idea that neoliberalism is a uniform set of principles. Those who denounced China's human rights record took an essentialist approach: they denied the idea that market transactions lead to bourgeois rights. They wanted Congress to deny China permanent NTR status, implying that the root cause of the dilemmas in China was something essential about the difference between China's lack of ability to grasp democracy and Western values. The CEOs, on the other hand, argued for an intimate "contact zone" (Pratt 1992) and a nonessentialist approach to the idea of change in China. Representative Nancy Johnson, supportive of the CEOs, asked that they comment on the issue of human rights in China. Following up on the testimony of several CEOs who claimed that their factories in China set positive examples for Chinese workers, Representative Johnson slid quickly from human rights to rights and responsibilities as individuals to the benefits that these companies offer, such as home ownership (100).[10] Representative Levin asked the pointed question of whether the Western values these companies bring include the right of workers to form labor unions. George Fischer, CEO of Eastman Kodak, replied that they bring "a basic value system . . . respect for the dignity of the individual, uncompromising integrity in everything all of our employees do, trust, credibility, continuous improvement" (91). Representative Charles Rangel then inserted a comment that almost appeared to be an aside: "If expanded trade with China is so important to move that great country into a democratic form of government, should not those same principles apply as it relates to Cuba?" (102). Chair Crane quickly crushed that point. But Levin's and Rangel's remarks highlight the unruliness of geopolitically informed economic action. No approach to neoliberalism that treats it as a set of logical and fixed principles can capture this unruliness.

John Sweeney of the AFL-CIO denounced China's treatment of workers and the Chinese government's repression of independent trade unions. He argued that China's accession agreement to the WTO — again sliding into the implicit agenda of the hearings — should include, in addition to monitoring its record on workers' rights, a safeguard provision against unpredicted import surges, provisions ensuring that parties other than the U.S. government can take action when imports cause market disruption, and a longer phase-out period on U.S. quotas for Chinese apparel and textiles. Representative Rangel again inserted what appeared to be a side note in response to Sweeney. While supporting the idea that the WTO should attend to labor rights, Rangel commented: "I don't know how in the world we could ever monitor that in China when we don't monitor that in Washington Heights in the Lower East Side [in New York City]. When we have prisoners — and one out of three black kids between 18 and 35 in this country ends up in the criminal justice system — we have them doing work competing with the private sector. We have sweatshops. We have welfare workers replacing civil servants right here in this country by the government making these decisions" (123). His comments were ignored. Both remarks, however, reflect the difficulty of deciding which principles should underlie neoliberalism. Sweeney's comments implicitly highlighted the difficulty of drawing nationalist borders around economic activity. The "imports" that Sweeney wanted to control include goods made for U.S. and other multinationals in Chinese factories either subcontracting to those companies or partially owned by them. Rangel's remarks about sweatshop and prison labor pinpoint the difficulty of discerning the difference between proper and immoral capitalist practices.

The testimony of several CEOs further accentuated these contingencies. Time and again in the hearings, the CEOs moved from discussion of trade to the fact that one of their main goals in support of NTR — and thus China's ability to join the WTO — was to protect their ability to establish factories and companies in China. George Fischer alluded to the fact that 80 percent of his company's "exports" from the United States go to one of their "foreign subsidiaries" for further work, "making overseas factories our best customers for made-in-USA products and materials" (63). In the written testimony he submitted to supplement his oral comments, Fischer was more precise: "In 1998 alone, we exported more than $100 million in goods and materials to China, mostly to our own facilities" (64). George David, of United Technologies Corporation, averred that his company's exports to China supported three thousand jobs in the United States. A few minutes later, he boasted that the company employed ten thousand people in China in twenty-one ventures (72–73). How, one wonders, does one make sense, any longer, of the categories "exports" and "imports" — not to mention "customers"? What, then, is the meaning of "trade"? Despite the economistic definitions of these terms in various trade agreements and laws that reach for pure forms, the messiness in the translation of these terms comes through in historically situated interpretations such as these hearings.

These hearings had about them the air of a foregone conclusion. More ritual than debate, they appeared to allow for the voicing of opinions even as they were stacked in favor of those who wanted to grant China permanent Normal Trade Relations status. As ritual, they preferred differing fantasies about "desiring China." Desiring China appears both open and seducible but also opaque and voracious. Still, no one in these hearings took Wang Hui's position: the very marketization of China has led to the abuses the members of Congress worried about. Nor did the hearings respond to a query voiced from developing countries in the recent past: Why are the northern states only concerned with the conditions of our workers now, when we are competitive with them?

In China, no such hearing occurred. Instead, China conducted its own familiar political ritual: an education campaign. Using the socialist narrative genre to laud market economy principles, the campaign set about to change people's consciousness about the WTO after central government leaders had already decided that China should join. A representative article from the November 1999 *Zhonghua Gongshang Shibao* (*China Industry and Commerce Times*), "Zhongguo Ru Shi Shi Da Hao-chu" ("China's Entry into the WTO: Ten Advantages,") quoted Professor Wu Yaotian, director of the Shanghai Research Center, explaining the advantages China would enjoy when it joins the WTO. These advantages create a vision of "desiring China" as emerging through the intimacies of economic encounters. Professor Wu states that China's accession to the WTO would increase the enthusiasm of foreign enterprises to invest in China; expand China's exports; benefit China's reforms, which are "inseparable from the outside environment"; benefit the reform of state-run enterprises, "which are like an only child, without cares or worries" (i.e, without competitive pressures); compel internal demand; increase the "consumer power of the masses"; and help resolve "the Taiwan problem" because Taiwan was also in the process of joining the WTO (as an independent customs territory) and their mutual accession would increase "interchange across the straits."

Professor Wu conducted his education campaign by weaving elements of everyday life into his narrative that made both "desiring China" and neoliberal trade appear as coherent, intertwined entities. The portrayal of China's reforms as inseparable from the "outside" recalls the revision of history I addressed in chapter 4, namely, the retrospective idea that China was "closed" under Maoism and this closure was partially responsible for Maoism's excesses (thus erasing the history of post-Bandung alliances). The representation of state-run enterprises as "only children" touched a sensitive nerve among Chinese citizens about how the one-child policy (for urban residents) is producing overweight, understimulated children who might not attain cosmopolitan features. The idea that consumers have power and that this power might enhance "the masses" reflects the postsocialist emphasis I discussed in chapter 5 that consumers have replaced workers as heroes of the nation. Finally, mention of the relationship with Taiwan invokes a mainland Chinese nationalism that, in turn, recalls the history of Japanese colonial occupation of Taiwan and U.S. American intervention in China's civil war during and after World War II. By weaving these elements into what otherwise appears to be a rather staid lecture to the newspaper's readers, the newspaper article, like numerous similar ones published during that period in China, conjures "desiring China" into existence as a coherent whole.

An extensive speech by Wu Yi, one of the main negotiators with the WTO, to government cadres, produced a "desiring China" that appears a bit less coherent and requires a great deal more work on the part of cadres to bring into existence. Her speech is exhortatory in the genre of socialist narratives. It reveals how political speech attempts to make the intimate articulation of economic policy and subjectivity. Wu Yi gave the speech to the Foreign Economic Trade Commission as China was on the verge of finalizing its WTO commitments. It was entitled "Base Ourselves on a New Starting Point, Shoulder a New Mission: Opening a New Phase in the Development of Foreign Economic Trade." Wu Yi begins with a lengthy review of the domestic economy's accomplishments. As with other political speeches of this genre, she arrives at the heart of the matter only near the end of the speech:

> Use entry into the WTO as a turning point. Energetically press for innovations in the economic system and changes in government. Conscientiously carry out the preparatory work of entering the WTO. This is one of the ten major tasks for the Central Foreign Economic Trade Commission's work for next year. We need to view with clarity the fact that entry into the WTO carries with it opportunities and battle-like challenges, advantages and drawbacks. It is not static, with no change allowed, but is relative and can be transformed. The key to how to turn the challenges into opportunities and the constraints into motivations lies with us. Each locale, each government bureau, especially the various foreign trade bureaus, must complete the preparatory work for entering the WTO, to place it in a top position for next year's work. (2001, 69)

Thus Wu Yi portrayed accession to the WTO as a transformative process for China but one that is also always in transformation. Her metaphor is strategic war rather than monotheistic religion. She envisions incessant repositionings rather than the fixity of logical principles. As she continued, she clarified that such constant maneuverings require a dual outlook, one toward the correct handling of foreigners and the other toward the masses:

We must do this work according to the evolution of negotiations for our country's entry into the WTO. There are procedures for each area, government bureau, and type of industry; time-dependent agreements our country needs to carry out. You need to become familiar with and research the WTO's rules and regulations . . . and establish a legal system concerning matters with foreigners that is in keeping with our country's realities and conforms with the WTO's regulations. Every bureau that has anything to do with foreign affairs needs to uphold the unity and transparency of economic policies concerning foreigners . . . Research and take advantage of the provisions in the WTO rules and regulations for new members and the exceptions for developing country members. Perfect the mechanisms for the accelerated system of foreign trade allowed by the WTO that will also protect our domestic industries . . . Work hard to raise up our great cadres, especially our leading cadres' level of familiarity and ability to put into practice the WTO's rules and regulations and the conventions of international trade. Spread knowledge of the WTO throughout society. Don't just have those in enterprise or scholarly circles master and be able to use the WTO's regulations. You need to ensure that the masses have a basic understanding of the WTO. Push forward a change in mentality, increase a more open consciousness, create the necessary social basis . . . Create an environment that will keep people tied here, establish mechanisms for allowing superior talent to be distinguished and for giving free rein to people's capabilities. (69)

Wu Yi's rhetoric mimics Mao's classic "On the Correct Handling of Contradictions" (1936) which addressed class relations among Chinese peasants in the countryside. Unlike Professor Wu's lecture, Wu Yi draws a clear line between foreigners and Chinese. Their desires are not intimately intertwined but need to be carefully distinguished. Cadres must handle foreigners' desires correctly, that is, they must accede to the letter of the WTO rules but also know that those rules are subject to exceptions and different interpretations. On the other side, however, lie the masses. In a rhetoric that sounds like a faint parody of the socialist past, Wu Yi exhorts cadres to educate the masses about the WTO. Why do they need this education? It appears that the answer lies in fashioning China's accession to the WTO into a coherent whole, from economic policy to individual consciousness. Wu Yi's speech implies that "desiring China" can only come into existence if these differing elements appear united.

But cadres also need to change their consciousness:

> The current moment is for reconstructing thought, study and work styles. This will guarantee continued advance in the transformation of government functions. In this regard, I want to emphasize some problems in thought and work styles.
>
> In our preparatory work to enter the WTO, many aspects have required exploration and creativity in the midst of practice. Any kind of thought that clings to the old system and is unwilling to forge ahead, any kind of formal subjectivism, any kind of dogmatism — all of these will be out of place with the new situation and demands after entry into the WTO . . . Go further in liberating your thinking, seek truth from facts, carry out these practices with courage, be innovative. Make sure your thoughts and ideas, work mentality, policy application, and concrete activities incessantly conform with world trends and that they make sense in the new era, which has bestowed on us this important historical responsibility . . . The work of foreign trade requires emphasizing reality, speaking the truth, carrying out authentic work, seeking credible results, and firmly conquering formalism and bureaucratism . . . In this way, the development of our foreign trade will bring forth the appearance of a new atmosphere. (69)

Here, Wu Yi's speech continues with its exhortatory commands. She is rousing cadres in time-honored socialist narrative style while pressing them to abandon time-honored socialist work styles. She frames joining the WTO as not only a historical inevitability but a historical responsibility. That responsibility is to the world, not just to Chinese citizens. But cadres need to transform both their consciousness and their conduct in order to shoulder this worldly responsibility. Wu Yi's speech expresses concern that cadres will cling to "formalism" (i.e., put forth false statistics under pressure to create pleasing appearances for the central government), "bureaucratism" (i.e., slow down economic change with bureaucratic measures invoked out of apprehension over blame and responsibility), and "dogmatism" (i.e., interpreting party rhetoric "literally"). Implicit in this speech, then, is a conversation within the party. Unlike the hearings in the U.S. Congress, which assumed the ability to construct knowledge of others, this narrative directs itself to the transformation of the self as that which is vital to become "desiring China" in the eyes of the world.

This speech could be viewed as a classic example of "governmentality," that is, of attention to the "conduct of conduct." Much has been written about Foucault's concept of governmentality (Burchell, Gordon, and Miller 1991). These writings have emphasized how power operates not just from the centralized locus of the state toward citizens but in a dispersed and diffused manner through experts, leading citizen-subjects to take it upon themselves to monitor their own conduct. Recently the concept has been used to develop the idea that neoliberalism is a form of governmentality, that economic policies, regimes of power/knowledge, and subjectivities structurally line up together in a coherent manner (see my introduction). Wu Yi's speech implicitly highlights the question of how "the state" reforms its own conduct. How do those who speak in the name of the state realize a form of conduct and get others who represent the state to reform their conduct? Wu Yi urges cadres to reform their conduct by presenting them with the relationship between neoliberal trade encounters, political consciousness, and subjectivities as if they were coherently connected. Her speech makes us realize we should not assume the coherence of these connections but search for how that coherence is made. It takes work. And Wu Yi is clearly not at all sure she will succeed. While Wu Yi certainly exhorts cadres to develop a new subjectivity, to conduct their conduct differently than before, the concept of governmentality fails to capture the subtle anxieties underlying the speech. The operation of power among cadre-officials is deeply entrenched. Their own modes of both adhering to and maneuvering around socialist bureaucratic life might not be so easy to change. Theories of neoliberal governmentality accept Foucault's emphasis on historical disjunctures (although Foucault also acknowledged continuities). While the production of "desiring China" presents a clear moment of historical transformation and perhaps marks a radical disjuncture, numerous cultural and political practices such as cadres' bureaucratic routines extend across the historical divide between the socialist and postsocialist periods. They live on not as historical anachronisms but as part of the postsocialist operation of power.

Through different routes and distinctive visions of neoliberal encounters, members of the United States Congress and Chinese cadres eventually converged toward the same goal, that of China's successful accession to the WTO. The United States has an overweening influence on the WTO, but the Chinese state is also a co-creator of these encounters. The Chinese government's construction of a "desiring China" that would legitimate the state and foster consumer fundamentalism meant adherence to a discourse that the United States first used to stake its claim to superiority. But subscription to this discourse did not obviate the ability to criticize American imperial aspirations, as China did when NATO bombed its Belgrade embassy, and has continued to do since, with the installation of American military bases in the former Soviet countries. Still, the final bilateral agreement between China and the United States, signed in November 1999, contained numerous concessions by China to lower its tariff and nontariff barriers in areas of concern to U.S. businesses, namely, automobiles, agriculture, and telecommunications. These levels were well below those agreed to by other members of the WTO. China also conceded to the United States' demand to maintain a special anti-surge safeguard mechanism against Chinese imports. Perhaps most astonishing of all, with regard to anti-dumping rules — a key provision in WTO agreements, as we will see — the United States insisted on the right to consider China a "non-market" economy for fifteen years after China's accession to the WTO. Since dumping decisions are based on fair market value, by definition China would be considered an "unfair" market, regardless of the actual circumstances of trade. The United States additionally abrogates to itself the right to monitor China's compliance with WTO regulations on an annual basis. This bilateral trade agreement is widely acknowledged to have been the key factor in paving China's entry into the WTO.[11]

WTO NEGOTIATIONS

It is easy to imagine that the WTO applies a universal set of rules and regulations to all countries in the same manner. The WTO itself makes this claim. It portrays itself as laying out the pure forms of neoliberal capitalism. If one thinks of WTO rules at the most general level — that trade should be "liberalized," for example — then perhaps this assertion appears credible. But a closer look at encounters structured through the WTO reveals that the organization regulates a plethora of detail particular to each country and that country's specific relations with other countries. The contentious economic and discursive encounters that develop over these details highlight the cultural production of an unstable process of heterogeneous neoliberal practices. They highlight how efforts to instill economic purification end up producing unexpected and, to use Mei Zhan's term, "unruly hybrids" (2005). Culture and history replace abstract universality in these encounters. In this section, I examine one of the central WTO documents that details the negotiations for China's accession. The "Report of the Working Party on the Accession of China" (Working Party 2001) (hereafter the "Report"), completed on October 1, 2001 (coincidentally the anniversary of the Chinese socialist revolution), spells out the final commitments China had to fulfill before being allowed to enter the WTO. I turn to this document rather than to the final agreement because it offers more insight into the processes of negotiating global capitalism.

The Report constitutes China as a special problem for world trade. It moves between assertions that China needs to become the same as other countries and endless deferrals of that sameness by constructing China's difference. In the case of China, the Report asserts that it is difficult to distinguish between the state and the market, that the Chinese government is both too controlling but then again not controlling enough, that China demonstrates only surface but not substantive compliance with WTO regulations, that there needs to be more heterogeneity in China's market practices but then again there is altogether too much heterogeneity within China, and that although China needs to become transparent (to investors), that goal might be only a distant reality since China is complex, inconsistent, and hard to fathom. I take up each of these paradoxical points in turn.

Early in the document, the Working Party concedes that China will continue to have "state-owned" and "state-invested" enterprises. But it wants to ensure that government involvement in market activity is constrained in particular ways. For example, Paragraph 44 states: "In light of the role that state-owned and state-invested enterprises played in China's economy, some members of the Working Party expressed concerns about the continuing governmental influence and guidance of the decisions and activities of such enterprises relating to the purchase and sale of goods and services. Such purchases and sales should be based solely on commercial considerations, without any governmental influence or application of discriminatory measures."

The WTO is asking the Chinese government to draw the fine line between state-based interests and market-based ones. Various state organs may own enterprises, but they should not use the state power at their disposal to influence the success of the enterprise, even if various state-run enterprises are in competition with one another. It is a shadow play, exchanging the visible hand of the state for the seemingly invisible hand of the market. But the WTO implicitly acknowledges that the growth of profit-making activity in China is historically specific. That history includes the central government's encouragement of and pressure on various state bureaucracies and local governments to become profitable and to procure their state budgets through their profit-making enterprises. As well, a large number of profit-oriented businesses are mixtures of local government ownership and private management (Oi and Walder 1999). In some cases, the local government is more adept than private investors at raising the capital that it then puts at the disposal of the enterprise. Far from dampening profit-making activity, state activities have fostered it.

Thus the undecidability between "government procurement" and "commercial sale": "any measure relating to state-owned and state-invested enterprises importing materials and machinery used in the assembly of goods, which were then exported or otherwise made available for commercial sale or use or for non-governmental purposes, would not be considered to be a measure relating to government procurement" (Paragraph 44).

That is to say, if the government were running an enterprise for non-commercial purposes, then its activities would come under the rubric "government procurement" and would not be subject to the same WTO rules and regulations as those activities geared toward making profits. But the development of China's economy, one of the world's fastest-growing economies, rests precisely on the deft imbrication of these activities.

One of the main goals of the Report is to ensure that China will hasten its withdrawal of government guidance from a wide range of activities that can make themselves available to schemes for seeking profit. Much of the Report, the Draft Protocol, and the final Accession Agreement are specifications of the dates by which the Chinese government must withdraw its involvement in specific activities, ranging from subsidies for various agricultural and industrial products to insurance to financial investment institutions. Throughout, the Report reaches for clear and indisputable distinctions between the state and the market. Time and again the Report falls back on acknowledgments that the history of China's postsocialism means such distinctions are not only impossible but that neoliberal capitalism has thrived in China precisely by blurring the division between the state and the market.

The Report seesaws back and forth between criticisms of China for too much government control and demands that China institute more government control. Paragraph 50, for example, criticizes excessive price controls:

> Some members of the Working Party noted that China had made extensive use of price controls, for example in the agricultural sector. Those members requested that China undertake specific commitments concerning its system of state pricing. In particular, those members stated that China should allow prices for traded goods and services in every sector to be determined by market forces, and multitier pricing practices for such goods and services should be eliminated. Those members noted, however, that China expected to maintain price controls on the goods and services listed in Annex 4 to the Draft Protocol and stated that such controls should be maintained in a manner consistent with the WTO Agreement, in particular Article III of GATT 1994 and Annex 2, paragraphs 3 and 4, of the Agreement on Agriculture.

Note that the WTO does not require the full elimination of price controls, only their elimination on goods and services of historical concern to other members, most particularly to the United States, such as agriculture.

Paragraph 80 focuses on control over imports and exports:

> Some members of the Working Party noted that China was in the process of liberalizing the availability of the right to import and export goods from China, but that such rights were now only available to some Chinese enterprises (totalling 35,000). In addition, foreign-invested enterprises had the right to trade, although this was restricted to the importation for production purposes and exportation, according to the enterprises' scope of business. Those members stated their view that such restrictions were inconsistent with WTO requirements . . . and welcomed China's commitment to progressively liber-

alize the availability and scope of the right to trade so that within three years after accession all enterprises would have the right to import and export all goods.

Here, we find concern with the history of China's postsocialist engagements with capitalism. The Chinese state, mindful of China's colonial history, had initially required foreign companies to share their technologies and production processes with their counterparts in China and not merely use China for cheap labor. They had also required a certain level of investment in China in return for the right to make profit there. In addition, the state had kept a tight grip on which state organs could profit from foreign trade. Finally, the state attempted to limit foreign disruption of Chinese markets.

The replies by the representative of China to these two demands (and throughout the document) reflected both compliance with the "orthodoxies" of WTO's neoliberal principles but also statements of "heterodoxy" that make those principles a matter of paradoxes that engender ongoing disputes. They show again the Chinese state to be a coauthor in the making of neoliberal encounters. In the former case of price controls, the representative moved toward heterodoxy by providing a long justification of the continued use of both "government prices" and "government guidance prices," the former more strictly established than the latter but both justified in terms of "having a direct bearing on the national economy and the basic needs of the people's livelihood, including those products that were scarce in China" (Paragraph 52). The WTO committee accepted his remarks and this heterodoxy was incorporated into the trade agreements. In the latter case, the representative from China strove for orthodoxy: he confirmed that China would liberalize the scope and availability of trading rights by eliminating export performance, trade balancing, foreign exchange balancing, and prior experience requirements; by reducing the minimum registered capital requirement for wholly Chinese-invested enterprises; and by granting full rights to trade to foreign-invested enterprises without requiring them to be established in any particular form.

If the Report criticizes China for too much state control, it also criticizes the central Chinese government for not having enough control in relation to local governments: "Some members of the Working Party also raised concerns that many non-tariff measures were imposed by sub-national authorities in China on a non-transparent, discretionary and discriminatory basis. Those members of the Working Party asked that China undertake a commitment to ensure that non-tariff measures would only be imposed by the central government or by sub-national authorities with clear authorization from the central government" (Paragraph 123).

In discussions of government control, the WTO committee itself moves between faithfulness to the orthodoxy of its neoliberal beliefs and acceptance of heterodox practices. For neoliberal trade to work, it actually needs both less and more government control. The WTO committee's approach to the case of China reflects a recognition that the answers to which situations need which kind of governance are historical rather than deduced from the political theory of neoliberalism. They also depend on how various Chinese actors come to engage with and translate these transnational encounters. Central government leaders of China might well have been happy to use this WTO provision to rein in local governments and reassert a measure of control the central government had lost. In its desire to uphold the sense of coherence in neoliberalism, however, the WTO needs to move paradoxically between sameness and difference: China should be the same but is endlessly different. Echoes of orientalism can be found in these maneuvers, as they repeat the colonial desire to present a particular set of cultural values as universal.

This orientalism becomes much less subtle when the discussion turns to the idea that China shows only surface compliance with the commitments it has already made. The Working Party repeatedly demands transparency:

> Some members of the Working Party raised concerns that the current investigations by the Chinese authority [i.e., the Chinese state has its own methods for judging trade disputes at the current moment] would be judged to be inconsistent with the Agreement on Implementation of Article VI of GATT 1994 ("Anti-Dumping Agreement") if China were a Member of the WTO today. In certain cases, the basis for calculating dumping margins for a preliminary affirmative determination was not disclosed to interested parties. Furthermore, the determination of injury and causation did not appear to have been made on an objective examination of sufficient evidence. In the views of these members, bringing the Chinese anti-dumping

rules into compliance with the WTO agreement on its face was not sufficient. WTO consistency had to be secured substantively as well. (Paragraph 147)

The distinction between the surface of the face and the depth of substance is familiar language. It echoes a long history of accusations by Western missionaries, diplomats, and writers that Chinese people hide their inscrutability behind their "face." Such accusations lie in the culturally specific body/soul dichotomy of Christianity. Postcolonial scholars have analyzed these accusations as comprising the history of the idea of national character (Liu 1995) and of Western imperialism (Hevia 1995). They have delineated the multiple notions of "face" in Chinese culture as that which constructs sociality (Kipnis 1997, Martin 2003). Historians have additionally traced the complexity of imperial Chinese notions of tactile, bodily surfaces as in fact the site where one finds the subject's depth (Zito 1994, 1997). But in the Report, this inscrutable difference appears to be nearly impossible to overcome. The Report repeatedly demands greater "transparency" from the Chinese government. One can see another effect of this repeated emphasis on government transparency. It allows the secrecy of foreign companies to remain unremarkable.

If China is inscrutable, it is also too unpredictable. There is too much heterogeneity in China. The desire for homogeneity as a means to have predictability in China is expressed in the document, as noted above, in the relationship between the central and local governments:

> Several members of the Working Party raised concerns about the continued presence of multiple trade instruments used by different levels of government within China. Those members considered that this situation resulted in a lessening of the security and predictability of access to the Chinese market. These members raised specific concerns regarding the authority of sub-national governments in the areas of fiscal, financial and budgetary activities, specifically with respect to subsidies, taxation, trade policy and other issues covered by the WTO Agreement and the Draft Protocol. In addition, some members expressed concerns about whether the central government could effectively ensure that trade-related measures introduced at the sub-national level would conform to China's commitments in the WTO Agreement and the Draft Protocol. (Paragraph 69)

In response the representative of China confirmed that all local governments would conform with China's obligations undertaken in the WTO agreements. But as will become clear in the next section, "predictability" as a logical and generalizable principle does not ensure a homogeneity of interpretation when faced with specific historical encounters over trade.

This repeated emphasis on China's difference from a universal norm of neoliberal practices meant that China was called upon to prove, with extraordinary measures, its ability to become a universal capitalist subject. Yet, even as the Report spoke in terms of a coherent set of neoliberal principles, it grappled with the messiness of culture and history. In doing so, it worked to produce "desiring China" simultaneously with neoliberalism. The Chinese government's voice was included in the Report. It co-created "desiring China" and neoliberalism with the WTO in the encounters over how to interpret such seemingly cut and dried issues as the relationship between the state and the market and principles of transparency and predictability.

In the final accession agreement China was compelled to cut average tariff levels for agricultural products to 15 percent and for industrial products to 8.9 percent; to eliminate all quotas and other nontariff barriers to imports no later than 2005; to allow direct foreign investment in telecommunications services; to substantially open its markets in banking, insurance, securities, fund management, and other financial services; to phase out restrictions on distribution services; to lift most restrictions on the provision of professional services; to limit domestic support for agricultural producers and remove nontariff barriers to agricultural imports; and finally, to bind all tariffs at the lowest statutory rates as they are phased in. These concessions far exceed those of other member countries.

UNIVERSAL COHERENCE AND ITS AFTERMATH: DUMPING

The WTO insists that there exist transparent and uniform definitions and understandings for such concepts and practices as "trade equality," "freedom from constraint," "fairness," "predictability," "full market economy," "distortion," and "dumping." This reach for the pure forms of neoliberal capitalism has had the ironic effect of producing a proliferating number of trade disputes. They center on the problem of dumping. Dumping has historically been the sine qua non of free trade, as under British colonialism, and at the same time its feared opposite. As a result, dumping accusations assert a claim rather than offer a description of a well-defined practice. Like its cousin "piracy," the history of dumping exempifies the rearrangement in the meanings and practices of transnational trade encounters. Dumping accusations reveal the proliferation of capitalist strategies that do not fit neatly into categories such as predictability, even as WTO members use these categories to advance their claims. From an annual average of thirty cases in the 1950s and 1960s, dumping disputes have risen to 2,284 cases from the founding of the WTO in 1995 to 2003 (leading to an annual average of 285 cases per year).[12]

The WTO defines dumping as (1) selling products at prices lower than their normal value and (2) causing damage to a country's national industries.[13] Just what is considered a "normal value" and what constitutes "damage" turn out to be anything but straightforward. Countries lodging accusations of dumping against other countries are allowed to impose temporary import duties until their own trade ministries make a final ruling in the case. Any country may then appeal these duties and rulings to the WTO. The WTO has established a dumping dispute resolution board. These seemingly clear legalistic rules and definitions about dumping contain a basic paradox: while capitalism is, by its nature, competitive and therefore disruptive, an importing country may impose tariffs or quotas if its "national industries" experience disruption and undue competition.

China is a special case with regard to dumping. Because China had to accede to the rubric of "non-market economy" for fifteen years after its accession, other WTO members have a much easier time accusing China of dumping. They can accuse the Chinese government of providing unfair subsidies for the export of various goods and therefore of illicit competition, even if the government had nothing whatsoever to do with the actual production of said goods.[14] Thirty-three countries have initiated 544 anti-dumping investigations against Chinese exports since China's accession to the WTO.[15] These dumping accusations mean that the route for producing "desiring China" through the WTO entails the "friction" (Tsing 2005) of competing interpretations of valid and proper capitalism. The disputes reflect the difficulties of adjudicating between sinners and the chosen ones, between moral and upright capitalist competitors and immoral and unacceptable players in the game. Dumping disputes are especially prolific in this regard because what one country or group of capitalists calls dumping another regards as creative business practice — the quintessence of successful capitalism. They thus provide another window onto the cultural production of neoliberal desires as an unstable, ceaseless process. They reflect as well how trade is war by other means.

One of the major set of dumping accusations against China involves textiles. Before turning to this well-known issue, however, it might be instructive to begin with another case that has received less attention but will help to put in relief the complexity of the textile disputes. This case deals with furniture. In the first year after China's accession to the WTO, imports of all household and office furniture from China rose by 38 percent. In the three-year period between 2000 and 2003, the U.S. furniture manufacturing industry lost 34,700 jobs.[16] The case seemed, at first, straightforward. American furniture manufacturers accused China of dumping furniture imports on the U.S. market. "The future of the domestic furniture industry is at stake," declared Paul Broyhill, spokesperson for the American Furniture Manufacturers Committee for Legal Trade, a newly formed coalition of fifteen producers.[17] Their accusation got the attention of the U.S. Department of Commerce, which initiated an investigation. John Bassett, CEO of the U.S. furniture maker Vaughan-Bassett and a driving force behind the new coalition, unintentionally invoked earlier histories of dispossession by declaring, "There's a stampede here, and there's about a dozen cowboys out here now trying to turn the herd."[18] Intriguingly, it is not entirely clear who plays the cowboys and who the herd. Bassett seems to mean that he and other furniture makers are the cowboys staving off the stampede of Chinese goods. Then again, one could turn the image around and interpret it as saying that Chinese companies are herding in and corralling American furniture manufacturers. Auggie Tantillo, a representative of the American Manufacturing Trade Action Coalition, for example, stated categorically that "China has the ability to consume most of the U.S. market if left unrestrained."[19] Other evidence was marshaled to support their case: China manipulates its currency, China plays fast and loose with trade rules, and the U.S. trade deficit with China is expected to reach $120 billion.

The story quickly became more complex. If imposed, anti-dumping duties are actually paid by the U.S. importers of Chinese goods — and eventually by the American consumer. Thus began a story about the anti-Chinese furniture campaign in the *South Florida Sun-Sentinel*: "Norma Purinton was surprised to learn that the pretty, pale-wood bedroom furniture she selected at a Fort Lauderdale City Furniture store was made in China. Destined for a guest room in her Pompano Beach home, the suite carried a modest price tag. Adding matching bookcases and cabinets, the furniture totaled $3,500. A good deal, Purinton thought. But she said she might balk if their price was higher" (December 21, 2003, 1). This story begins to raise the contradictions between the WTO's mission to foster consumption and the interests of American furniture manufacturers. Who, then, represents the proper capitalist interests?

This type of consumer narrative emboldened furniture retailers in the United States to mount a counteroffensive against the furniture manufacturers. They organized the Furniture Retailers Group, which defended China. They argued that China has cheap labor and low production costs and therefore is not selling at unfairly low prices. They threatened to look elsewhere, such as Vietnam, for inexpensive furniture if the United States imposed anti-dumping tariffs. Several of the retailers even announced they would stop buying furniture from the American companies calling for the duties.

The final twist to the story emerged when one of the furniture manufacturing companies decided to withdraw from the American Furniture Manufacturers Committee for Legal Trade. Under pressure from the retailers, Hooker Furniture Corporation, located in Virginia, had to admit that its revenue growth in recent years was largely tied to its own imports of Chinese furniture.[20] Like Hooker, many U.S.-based manufacturing companies either have factories or subcontract with factories in China to cut down on their labor costs. These factories send parts or finished goods back to the United States. The question of how to label these imports by nationality or how to define their travel route thus becomes increasingly blurred. Are they imports, exports, or none of the above? Even when they are labeled imports, this category does not tell us about ownership. Nonetheless, in January 2004 the U.S. International Trade Commission announced a tentative ruling that there was "reasonable indication" that U.S. furniture manufacturers were hurt by bedroom furniture imported from China at less than fair value. The U.S. Commerce Department imposed preliminary duties of 4.9 to 24.34 percent on China's largest factories and duties of up to 198 percent on the smaller ones.

The furniture dispute reveals how the WTO's universal rules create competing interpretations about whose interests serve the interests of neoliberalism. They also construct a necessarily contested "desiring China," as the desires that traverse China through transnational trade are multiple and conflicting.

Lest one conclude that the United States is the only country accusing China of dumping, it is instructive to note that since China's entry into the WTO, Zimbabwe has accused China of dumping substandard footwear, India has accused China of dumping raw silk, Malaysia has accused China of dumping bicycles, and Mexico has accused China of dumping clothing. Thus, the WTO might be dominated by north-south inequalities, but it has also created south-south trade relations of contested power.

Wedded to producing "desiring China" through the WTO, various entrepreneurs, government officials, and lawyers in China have learned how to maneuver in the post-WTO world of anti-dumping accusations as well. Chinese companies successfully fought the first U.S. anti-dumping case brought against them after their entry into the WTO. It concerned ball bearings. In February 2002, the American Bearing Manufacturers' Association accused China of selling bearings on the U.S. market at prices lower than ordinary export prices and demanded an anti-dumping investigation. The investigation, by the U.S. International Trade Commission, covered 253 bearing enterprises in China's twenty-eight provinces and municipalities. According to the Chinese Xinhua News Agency (a government agency), at the time of this case, "In sharp contrast to their competitors who were well-versed in WTO rules of the game, many Chinese enterprises did not know what anti-dumping was, were always scared stiff by international lawsuits, and would automatically give up the right to challenge the lawsuits, thereby providing their rivals a chance to beat up and pressure Chinese enterprises."[21] But then the Chinese Chamber of Commerce for Importers and Exporters of Electrical and Mechanical Products held an emergency meeting with more than eighty bearing producers to discuss how to challenge the lawsuit. Eventually some fifty enterprises decided to participate in the class action suit in order to defend the U.S. market. The Xinhua article continues: "After braving the storms in the international market, some Chinese enterprises are no longer resigned to being taken advantage of by other people. Peer Bearing Company . . . after receiving the notice of the investigation . . . spent $1 million hiring a US lawyer, established an anti-dumping work group of a dozen or so full-time staff and completed the questionnaires under the lawyer's direction. Due to its adequate preparations and detailed and credible data in the preliminary notice of determination published by the US Department of Commerce in October last year, Peer Company had the lowest dumping margin . . . Past lawsuits show that challenging lawsuits is a travel permit in the market."[22]

Lawyers in China have begun to specialize in how to fight dumping disputes at the WTO. Wang Xuehua, for example, one of the founding partners of the law firm Beijing Huanzhong and Partners, was extensively involved in the trade dispute with the United States over imported steel. The United States lost its case before the WTO for protected steel tariffs. Wang felt that his experience in that case taught him "how to play by WTO rules."[23] He also recently won a U.S. anti-dumping case against Chinese apple juice imported into the United States. His firm has since handled seventeen of the twenty-seven anti-dumping cases filed in Chinese courts. "At the beginning," Wang said, "people felt panicked, bewildered and even outraged at any news that an anti-dumping case was raised against China. Many Chinese enterprises complain that the anti-dumping accusations against them are often unfair . . . But as experience grows, Chinese entrepreneurs know they have to face anti-dumping charges and have to handle them." Wang said that he now treats anti-dumping cases as "normal business." He offered the following advice: "All parties involved in foreign trade should study these matters to some extent, if they want to have the advantage in any potential disputes . . . the Chinese side should improve its awareness about the dumping activities of foreign exports [to China.] Chinese farmers are particularly vulnerable in this matter . . . Lots of people know a great deal about the WTO on the macro level, but we need more who are very familiar with the concrete rules."[24]

Since its entry into the WTO, China has launched a total of fifteen anti-dumping cases involving twenty-two countries, targeting products including iron and steel, chemicals, light industry products, textiles, and telecommunications. China has brought accusations against Japan, South Korea, Taiwan, and Thailand for dumping PVCs; against Japan, South Korea, and the United States for dumping art paper; against Taiwan for dumping steel; against Japan, South Korea, Taiwan, and the United States for dumping phenol, a chemical compound used in resins, plastics, and pharmaceuticals; and against the United States, South Korea, and Thailand for dumping unbleached Kraft liner and board. Playing the dumping and anti-dumping game of neoliberalism has paved a contentious route toward "desiring China." Even as it appears to be the only church in town, the WTO cannot rein in schisms in belief and practice.

THE ERASURE OF HISTORY AND ITS AFTERMATH:
MORE DUMPING

If the language of universality pervasive in the WTO has difficulty moving unimpeded across geopolitical space, it also has to move through time by addressing multiple histories of worldly encounters. Both time and space shape the "desiring China" coming into existence through the WTO. A different operation takes place with temporality, though. Since the WTO's mission is to spread neoliberal trade rules throughout the globe, it must incorporate spatial categories into its language and practice. The language of temporality, however, especially the recognition of specific histories of unequal trade, hinders the WTO's mission. Thus, the strategy is to ignore those histories rather than to incorporate them. Only the most recent history, and only a selective portion of it, is relevant. Witness the mission statement and brief history of the WTO:

> The World Trade Organization is the only international organization dealing with the global rules of trade between nations. Its main function is to ensure that trade flows as smoothly, predictably and freely as possible. The World Trade Organization came into being in 1995. One of the youngest of the international organizations, the WTO is the successor to the General Agreement on Tariffs and Trade (GATT) established in the wake of the Second World War. So while the WTO is

still young, the multilateral trading system that was originally set up under GATT is well over 50 years old.

The past 50 years have seen an exceptional growth in world trade. Merchandise exports grew on average by 6% annually. Total trade in 1997 was 14-times the level of 1950. GATT and the WTO have helped to create a strong and prosperous trading system contributing to unprecedented growth. (WTO n.d., 7)

World systems scholars might take issue with this timeline. Their timeline for world trading systems dates back to the thirteenth century (Abu-Lughod 1989) and for world capitalist relations back to the sixteenth century. Historians of colonialism would also remind us of the international divisions of production and consumption and their relations of dependency that supported colonial power. The WTO does not exactly deny these histories, but it treats them as irrelevant to the fantasy of the trade order they wish to establish. One might be curious, then, about the mapping of those WTO-cited trade relations in the immediate postwar period and the imagined world they portray. One might suppose that such a map would have a distant relationship to not only the Soviet networks of trade and their very different rules of interlinkage and mutual aid but also to many of the newly independent African nations that were marginalized by their former colonial rulers.

In addition to the partial erasure of alternative timelines, the WTO's universalist categories have multiple rhetorical effects in relation to temporality that are paradoxical: they imply an "end of history" perspective in which nothing but the most recent past has any significance and nothing but the most recent capitalist practices are proper and licit.[25] Working through the plethora of detail necessary for each country's accession to the WTO, however, necessarily means that WTO members must grapple with the histories of trade in particular products that implicitly betray other notions of history.

The negotiations over textiles are illuminating in this regard. The Report on China's accession to the WTO contains a short section on textiles that both hints at and ignores the long history of textile production in China. That history tied China to a world system of trade since at least the thirteenth century, and in the nineteenth century to the British empire, which spread its imperial rule through a multicountry nexus of textile production and consumption. The section begins:

Some members of the Working Party proposed and the representative of China accepted that the quantitative restrictions maintained by WTO Members on imports of textiles and apparel products originating in China that were in force on the date prior to the date of China's accession should be notified to the Textiles Monitoring Body ("TMB") as being the base levels for the purpose of application of Articles 2 and 3 of the WTO Agreement on Textiles and Clothing ("ATC"). (Paragraph 241)

In other words, those countries that already had import quotas on Chinese textiles in place prior to China's accession would be allowed to keep those quotas as base levels that would be phased out only after 2005. The representative of China agreed to set up an orderly process of consultation with WTO members who believe that Chinese textile imports were "threatening to impede the orderly development of trade in these products" (Paragraph 242, subsection [a]).

This bureaucratic language begins to hint that a history of production and trade in textiles pertained prior to China's entry into the WTO. Certainly, it refers most immediately to the import quotas of the 1980s and 1990s. But the history of China's textile production from the early part of the twentieth century hovers in the background of this recent past. China picked up its textile production in the 1980s basically where it left off at the time of the 1949 socialist revolution, following the same previous routes of trade and consumption. Most of the other agreements in the Report address the need for China to lower its barriers to foreign investment in China. With textiles, it is the other way around. Since textiles have long been one of China's main exports, the goal of the WTO was to create restraints on these exports.

It might be instructive to recall the history of British colonial textile networks that made China part of an interconnected and unequal world of textile production and trade. For the traces of this history persist in the unevenness and divisions of textile production and consumption of the WTO world. The British colonial textile industry also operated under a system of so-called free trade among its colonies. The British imperial version of free trade, combined with its political rule, allowed the British textile industry to dominate the world market. The British empire established a broad, multicountry network in textiles, including both cotton and silk, in order to extract the raw materials from its colonies, weave the clothing in England, and then export the finished cloth and garments to those same colonies. This broad network spanned slavery and cotton production in the United States, household silkworm cultivation, spinning and weaving in China, cotton handicraft weaving in India, and later the mechanical processes introduced by Britain into China and India in its search for cheaper labor that disrupted both its own Manchester textile industry and indigenous industries (Pomeranz 2000). Britain fostered this imperial domination in textiles through protective tariffs for its fledgling textile industry in the metropole, coupled with nonprotected trade to its colonies. With regard to India, for example, the British government carefully studied the varieties of clothing and fashion produced within India and then systematically proceeded to displace native weavers, especially those who produced middle-level Indian cloth and clothing (Harnetty 1991).[26] In addition, they instituted certain regulations for proper dress for those natives who worked within British firms and households (Cohn 1996). The British imperial textile industry also disrupted India's previously widespread global exports, the latter reviving only after the decline of the British empire. India's mechanized textile industry only got off the ground when the Indian National Congress insisted on protective tariffs in relation to Britain (Breman 2004).

In a sense, then, textiles signified colonial domination. Textile production and trade was a lightning rod for anti-colonial sentiment and nationalist organizing in both China and India. China's May 4th Movement of 1919 called for boycotts of British and Japanese textiles, while Gandhi's famous swadeshi movement to boycott British cloth and wear only indigenously produced clothing galvanized India's independence movement.[27] Both Chinese and Indian anti-colonial nationalists argued that their native textile handicrafts industries had been crushed by the inflow — or should I say dumping — of foreign manufactured goods.[28] The implementation of protective tariffs on textiles was one of the major planks of India's National Congress, while the Chinese communist party immediately nationalized the textile industry upon taking power.

It is worth remembering that China and India established their independent nation-states after World War II, the very date the WTO uses to found its own progressive history.[29] This colonial history and the nationalism it spawned continue to reverberate in the relations among these former British colonies that pertain under the WTO. China, for example, has reinvigorated its role as one of the primary sites of textile production. In the 1980s, at the beginning of economic reform, it was one of the few routes through which China could successfully enter transnational capitalist trade relations. The colonial histories of India and Malaysia, other primary sites of textile production, echo in their concerns about yet again facing damage to their textile industries.[30] The United States, also long tied into world networks of textiles, has experienced decline in its textile industry as most of that industry has located offshore — in China. In this regard, it mirrors British colonial history.

The WTO does not acknowledge these histories. It treats member countries as if they were equal and equivalent trading partners. But traces of these histories are found nonetheless in the otherwise bland issue of quotas. This history implicitly informs current dumping disputes. In June of 2003 the six largest U.S. textile trade associations began a lobbying campaign to restrict imports from China, specifically bras, nightwear, gloves, and knit fabrics. In response, the China Textile Industry Association said that if the United States implemented restrictions, they would also ask the Chinese government for countermeasures to protect Chinese textile manufacturers.[31] The United States did impose restrictions, to which the China Textile Association responded: "the increase in the exports of Chinese textile products to the United States is normal after the United States — which had imposed quotas on textile products — abolished such quotas. It is the result of the U.S. textile industry's readjustment. The U.S. side's restrictive measures against Chinese textile products is wholly an act of protectionism and unfair to China's textile industry."[32] The aftermath of British imperial history has left a clear path of dumping disputes. India and Malaysia have also brought charges against the Chinese textile industry for dumping. Thus, multiple histories of translocal and unequal trade traverse the imagined WTO world of free trade relations.

WTO'S FRAMEWORK OF EXCLUSIONS: LABOR

When I first learned about the proliferation of dumping charges against China, I had assumed that most Chinese citizens would be upset about the charges and their patent unfairness. Many entrepreneurs in China have reacted angrily and, as I discussed earlier, they have begun to fight these charges. Official state media also condemn the disputes. I was surprised, however, to learn of another undercurrent of conversation not caught in the discourse of free trade. Some Chinese citizens, it turns out, think the dumping charges are a good thing. Contrary to the strange assumption that national entities are the only players in these disputes, these citizens hope that dumping charges against China will force foreign as well as Chinese factory owners in China to raise the wages of factory workers and curtail the sweatshop conditions that have grown along with dumping disputes.[33] Their view reminds us of the conjuring act the WTO has to perform to entice members to sign on to its beliefs. The WTO conjures images of prosperity for all. Its mission statement proudly proclaims that its regulation of trade will lead to "a more prosperous, peaceful and accountable economic world" (WTO n.d., 1). "Desiring China" has come into existence through this fantasy. Yet the "phantom of production," to borrow Pun Ngai's term (2003), haunts this celebration of consumption.

The vast majority of labor in sweatshops and other multinational factories is performed by rural migrant women (Lee 1998, Pun 2005, Tan 2004, Wang 2000, Yan 2003a and b). As I discussed in chapter 4, since the beginning of economic reform, the migration of workers from the countryside to the city has increased exponentially. Some estimate that at any one time, one-tenth of the rural population migrates (Wang 2004). Approximately three million migrants work in the city of Shenzhen, the first "special economic zone" (SEZ) established in 1980 to attract foreign investment (Pun 2005). All the coastal cities and coastal economic zones have attracted similar numbers of migrants.[34] These migrant laborers are treated more like illegal immigrants than legitimate citizens. They do not have legal access to state welfare benefits, such as medical care, nor do they have access to education for their children.[35] Recently, the central Chinese government has begun to lift some of these restrictions. Nonetheless, it remains the case that the gap between rural and urban life continues to grow. In China, urban incomes are four times higher than rural incomes, a ratio that exceeds that of most other countries. Migrant workers in sweatshops and other factories earn about Y600 or US$75/month.[36] Scholars in China have termed this situation a crisis of uneven development. This uneven development is structured by the articulation of a desiring China with neoliberal capitalism.

The negotiations over China's entry into the WTO illuminate the historically and culturally specific encounters over how to constitute "desiring China." As co-creator of these encounters, the Chinese state, along with numerous entrepreneurs and other citizens of China, have pulled China into the WTO fantasy of the world. Doing so has enabled the Chinese state to present neoliberalism as if it were a unified phenomenon that would produce in China not simply economic wealth but new kinds of persons. This neoliberal dream appeared concretely through the negotiations over China's accession and the aftermath of dumping disputes. Those disputes reveal the unruly heterogeneity of practices that a term like "neoliberal governmentality" might otherwise obscure. They highlight the fact that historical forms of world capitalism have always been the outcome of diverse conjunctures. These conjunctures allow for creative movements for social justice.

I was reminded of these creative gaps in a conversation with a Chinese social scientist who has befriended me over many years. I asked her views on China's entry into the WTO. She explained the ironies as she saw them: "The position of those in favor of neoliberalism and free trade," she said, "seems to support foreign domination of China, especially by the United States. But they do so because they want to challenge the authoritarian power of the Chinese government." She paused and then continued, "Some of those on the New Left [in China], on the other hand, who are critical of the United States and of capitalism, have rightly pointed out the social ills in the growing gap between rural and urban life and the treatment of workers. But they do so by emphasizing the need for more government involvement and some speak from the position of nationalism. In some ways, the government likes their position." I thought she would finish here with her explanation, having set up this neat and ironic dichotomy. But she continued, "Meanwhile, a few multinational corporations, due to pressure from global social movements on corporate responsibility, have introduced 'socially responsible contracts' for workers in their factories.[37] We know that of course these multinationals are hypocritical but the government is sensitive to the 'human rights' language of these contracts. And the government is weak in relation to both international and domestic capital in carrying out its own labor laws; they basically speak for capitalists. The WTO stands above the Chinese government and so provides some restraint on the government. This is the irony: relying on one social injustice [i.e., WTO-style capitalism] to change another social injustice [i.e., the authoritarian government]."

*I*t might seem difficult to find hope in these times. Those who tout the triumphs of neoliberal capitalism appear poised for success in convincing the rest of us that no other dreams exist or are worth having. For this reason, I feel it is imperative that progressive scholars and activists find other ways to describe the world today. Merely to turn the triumphalist narrative upside down, to say that it is bad instead of good, will not be sufficient. In so doing, we have already accepted their vision. To find another vision does not mean ignoring the powerful and murderous exclusions taking place. It means that we do not have to think of these exclusions as inevitable.

For this reason, I have shown an alternative to thinking that neoliberalism and global capitalism exist as coherent totalities. I have shown the imaginative dimensions that have made citizens in China develop a self-conscious enthusiasm for coherence in their search for a new cosmopolitan humanity. This imagination was not first erected and then put into social practice. Rather, it emerged out of the upheavals and excitement within the uncertainties of social life. The transcultural encounters suffusing this social life led Chinese citizens to create a "desiring China" that would, they hoped, guide them out of the ruins of Maoist socialism, beyond the reminders of China's colonial history, and into a world of freedom. The "desiring China" that state officials, entrepreneurs, and ordinary citizens have pieced together from public culture phenomena, state policies, and corporate strategies gives the appearance that a new era has emerged with a new desiring subject at its core that will lead the way. Public culture has played the most prominent role in this regard. The soap opera *Yearnings* encouraged the art of longing, while the women's museum mirrored a desire for a postsocialist gender identity that rejects Maoist feminism. Those who have embraced a gay identity debated how to be properly gay by combining their engagement with transnational gay networks and a desire for cultural citizenship within Chineseness. They contributed yet another piece to the construction of "desiring China." Urban professional young women learned how to embody cosmopolitanism through consumption, sex, and fashion. In the process, they were pulled into a series of structured remembrances and forgettings that encouraged them to reinvent a past they could leave behind. Legal cases and legalistic public debates triangulated repression, interests, and passions to teach citizens how to distinguish licit from illicit desires. Finally, the negotiations over China's entry into the WTO made "desiring China" into a co-creator of neoliberal practices. Each of these public culture events demonstrates the disparate quality of the pieces of cultural, social, and economic life that did not present themselves, in the first instance, as a unified whole. If they came together into an entity I call "desiring China," this articulation resulted from historical and cultural work to bring them into some kind of coherence.

This coherence was often momentary. "Desiring China" created as many ambivalences and exclusions as inclusions. "Desire" as a social force has been difficult to confine along one path. This difficulty does not come from an essence in desire that is inherently deterritorializing or flow-like, as Deleuze and Guattari (1983) would have it. Rather "desire" in China has been assigned the weight of throwing off historical constraints and of creating a new cosmopolitan human nature in the contingent context of postsocialist experiments and post–Cold War global politics. With such a venture as its purview, "desire" could not be confined in advance. Such a historically and culturally specific assignment thus opened up a terrain of potentially unknown consequences.

Hence the ambivalences about homoerotic desire. And hence the instability in the exclusionary boundaries that marked certain kinds of people as either incapable of embodying desires properly, such as rural migrants, or as displaying passions that turned them into "low quality" persons, such as money boys. Does homosexuality represent the quintessence of a desire which will effectively overcome the socialist past or will it impede China's neoliberal hopes? Does it represent the avant-garde of cosmopolitanism or the contamination of Chinese morality?

The answer is continuously deferred, as both positions flourish in China. Gay men and lesbians in China have asserted that they are at the forefront of cosmopolitan humanity. They are self-reflective and innovative about desire and their networks have always been transnational, since the inception of gay identity politics in the 1990s in China. Many others in China support this view, even though they say they have difficulty imagining what homoerotic desire is like. But they clearly believe that homosexuality must be part of any cosmopolitan human nature.

Rural migrants and money boys, in turn, have challenged their exclusions. Reaching across gender lines, money boys insist that their lives resemble those of women who get taken care of by their boyfriends and husbands. They thus blur the line between sex for money and sex for love. They believe that the discomfort of this blurring leads other gay men, who wish to appear as autonomous middle-class individuals, to shun them. Money boys share some of the marginalizations of other rural migrants, as many of them come from small towns and rural areas outside the big cities. These migrants, mainly young women working as domestic servants or in other low-paying service jobs, are well aware of the disdain with which more established urban residents view them. They, in turn, are quite articulate in describing the pretense of the urban middle class that the intimacy they share with these migrant women in their daily lives does not exist. Sometimes these young women manage to turn around that disdain and invisibility, insisting on their right to yearn for the proper embodiment of a cosmopolitan subjectivity.

Only by tracing these historical contingencies can we find a route to social justice that gives us hope. Such hope has the best chance of success, I believe, if we do not treat neoliberalism (or, for that matter liberalism or global capitalism) as a set of coherent, a priori principles that devolve, in deterministic fashion, onto social life. A totalizing view of neoliberalism, one that accepts theoretical proponents' writings as a description of social life, misses these kinds of social and cultural struggles. That approach has the implicit problem of treating these social and economic practices as if they first evolve fully formed in the West (assuming the coherence of that entity as well) and then spread to the rest of the world. The sly Eurocentrism embedded in this approach elides itself only partially by treating nation-states in the global south as equivalent in their abilities to embody neoliberal principles. The recent anthropology that has theorized the central role of encounters to replace the notion of spread or flows gives us a more thoroughly postcolonial vision of how social transformation occurs. Only by theorizing how differences become articulated in transnational encounters and how power is produced in interactions across varied boundaries, both social and geopolitical, can we see how neoliberalism exists as disparate practices across the globe.

China has participated in the excitement and the pressures to appear as a full neoliberal subject. "Desiring China" is both the object and the subject of these encounters. The unexpected cultural struggles over licit and illicit desires in China should alert us to the peculiarity of the assumption that neoliberalism has coherent meaning across all realms of social life. Highlighting this strangeness can give us hope of imagining other worlds.

I conclude with two recent films in China that offer such hope. They demonstrate how "desiring China" is heterogeneous rather than merely whole, how the transcultural encounters through which it has come into being provide unexpected perspectives. The first film, directed by He Yi, is *The Postman* (*Youchai*), and the second, directed by Wang Jianwei, is *Living Elsewhere* (*Shenghuo zai biechu*). These films use different genres, address quite different topics, and have followed different transcultural routes. Yet together they challenge the naturalization of neoliberal practices. *The Postman* is a fictional experimental film that has been shown in underground venues and has not had any distribution. Wang Jianwei, on the other hand, is well known as an avant-garde artist whose work has been exhibited throughout the West. In *Living Elsewhere* he uses a seemingly conventional genre of social documentary but displays an unconventional theme. Because of his other avant-garde art work, this film has been exhibited internationally and received accolades. Together these two films provide alternative visions of how to imagine a new world order.

I was fortunate to view He Yi's *The Postman* during one of my visits to Beijing. Cui Zi'en (whom I mention in chapter 3) invited me to his home to show me recent films made by his students. Cui Zi'en, you may recall, is a well-known queer (he prefers this term) filmmaker and novelist living in Beijing. The context of my viewing this film and Cui Zi's excitement about it have influenced my interpretation.[1]

The Postman raises existential questions about the difficulties of human intimacy and communication. Perversion plays a role in this film but exists alongside seemingly "normal" lives that share equally in the same alienation as perverse desires. The film begins with a young man, Xiao Dou, who lands a promotion in his neighborhood post office and begins a mail delivery route. Xiao Dou is quiet and shy; he lives with his sister, who has raised him since their parents died when they were both young. One day, as he delivers the mail to an apartment building, he notices that one of the mailboxes is always left unlocked and that the mail he delivered there the previous day has not been picked up. He takes all the letters home and reads them. He discovers that a married woman is having an affair with a married man. She thanks him for saving her from a cruel and meaningless existence with her husband. Xiao Dou decides to intervene. The viewer is not told the reasons for his intervention, for we are not privy to Xiao Dou's thoughts (i.e., there is no voice-over and little dialogue). Xiao Dou writes a letter threatening the man with unstated consequences unless he hands over all the letters between the two lovers. Xiao Dou picks up the letters and spends his evenings at home reading through them. He does nothing else to the man.

Xiao Dou begins to pick up the mail, not to deliver it but to take it home and keep for himself to read through. He continues to discover other perversions and alienations in his neighborhood. He learns about a doctor who introduces clients to a prostitute. Xiao Dou first approaches the doctor's office and then visits the prostitute, claiming the doctor sent him. But he rushes out after she hands him a condom. Then he reads letters from a young couple, living far away, writing to their parents to announce their impending suicide. Xiao Dou rides by the home of the elderly parents, watches them happily going off for a walk with their birds, and then goes home to rewrite the letters to say how happy the young couple are in their lives.

One night, late at the post office with a fellow female worker, Xiao Dou responds to her advances; they fall into one another's arms and make love. Then she tells him that she had had the same experience with the man who used to have his job. Xiao Dou continues with his life, stuffing more and more undelivered letters into his desk at home. One of his few spoken lines comes at this point, when at work he remarks to his fellow worker that people seem to have difficulty talking with one another in person and can only say things through writing letters.

The last intervention Xiao Dou makes involves two young men in love with one another. Xiao Dou has been withholding their letters, even as they keep writing to one another asking why the other has not communicated. Xiao Dou visits one of the men, pays his overdue rent the landlady there demands, and then enters the apartment. He spies the drug paraphenalia just as the young man returns. The young man casually sits down and begins to describe the intensity of his intimate experiences with his male friend when they used to take drugs together. He pines for his friend. Xiao Dou gets up and leaves before the young man finishes his story. The next scene shows us the young man brought out on a stretcher, presumably dead from an overdose.

Xiao Dou has no friends. The only human intimacy in his life is with his sister. His sister marries near the end of the film and has a wedding dinner completely lacking in celebratory joy. Though married, she refuses to leave Xiao Dou and move with her husband until Xiao Dou has found a spouse as well. Earlier in the film, brother and sister chatted about a peach orchard they remember from their youth and their failure to taste a peach despite their attempts to steal one. (The peach is a symbol for sex in classical Chinese literature.) As the film draws to an end, we find Xiao Dou and his sister making love in a bed meant for the sister and her husband. His sister then admits that she was once in the orchard without Xiao Dou and tasted a peach after all.

In *The Postman*, He Yi juxtaposes mediated communications through writing and the gaze with sexual perversions and lack of human intimacy. The implicit backdrop is the social transformations wrought by economic reform. New buildings go up, some people drive cars, and everyone is free to go their own way. Yet no one has anywhere in particular to go. Xiao Dou's voyeurism echoes Maoist state interventions. It recalls visions of Maoism when all citizens were supposed to open every aspect of their lives for political inspection. But Xiao Dou draws back from exercising the power of his voyeurism to its ultimate limit. His voyeurism is not motivated by politics. Instead, he both yearns for and shuns human intimacy. His interventions are both destructive and seemingly constructive. His perversion of voyeurism is juxtaposed with other perversions, ranging from the rather mild perversion of adultery to the more serious issue of homosexuality to the extreme limit of incest.

The fact that Xiao Dou draws back from the potential for disruptive intervention into these perverse desires leaves open the possibilities for another kind of relationship to power. From one perspective, the film might appear to be a simple matter of citizens resisting the state's power. But the film has less a celebratory tone than one of anomie. The film presents the different scenes of perversion as if they are the stuff of everyday life. They do not symbolize a social danger to the polity but neither do they necessarily provide the answers to the dilemma of leading a meaningful life. Yet, in a world where a state-sponsored gaze still penetrates, perversions that harm no one are not allowed to flourish. Here, He Yi pushes on the limits of "desiring China." His film extends the ambivalences about the limits of desire that fuel the divisions within desiring China. Moreover, he pries apart the perversions from their installation in state or corporate strategies. He Yi refuses to adjudicate between licit and illicit desires. Nor does he present "desire" as the eschatological answer. It is enfolded into ongoing challenges wrought by upending previous beliefs. He Yi's banner might read, Let a hundred perversions bloom. But such a banner will not be contained by the new era's versions of desire.

The second film, Wang Jianwei's *Living Elsewhere*, tracks a very different subject. *Living Elsewhere* follows the lives of four peasant families living in abandoned, half-constructed villas on the outskirts of Chengdu. This is the fringe zone where rural and urban meet, where peasants, the former backbone of Maoist China, encounter the possibility of redefining themselves. The film begins with Wang Jianwei's slow camerawork allowing us to see the half-finished villas without anyone in them. Some do not have roofs, others have only half-finished walls. These unfinished villas, with their gaps, allow us to imagine the emergence of a gated community for wealthy elites. Many such communities have been built outside China's major cities. They intimate the luxuries of suburban living. The advertisements for such communities proliferate in newspapers and are plastered on billboards. Real estate is one of the fastest roads to wealth in China; the temptations to build rapidly are high. Of course, to build such a community means the displacement of the rural residents who used to live on that land. Wang Jianwei's half-constructed villas display the signs of being situated in between rural and urban worlds. The land surrounding this conglomeration of villas is planted with grains; closer up, we see the mud and unfinished ground between each villa.

The viewer is unsure, at first, whether the project is nearing completion or has been abandoned. Only gradually does Wang Jianwei let us see the people who currently inhabit the villas. They are not elites but poor peasants who have taken over the buildings. They live between the walls, with no roofs over their heads. But they have begun to build a life for themselves there. They have set up their coal-burning stoves and their beds. And they have begun to plant vegetable gardens alongside the buildings. We can imagine that perhaps they were the original residents who were displaced by the building project.

Wang Jianwei lets us witness their everyday lives. They try to scrounge for a living, poking around in the remains of the building materials to see if there is something to sell. They fight with one another, as they sit huddled over their stoves. They try to make their lives have some kind of direction and coherence. In one memorable scene, the different peasant residents stand together near the edge of the unfinished gated community and look at a distant highway being built. They know that their lives have been irrevocably altered by these transformations. They have lost a great deal of previous government support that enabled them to live just above, rather than below, the poverty line. But in this case, at least, they have also managed to redirect and use the resources from elite-driven projects gone awry.

One of the main sources of discontent and violent protests between peasants and their local governments in China is the issue of land use. Land is still categorized as state property. Individual peasant households are allowed to lease land long-term but not sell it. Many local officials, however, have confiscated land from peasants and sold it to private companies for development, holding onto the profit for themselves. Wang Jianwei's film shows us a small movement in the opposite direction. The film's point of view leads us, the viewers, to applaud this small victory.

Neither *The Postman* nor *Living Elsewhere* uses a celebratory tone to examine the lives of those who have been marginalized by neoliberal reforms. These films do not flinch from representing the depradations and hardships of being forced to live on the edges of the new world that China has become. Yet both films together remind us of other perspectives on the new cosmopolitan humanity. It is the fact of their having both been made that should give us hope.

Introduction

1. See Rofel (1999). Gail Hershatter (2002) provides a critical corrective to the assumption that state-sponsored campaigns defined the temporality of everyone's lives in China. Her research on rural women who lived through the early years of socialism demonstrates that these women did not always use what Hershatter calls "campaign time" to mark the key moments in their lives.

2. For an early rendering of these transformations in gender politics, see Honig and Hershatter (1988).

3. For an insightful analysis of the gender and sexual politics of these hotlines, see Erwin (2000).

4. See Kondo (1990b) for an inspiring ethnography that addresses this question.

5. Farquhar (2002) offers a nuanced interpretive analysis of what she calls "appetites," or embodied pleasures, with which my analysis resonates. Farquhar focuses on texts that range over domains conventionally kept apart — food, sex, health, and medicine — in order to historicize and pluralize embodiment. Farquhar convincingly argues that these appetites are intimately connected in the manner in which they articulate desires for a healthful body as informed by traditional Chinese medicine with a rejection of Maoist politics through a passionate embrace of pleasure. My book examines different types of texts and delves a bit more into the ethnography of everyday life. I am grateful for the trail Farquhar has blazed in the ethnography of Chinese public culture.

6. Various rubrics have been used in official, intellectual, and popular discourses in China to gloss these changes, including "economic reform," "socialism with Chinese characteristics," "market economy," "capitalism," and "neoliberalism."

7. Wang Hui further argues that: "using the existence of state interference in the economy to prove — as some have done — that there is no neoliberal hegemony in China is really beside the point, as the hegemonic position of neoliberalism in China was established precisely from within a domestic process during which the state's crisis of legitimacy was overcome through economic reform itself" (2004, 8). My arguments here owe a great debt to Wang's trenchant analysis.

8. For U.S. capitalists neoliberalism means weakening other countries' states. Thus, U.S. pundits tend to use the continued existence of Chinese state involvement in the economy as "proof" that China still lacks the "liberty" and "freedom" of proper capitalism.

9. In contrast to some of the sub-Saharan African, Latin American, and Southeast Asian nations, neither the World Bank nor the IMF, nor the periodic threats from or military dominance of the United States, nor a calculated financial crisis such as that experienced by numerous Asian nations in 1997 has managed to turn the Chinese state into a weak specter for the purposes of "free trade." Recently, however, Chinese economists trained in the United States have pushed for the kinds of neoliberal policies that the United States government favors. See Unger (2002).

10. See Tadiar (2004) for a theoretically insightful and politically engaged critique of the Philippine experience of what Tadiar calls the new world order. The contrast between the imbrication of the Philippines and China into transnational capitalism highlights my argument that neoliberalism is not a fully packaged deal that countries simply embrace.

11. Again, I follow Wang Hui's (2004) insightful outline of these policies.

12. Maoist socialist policies had transferred much of the agricultural surplus to the cities to support urban industrialization while simultaneously instituting a resident permit system that made it virtually impossible to move from the countryside to the cities without official permission. Economic reform did not abolish the residence permit system but addressed instead the need to develop the rural economy.

13. See Nan Lin (1995), Oi and Walder (1999), and Unger (2002).

14. For important studies on this migration, see Gaetano and Jacka (2004), Solinger (1999), Yan (2003b), and Zhang (2001). Pun Ngai (2005) has written a searing critique of sweatshop labor performed by migrant women. Julie Chu (forthcoming) offers a terrific cultural analysis of the category "mobility" among Fujianese who hope to migrate abroad.

15. These debates implicitly highlight the fact that the distinctions between licit and illicit, moral and immoral capitalist practices of profitseeking require certain legal fictions that only partially forestall the blurring of these boundaries. See chapter 5.

16. The 1989 social mobilizations were more complex. As Wang Hui (2004) argues, there were contradictory elements in the movement. Those who had been big winners in the reforms wanted to push for more privatization. They, too, participated in the movement.

17. This process of neoliberalism also became known as neoconservatism or neo-authoritarianism in China because of the continued close involvement of the state in the market as well as the close links between certain state sectors and the formation of elite social classes.

18.	The essays in Oi and Walder (1999) document the widely varied practices through which local governments contract or lease public assets to entrepreneurs who share in the risks and profits of the business. Local governments have also maintained full control over their township and village enterprises, though in the 1990s they also increasingly sold or "privatized" their unprofitable assets. These sales include illicit transfer of ownership to local elites.

19.	One of my favorite examples is the massage parlor (with sexual services included) located on the corner of a well-trafficked area on the east side of Beijing, which is run by the Retired Government Cadres Bureau. These efforts to garner more revenue also include a great deal of rent-seeking activities, which have given rise to numerous farmer protests. See Bernstein (1999).

20.	This situation might change as, post-WTO, foreign investors will be allowed to open up their own banking and investment firms in China.

21.	Gallagher (2005) argues that the central government has pursued a policy of "state-led capitalist developmentalism," modeling these large cartels after South Korea. Despite the effects of the Asian financial crisis in South Korea, Gallagher argues that central leaders concluded the problem lay not in large cartels but in overdiversification (143).

22.	The plethora of recent scholarship on the political economy of China converges on the conclusion that China is witnessing a creative construction of a profit-making world that, while recognizably capitalist, should not be measured against normative definitions of "the market," "finance capital," or "privatization." These conclusions are reached even by those scholars who might not be critical of capitalism or who take for granted certain ideological assumptions about economic relations derived from liberal and neoliberal theories about capitalism. Kellee S. Tsai (2002), for example, in her ethnographic research on the financing of private businesses that have opened in China since 1978, demonstrates that, since official state banks extend credit largely to state and collective enterprises, private entrepreneurs have resorted to a varied array of informal financing practices that help the economy flourish, even as they are not always legal. Tsai concludes that Western economic theories' emphasis on private property rights as the sine qua non of capitalist growth cannot explain China's dramatic economic growth because they oversimplify the political and social contexts of what she calls "real-life interactions" (4). Tsai concludes that informal finance is not always market-driven, but rather access to social and political capital mediates access to finance capital. Oi and Walder (1999) similarly maintain that the authors' approach in their edited volume on what they call "property rights" is empirical and historical rather than axiomatic and deductive. They conclude that China now has what they term "hybrid" forms of property rights, with the "rights" of control, income, and transfer of assets quite varied and complex by region, including the way local governments shield private firms by listing them as collective, the formation of shareholding cooperatives by local governments to mobilize investments, sometimes on behalf of small-scale family firms, and the "hollowing" out of public property through the transfer of public assets to elites and the diversion of public capital by bureaucracies into firms they register as "private." Unger (2002) describes the continuation of certain collectivist attitudes toward landholding in rural areas even as these combine with individual households' profit-making activities. Unger finds that even with decollectivization to individual households, villages, which still own the land, reallocate it regularly to accommodate changes in family size. Ironically, in the 1990s, the central government instituted strict measures to halt these reallocations, insisting on strict adherence to their regulation that land tenure should be frozen for a period of thirty years. Lin (2001) argues that the abstract concept of "the market" is not useful for understanding how economic growth in China has evolved from the mutually accommodating relations between entrepreneurs and state agents, as the former seek favors from the latter. Moreover, this favor seeking has spread the effects of ad hoc changes to allow for more growth than formal rules might have otherwise.

23. Wang and Hu (1999) document the regional disparities in wealth and poverty. They argue that in the Mao era the central government addressed regional disparities by transferring wealth from the richer coastal provinces to the poorer inland provinces. This redistribution, they conclude, succeeded in creating greater equity in income and consumption, though perhaps at the cost of overall efficiencies in economic growth. In the economic reform era, regional disparities reappeared and grew, after the central government favored the eastern coastal regions with the express purpose of fostering rapid growth and simultaneously devolved fiscal control to local levels. Other scholars agree that economic reform has led to regional disparities but disagree about the Maoist period, arguing that Maoist policies also led to income disparities among rural districts (Unger 2002, 120).

24. Unger (2002) finds that migrant labor to wealthier rural areas has increased, with discriminatory practices toward those not considered natives of the area.

25. On the privatization of housing, see Zhang (2004).

26. Gallagher provocatively contends that the central government used FDI to encourage greater economic competitiveness while simultaneously keeping an incipient domestic entrepreneurial class weak, thus managing to enhance its staying power and keep labor unrest from destabilizing the government. She emphasizes, however, that FDI liberalization was dynamic and gradual, reflecting practices on the ground. Indeed, she argues that its momentum was often from below, especially the convergence of the interests of foreign investors and local officials. Nevertheless, she argues that FDI liberalization played three crucial roles in this process: (1) it placed competitive pressures on regions and firms to reconceptualize labor practices and regulations; (2) it served as a

laboratory for politically sensitive reforms; and (3) it shifted the debate from public ownership to national ownership. That is, the Chinese Communist Party successfully redirected the debate about socialism and state-owned industry away from the public/private dichotomy toward a debate over the need for Chinese national industry amid foreign competition, even as they continued to depend on foreign investment to develop China's economy. She concludes that this ideological transition has shaped the content and form of labor protests in China.

27. As of 1997 Hong Kong belongs to the People's Republic of China. See Mei Zhan (forthcoming) for an insightful ethnography of this transition in China's global commitments in relation to medicine.

28. Yasheng Huang (2003) argues that foreign direct investment in China has certain characteristics not shared by FDI in other countries: relative to other countries, Huang asserts that China's dependence on FDI versus domestic investments is high; that foreign invested enterprises have replaced contractual alliances between foreign and domestic firms; that the dominance of foreign invested enterprises in labor-intensive and export-oriented industries is far more substantial than their presence in other Asian economies; that they are spread throughout many industries and regions, in contrast to other countries, where FDI is usually concentrated in a few industries; and finally, that most FDI projects in China are investments by small and medium-sized foreign companies rather than by multinational corporations.

29. Many Chinese citizens watched these wars as well to learn how an empire gets built. For that reason, some supported the United States, not because they thought the U.S. represents democracy but rather because they thought it might set an interesting example for how China could build its strength as well.

30. The official declaration that class struggle was no longer relevant for China extended to the idea that social relations of inequality should not become a public focus of analysis or politics. Similarly, official discourse described economic reform as a "transition" toward "socialism with Chinese characteristics." The state hopes this mythology of transition will allow it to grapple with the self-evident contradiction of a communist party fostering capitalist practices that have led to massive unemployment, increased poverty, a decline in social security, and a wide swathe of transnational sweatshop life for rural migrant workers.

31. Harriett Evans (1997) usefully reminds us that foundational assumptions about "women's nature" persisted throughout the revolutionary and reform periods.

32. "Desiring China" makes "neoliberalism" appear as a new era producing a new kind of humanity. Although the content of this transformation is quite distinct from Maoist socialism, its manner of attempting to fasten together economic

policies, moral evaluations of social life, and the emergence of new kinds of persons closely resembles the earlier socialist articulations of power, knowledge, and subjectivity.

33. Rose has done us the great service of offering a careful reading of Friedrich von Hayek, Alexander Rüstow, and others who are frequently credited with elaborating neoliberal ideology.

34. Here, Rose refers to the influential work of Friedrich von Hayek (1944) and the work of those associated with the journal *Ordo*.

35. This quotation is actually from Lemke's (2001) discussion of Foucault, as quoted in Brown. Brown extends Lemke/Foucault into contemporary U.S. politics and political theory.

36. Ong's argument is partially motivated by her deft refutation of Samuel Huntington's "clash of civilizations" thesis (1997) that "Confucian cultures" do not have the liberal values of the West. Ong refutes Huntington by pinpointing the regulative aspects of liberalism, the misleading opposition between the market economy and cultural values in Huntington, and the history of European colonialism in Asia.

37. My ability to make this analytical move is inspired by Anna Tsing's creative reconceptualization of universals (2005), Timothy Mitchell's postcolonial deconstruction of social science universals (2002), and Sylvia Yanagisako's analysis of the cultural specificities of the forces that motivate capitalists (2002). Tsing argues that universals become universals through the means by which they get taken up and reworked in the "friction" of encounters across regions, classes, and ethnicities. Mitchell demonstrates that the way social theory typically operates, by relating particular cases to a generalizable pattern or process, is itself a product of postcolonial modernity and works together with and creates the conditions of possibility for, rather than against, the reach of its power. Yanagisako refuses the abstractions of capitalism, arguing instead that we must always situate capitalist desires.

38. For Harvey, neoliberalization (as opposed to neoliberalism) entails moves by economic elites to regain a greater share of the wealth that they had been constrained from grabbing by post–World War II social welfare programs. In contrast to the Foucauldian approach to governmentality that moves the analytical attention away from the state, Harvey argues that the state plays a large role in this process. Where I depart from Harvey is in my interest in how these claims to coherence have traction. I also depart from Harvey's classical Marxist approach to questions of desire, pleasure, and sexuality. Harvey is suspicious about all forms of desire. He invokes a sweeping condemnation of desire as capitalist mystification for the masses. He thus leaves unexamined his own heteronormative desires concerning questions of marriage, pornography, prostitution, homosexuality, and nonnormative sexual practices. The question

to pose to Harvey, of course, is why he fixates on sex. Why does he not put, for example, food at the center of his condemnation of pleasure?

39. Charles Hale (2002, 2005) has shown how economic policies he calls neo-liberal can co-exist with an endorsement of the principle of intercultural equal-ity and collective rights for indigenous peoples in Central America. In his view, neoliberalism does not necessarily need to create discrete individuals. As he points out, of course, the limits to support for these collective rights lie in the actual rearrangement of resources such as land.

40. I am inspired in this argument by Neferti Tadiar (2004), who reminds us that these desiring-actions are constitutive of transnational capitalist practices rather than the property of autonomous subjects or nation-states. Tadiar's analysis focuses on the role of the imagination in constituting the Philippines as part of the world capitalist system. Inasmuch as the Philippines is a supplier of global labor, Tadiar argues that its material dreams are the consequences of — as well as bear consequences for — an international order of political and economic dreamwork, which she calls "fantasy-production."

41. It is instructive to remember that for a long time post-Enlightenment theory sought positivist definitions of humanity. These definitions were wrought in the contexts of colonial encounters and the rise of first mercantile and then industrial capitalism. Karl Marx, for example, argued that "labor" — that is, a sensuous engagement with the material and natural world to satisfy human needs and thereby produce new ones — defines humans' species-being. For Émile Durkheim, collective effervescence, or the "social," underlies humanity. Sigmund Freud delineated how desire and the life of the unconscious lies at the heart of that which makes us human. Finally, for liberal philosophers, reason is that which defines Man. As numerous histories of colonialism and its after-math attest, these definitions constructed a difference between those deemed truly human and those others — the racially marked, the colonized, women — marked as incapable of fully embodying this humanity. Counterhistories have, in parallel fashion, engaged these definitions to prove otherwise.

42. Class never fully replaced kinship as defining one's humanity, though nu-merous political campaigns defined their goal as such.

43. My approach to desire could be seen as an engagement with both Deleuze and Guattari (1983, 1987) and Foucault (1985). Deleuze and Guattari emphasize that desire is produced not simply within the individual but through social worlds. They specifically argue that desire's heterogeneous, productive, poly-vocal, synthetic, and "nomadic" qualities were unleashed by the "capitalist machine." But at the same time, capitalism sets limits to and regulates the directions desire can take, even as desire always partially escapes these stric-tures. Thus, they see capitalist "flows" and "flows" of desire as one and the same economy; desiring production and relations of production are immanent

to one another. As against psychoanalysis, especially the yoke of Oedipus that establishes a totalizing subjectivity, represses the multiplicity of desire, and defines desire as lack, Deleuze and Guattari stress the need to see desire as productive flows rather than unities and as excessive mobility rather than sedentary stasis. "Lack" is not the product of an Oedipal complex but the creation of a dominant class in a market economy.

Deleuze and Guattari treat desire as a site of both oppression and potential liberation. They try to imagine how desire, or "desiring-production" as they call it, can lead humanity beyond power. Hence their interest in tracing those desiring flows that escape codification. They further seek to "de-normalize" and "de-individualize" desire by searching for the multiplicity of collective arrangements against power. Deleuze and Guattari put a great deal of hope in desire as that which can overthrow the established order, because in their view desire is ultimately a proliferating force.

Foucault, on the other hand, never theorizes anything as standing outside of, or escaping, power. For Foucault, "desire" is that site through which individuals make themselves subjects of specific regimes of power/knowledge. Rather than decide desire's qualities in the abstract, Foucault eschews this philosophical approach, with its assumption that desire is a constant. In its place he adopts a genealogical method in which he traces how, in different historical moments, various cultural epistemes led people to search for the truth of their being in desire. Foucault is particularly concerned with the question of why the activities and pleasures associated with sexual conduct became an object of ethical concern. Why was sexual desire problematized?

In his study of classical Greek culture, for example, Foucault argues that this ethical concern manifested in the articulations among problematizations of the life of the body, the institution of marriage, relations between men, and the existence of wisdom. These articulations, with their "ethics-oriented" moralities, led to a valorization of sexual austerity despite the absence of prohibitions in the exercise of sexual pleasures. The exercise of restraint in the practice of pleasures was not because Greek men hoped to regain an original innocence or purity but because they viewed it as the route toward freedom. .

Thus, Deleuze and Guattari approach "desire" as both an essence that defines humanity and as a social, political, and economic force. In contrast, Foucault eschews this universalizing essentialism, seeking instead to understand how and when Western societies defined it as such in their search for the truth of their humanity. On the other hand, Deleuze and Guattari are interested in the relationship between multiple desires and capitalism. Foucault has no interest in capitalism. Furthermore, he tends to narrow the meaning of desire to sexual desire, whereas Deleuze and Guattari consider "desire" to encompass a broad range of social practices and relations. My approach to desire combines Foucault's anti-essentialism with Deleuze and Guattari's opening out of the category.

44. In the recent special issue of *Social Text*, "What's Queer about Queer Studies Now?" (Eng, Halberstam, and Muñoz 2005) the contributors argue that these normalizations and exclusions occur within queer studies as well. In their introduction to the issue, Eng, Halberstam, and Muñoz warn of the "queer liberalism" that has deflected more radical critique and that fosters a convergence of U.S. imperial interests with certain forms of gay rights.

45. My indebtedness to Foucault (1978, 1979, 1980) in thinking about power is undoubtedly clear at this point. His discussions about the diffuse and polyvalent operations of power in the modern world, the interconnections between power, knowledge, and norms, and the "techniques of the self" by which individuals make themselves into subjects in and through their bodies inform the essays that follow. But I also avoid certain applications of his approach that have hardened these processes and left them less mobile, contingent, or porous than I believe he intended. See David Hoy (2004) for an inspiring discussion of what he calls "critical resistance" in relation to Foucault as well as other contemporary French theorists.

1. Yearnings

1. Field research for my first book (Rofel 1999), conducted from 1984 to 1986, focused on the effects of the imaginary of political economic reform in China on the subjectivities of Chinese workers.

2. A cultural critic in Hong Kong, for example, sardonically pinpointed *Yearnings* as an effective apolitical means through which people could be led away from reflection on the political issue of democracy (Chu 1991).

3. For an inspiring ethnography of these contestations over national identity in relation to race politics in England, see Brown (2005). Homi Bhabha (1990) has indicated this direction in his argument that the idea of the nation and of "the people" that nation is said to represent is continuously emergent (in Raymond Williams's [1977] terms) through the process of narration. This process allows people on the margins of the nation-space to force open the boundaries of that imagined community. An analysis of *Yearnings* supports Bhabha's attention to narrative in creating nation-ness, but the arguments it engendered point to distinct marginalized subjects differentiated through class and gender who do not homogenize into a single marginal group, as Bhabha seems to imply. For an incisive critique of the way the specificities of gender are effaced in Bhabha's as well as others' discussions of nationalism, see Liu (1995).

4. During the 1980s, political study sessions, at least in the factories, were per-

functory. They informed workers of the latest government directives but were not used to stir political struggle. After June 4th, the state required all work units to conduct political study sessions in the old manner in order to seek political "confessions." Their tenor varied; many work unit leaders had supported the demonstrations and held pro forma sessions. Others required written confessions. The following year, however, these sessions once again withered.

5. Stuart Hall (1981) offers a critical discussion of the definition of "the popular" in which he argues that the definition depends not simply on content but on the social context in which what counts as "the popular" is always opposed to something which is located outside of or higher than that realm. What counts as "the popular," then (and by contrast "the canon"), is always the site of cultural struggle. In China, the term "popular culture" would have made little sense in the Maoist era, for official culture constituted what was popular. The post-Mao period, however, has witnessed an increasing division between "serious" and "avant-garde" art and "popular entertainment." See the well-known literary critic Li Tuo's (1991b) brief literary history of the contemporary period for his slightly different emphasis on the "popular" quality of Maoist aesthetic standards.

6. My thinking on these issues is indebted to Henry Jenkins, who patiently reviewed these debates with me; Kathleen Biddick and Sandra Joshel, who tightened my critique; and Purnima Mankekar's (1999) insightful discussion of this literature.

7. I have borrowed this concept from Rowe and Schelling (1991).

8. For the classic statement on the symbolic images of the state, see Geertz (1980).

9. Thanks to Ann Anagnost for reminding me of this point.

10. "Commercial" here means sales of ads but also sales of the show itself to other television stations that were just beginning to appear in counties outside major cities.

11. Subtle irony coupled with political allegory, as I argue below, exist as part of the multivalent meanings in this melodrama, but it is impossible to discern the extent to which they were intended by the authors. Even should one have a clear vision of authorial intention, such knowledge would not resolve the ethnographic challenge of analyzing the varied interpretations of *Yearnings*. Despite the efforts of at least a segment of intellectuals in China to portray themselves as humanist creators of imaginary meanings, one must remember that they, as well as their audience, operate within a cultural field of structured meanings. This, I believe, is what Foucault (1977) meant by the concept of author-function, in his critique of theories of originality.

12. The representation of domestic space itself is no exception. The enclosure of *Yearnings* into a wholly domestic arena was much remarked upon and indeed the notion of the "domestic drama" gave its name to a new genre of television programming in China. Ironically, then, even as people experience home view-

ing as a haven from the heartless postsocialist market world, the "domestic space," in being brought into representation, is also opened to the gaze of the state, made subject to discourse, and thus opened to the reach of power to colonize there.

13. I do not mean to imply that the melodramatic sensibility in China developed wholly out of socialist realism. Certainly the earlier part of the twentieth century and before witnessed melodramatic fiction about morality and love (Chow 1991a). Nor do I mean to conflate all socialist realism in China with melodrama. A socialist realist drama becomes melodramatic when the drama plays off of the realism through a heightening or exaggeration of the emotions, an emphasis upon the metaphysical dimension of moral conflict, an assertion of how things ought to be rather than merely how things are, and, finally, a melding of these elements into spectacle. The few examples I have chosen reflect these qualities. These sensibilities in literature, drama, and film produced after the 1949 socialist revolution are obviously a syncretism of Soviet realism and earlier Chinese morality tales.

14. Anderson (1983) perceptibly argues that conceptions of simultaneity in homogeneous, empty time that pervade the structure of the nineteenth-century realist novel are a key cultural component of the idea of the nation. One can easily extend his argument to television melodramas. Clearly the national community is the imagined referent in the links among the simultaneous plots. However, as I argue below, beyond this formal homology, the cultural specificities in the narrative form of *Yearnings* more pointedly evoke national identity.

15. See Faye D. Ginsburg (1989) for her insightful analysis of life stories among anti-abortion activists and their importance in moving others to take up political action.

16. See Anagnost (1997) for an insightful discussion that focuses on speaking bitterness narratives to question the conventional fieldwork assumptions in China that a popular voice unmediated by official discourse can be found. My point differs in that I am extending the form of speaking bitterness from its enactment in the 1950s period, with which it is conventionally associated, into the economic reform moment.

17. The Cultural Revolution was perhaps filled with formulaic accusations, not always by those who had actually suffered. But in the factories I researched, workers confronted managers directly and, as with the land reform campaigns, then assumed control.

18. This term is derived from a story of the same name by Lu Xinhua, one of the first in this genre (translated in Barme and Lee 1979). This genre was followed by Cultural Revolution memoirs written directly in English for an American audience (see Gao 1987, Nien 1986, Yue and Wakeman 1985).

19. See Barlow (1991) for a provocative historical archaeology on the construction of "intellectual" as a state category under Chinese communism and Chi-

nese intellectuals' continued implication of themselves in this statist project in the post-Mao era.

20. By contrast, workers under economic reform used a more informal mode of speaking bitterness to contest the official discourse on workers that decentered them as the vanguard of the nation. They complained about the bitterness they had to eat with increased pressures to be "productive" (see Rofel 1999).

21. Rey Chow (1991b) has traced a related aesthetic formation of national culture in the literature of the 1920s and 1930s, prior to the communist revolution. There, the conception of national culture took the form of a literary pre-occupation with various figures who connoted powerlessness.

22. All the names in this essay, as well as in the other essays, are pseudonyms.

23. It goes without saying that intellectuals were not the only audience for this first part of the melodrama. More broadly, it reconfirmed an official history of the Cultural Revolution as a senseless mess that ruined the country and delayed its economic development.

24. It is critical to the ambivalence that follows that those we might label "working class" are never referred to as such, though they carry all the telltale signs: factory work, cramped homes, etc. The melodrama assiduously avoids this label, as class labels reminiscent of Maoist politics were officially erased in 1978, when intellectuals were declared part of the working class. The ambivalence I describe below depends on this obfuscation.

25. See Foucault (1980) on the relation of resistance to power/knowledge. For one of the most controversial examples in literature, see Dai (1985). See also selections in Barme and Minford (1986). There is much argument among Chinese intellectuals both in China and in diaspora about this embrace of humanism in light of the poststructuralist critique of humanism in Europe and the United States. See Tang (1991), Li (1991a), and recent articles in the Chinese film theory journal *Film and Literature (Dianying wenxue)*.

26. For more detailed discussions of marriage and family relations in socialist China, see Evans (1997), Honig and Hershatter (1988), Johnson (1983), Wolf (1985).

27. It seems more than likely that the ambivalence also involves a very subtle parody by the main authors. Wang Shuo is well known for subtle satire that appears innocently apolitical on the surface and therefore has eluded official criticism.

28. The fact that there was no singular, fixed meaning to the text does not imply that the ambivalence occurred only "inside" the text. In contrast to the claims of certain forms of academic deconstruction, the indeterminacy of *Yearnings* was not a purely linguistic event. It was a point of fierce contestation of power. See Volosinov (1973) for a fuller discussion of the relationship between politics and the multivocality of linguistic signs.

29. The idea that she would have had a more comfortable life with a working-class

man continued the Cultural Revolution's class politics. This message was complicated, however. For viewers situated in the early years of the post-Mao era, marrying an intellectual was seen as marrying up. That, too, is no longer the case.

30. One could argue that self-sacrifice was the ground on which the party continued to construct the domain of good citizenship in the early years of reform. In this sense, Huifang could be seen as fostering a socialist sense of social responsibility that transcends one's own kin and family. Granting that the striking lack of blood tie with her daughter provides one means through which Huifang can be considered self-sacrificing, I would still argue that the incorporation of this daughter into kinship relations and the unfolding of the drama completely within that realm calls into question any direct homology with socialist politics.

31. Thanks to Gail Kligman for pointing this out to me.

32. I concur wholeheartedly with Ahmad's (1987) critique of Jameson's insistence that all third world literature operates as national allegories. Jameson's essentializing, orientalist assumptions unfortunately mar some otherwise interesting insights into specific Chinese literary texts. Though I believe that in China the sense of national identity is in crisis, I do not think this crisis necessarily informs all contemporary cultural productions.

33. Space limitations forbid an elaboration of the feminist film theorists who have influenced this essay. They have clarified dynamics of visual objectification by examining how the technical apparatus of cinema and television structures gendered relations of viewing that frame the position of women as objects of the masculine gaze. See de Lauretis (1984), Kaplan (1987), Doane et al. (1984), and the pathbreaking work of Mulvey (1989). Discussion of female spectatorship and reception has supplemented the earlier work, though I still find much of it narrowly focused on the single text of the film or television program (see Pribram [1988], Rabinowitz [1990]). For an excellent exception that addresses gender and race, see Bobo (1988). Chris Berry (1991) offers a suggestive alternative reading of these conventions in Chinese cinema.

34. The collective group of (male) scriptwriters clarifies any doubts on this score. Midway through *Yearnings*'s denouement, they declared in the media that their purpose was to create a female heroine whom male viewers would find appealing (*Hangzhou Radio and Television Weekly* 1991). It should also be noted that these masculine fantasies are constructed as oppositional practices to state power; see Zhong (2000).

35. Gender politics in the post-Mao period are more complicated than I have the space to go into here. I address them further in the next chapter. For example, women's studies scholars in the late 1980s and 1990s embraced "difference" from men as a key way to advance their cause against what they perceived as the "sameness" created by the state. That is, they created meanings for woman

that build distance from the state. Their notion of difference is not necessarily predicated on any view of its naturalness. See Dai Jinhua (1995b, 1999, 2002) and my discussion of Li Xiaojiang in the next chapter. For Li's writings, see Li Xiaojiang (1989, 1990, 1999). Women writers have similarly created a space for difference in their writings (Li Ziyun 1994). See Barlow's (2004) thorough and insightful discussion of these theorists. On the other hand, male writers in search of a Chinese masculinity have essentialized woman as the grounds upon which they can find themselves as men. See Zhang Xianliang (1986) and the last section of this essay.

36. Bobo eloquently makes this point in reference to African American women who enjoyed the film version of *The Color Purple* despite criticisms of Steven Spielberg's directorial editing, on the one hand, and elements of the story by certain African American male critics, on the other.

37. Such a marriage in the context of post-Mao social politics could also be seen as a sacrifice. Intellectuals criticized the class-based marriages of the Cultural Revolution, in which they (retrospectively) felt forced to marry workers out of political consideration and not for love and certainly not "compatibility."

38. Thus, his repeated assertions to Yaru that they should forget past wrongs implies not only those between each other but those of the socialist state.

39. For examples of this kind of literature, see Zhang Xianliang (1986), Zhang Chengzhi (1990), and Zhu Hong (1988).

40. The Hong Kong writer Sun Longji, in his popular and widely read study (1983) *The Deep Structure of Chinese Culture*, borrows from Lévi-Strauss to attribute this problem of what he labels the "eunuchization" of Chinese men to Chinese culture tout court.

41. Though not explicitly theorized in either sympathetic or critical analyses of these works, the masculinity being created is imagined in the context of a global cultural economy in which China, and Chinese men, have been feminized in relation to the masculine West. See Chow (1991a) for a more general theorization of this issue.

42. As Zhong Xueping (2000) has argued about Zhang Xianliang's *Half of Man Is Woman* (1986), the story equates male suffering — i.e., the inability to possess a woman and therefore the inability to possess the body politic — with the suffering of the entire nation. Much of this genre plays out a masculinist politics over women's bodies.

43. The question of the future touches on the character of the child. The end of the melodrama implies that the young girl has inherited the necessary sense of self-sacrifice from her mother while acquiring the essential intellectual yearnings of her father. She, too, may represent China's future possibilities. Having children in China is enormously fraught, given the one-child policy. Yet the lack of explicit commentary about the child indicates that perhaps the child allays an

anxiety rather than stirs one up. With the one-child policy, one child—even a girl—can perhaps resolve all of her parents' painful yearnings.

44. Teresa de Lauretis describes this process as one in which a person "perceives and comprehends as subjective (referring to, even originating in, oneself) those relations—material, economic, and interpersonal—which are in fact social and, in a larger perspective, historical" (1984,159). See also Joan W. Scott's critique of assumptions about unmediated "experience" (1992, 22–40) and Susan Friend Harding's (2000) creative exploration of how biblical discourses "speak" their believers.

45. My point here is that the ideological effectivity of discourse operates on the very frames through which we construct the world and that those spheres in China scrutinized by scholars as potential havens from the state are in themselves part of that ideological effect. This should make us pause before the explosion of research on the issue of "civil society" in China. See Gold (1990) and Strand (1991). See also Chatterjee (1990) on the problems of applying the concept of "civil society" outside its Euro-American historical context.

2. *Museum as Women's Space*

1. For an elaboration of this point, see Gail Hershatter's (2004) incisive review of the literature on women in China during what she calls "China's long twentieth century." See also Liu (1995).

2. I want to emphasize that Li is not merely a "local" feminist who has not had the opportunity to or who refuses to engage with feminism in the West. She has traveled and spoken at numerous conferences in the United States, Canada, Mexico, and Europe. At one conference I co-organized at Harvard in 1992, Li argued vociferously with Chinese feminists studying in the United States about the usefulness of Western feminism for China. To read her own explication of these debates, see Li (1996, 1999).

3. See Tani Barlow (2004a) for an elaborate and nuanced analysis of Li Xiaojiang's multiple theoretical positions.

4. See Yang (1999) for an overview of women's activities in postsocialist public space that contextualizes Li Xiaojiang's museum along with women's hotlines, women's media productions, and women's fiction. See also Shou (2004).

5. At the time Li Xiaojiang wrote, the proliferation of multinational sweatshops and the enormous migration of rural women to work in them had not yet occurred.

6. The "cultural fever" debates of the late 1980s recreated China's identity by rewriting Chinese history. Participants in the debates searched through the history of Chinese culture for answers that might lead to the future regeneration of China's precolonial imperial stature (Wang 1996). One position, as

played out in the infamous television series *River Elegy*, contended that China had lost its opportunity to reach a status as a world power on a par with the West when the Chinese imperium turned away from seafaring and bent its gaze inward to build power on land rather than outward overseas (as had Western colonialists) (Su and Wang 1991). In the 1990s, this cultural fever transformed into cultural nationalism.

7. This province is to the south of Henan province, where the women's museum is located.

8. When I saw it the museum was still a work in progress. It did not have explanatory texts, for example, of the exhibits.

9. Taussig (1993), Bhabha (1994), Tsing (1995) and others have revitalized the concepts of mimesis and alterity, turning them back against their Enlightenment origins. Earlier ideas of mimesis as a symptom of realism, as an endeavor to craft an exact replica of the social world, have been reconceptualized by these authors in a poststructuralist manner to signal actions and representations of similitude that, in attempting to copy the original, end up subverting it, or making the copy more "original" than the original, or exposing the provisional and strategic constructions of subjects and objects and the orders of power involved in those constructions. Mimesis, in their theories, depends on a relation between a knower and its object, or a relation of alterity, of making a thing or person into an "other." Taussig draws from the Frankfurt School, Bhabha from psychoanalytic theory, and Tsing from postcolonial, minority discourse and feminist theories. All of them emphasize the importance of colonialism in the dynamics of mimesis and alterity. They all use concepts of mimesis and alterity, then, to conceptualize dynamics of domination and its possible subversions.

10. One finds alterity, by contrast, in museums constructed by colonizers to display the native peoples they have conquered, or in history museums that produce replicas of the quaint "traditions" of "our forefathers" that reassure us about our modernity. The women's museum, with the exception of minority women, does not display a set of contrasts against which the subject gazing upon the exhibit can be reassured about the normative nature of their subjectivity.

11. When I first wrote this essay, I had in mind lesbian and gay cultural productions in the United States. Since the early 1990s, as will become evident in the next chapter, lesbians and gay men in China have put on cultural productions that are in dialogue with a transnational gay network but do not merely replicate U.S. identities.

3. *Qualities of Desire*

1. This essay speaks mainly about gay men. At the time I began this project, in the summer of 1997, the few lesbians I knew in China asked me not to write about them. Since then, I have interviewed a number of lesbians but feel it is best for

the purposes of this essay to direct my argument to the majority of those with whom I have spoken about these questions.

2. They almost always use the English word "gay." The Chinese word for "homosexuality" is *tongxinglian* and carries connotations of medical abnormality. As I describe in the essay, the term "comrade" has also become popular.

3. See Kang (2006), Ng (1990), Sang (2003), Vitiello (1996, 2000), Volpp (2001) for discussions of same-sex desire in earlier periods of Chinese history.

4. Italics indicate that these terms were said in English.

5. Lydia Liu (1995) coins the term "translingual practice" to highlight how the politics of crossing categories and concepts over language boundaries can lead to fraught confrontations charged with contentious claims to power. My use of "transcultural practices" stems from Liu's conceptualization, though I am tempted to keep her felicitous phrase for use in an analysis of sexuality. I explain cultural citizenship below.

6. David Halperin's (1998) exquisite rendering of the historical and cultural specificity in Foucault's study of sexuality — which moves us beyond the acts-versus-identities dichotomy — is a model of what I have in mind.

7. Altman has written a more elaborate version of this argument in his monograph, *Global Sex* (2001).

8. See also Strongman (2002) for a related critique.

9. As Thomas Boellstorff (1999) points out, this inattention naturalizes heterosexual practices in other cultures. See also Morgensen (2002) and Elliston (1995).

10. For recent examples of the work I allude to, see Boellstorff (2005), Cohen (1995), Manalansan (2003), Morris (1997), and Povinelli (2002).

11. Kath Weston (1995) has argued this point beautifully in her essay on gay urban/rural imaginaries in the United States.

12. I use Stuart Hall's (1985) concept of articulation, by which he means that connections are not given but appear only under particular conditions and must be constantly renewed. An articulation of different practices means not that they become identical but that they function together.

13. See Gopinath (2005) and Manalansan (2003) for leading the way in this critique in relation to queer politics and culture.

14. I suspect that homosexuality is exempt in part because its major faultline of difference lies not between itself and heterosexuality but between itself and homosociality. Unlike the homosociality that Sedgwick (1985, 1990) so perceptively excavated, homosociality in China is public, intimate, and the norm. Many men I have spoken with, both gay and umarked as gay, feel that sex among men may be seen as a natural outgrowth of friendship among men, at least until they marry. Love between men is seen as normal.

15. Wan Yanhai is his real name, which I use because he became internationally famous after he was jailed by the government in 2000 for exposing the prob-

lem of AIDS among poor rural farmers. He then went into exile in the United States. Since that time, he has been allowed to return to China, and he works on public health issues with the support of NGO funding.

16. Indeed, one could argue that human rights discourse is similar to gay identity in that both circulate globally and both are translated with ambivalence.

17. Cui Zi'en is his real name, which I use because he has an international reputation and regularly attends film festivals and academic conferences. Other than Cui Zi'en and Wan Yanhai, the names in this essay are pseudonyms.

18. As Fuss explains, "Identification is a process that keeps identity at a distance, that prevents identity from ever approximating the status of an ontological given, even as it makes possible the formation of an *illusion* of identity as immediate, secure, and totalizable" (1995, 2).

19. Manalansan (2003) portrays the specificities of this Filipino identification, which is termed *bakla*, both in the Philippines and in the Filipino diaspora. Manalansan argues that *bakla* is socially constructed as that of the male body with a female heart. This identity has less to do with cross-dressing or effeminacy than with being able to express emotions and desires conventionally associated with women. Few of those who identify as *bakla* want to have sex with other *bakla;* instead they look for straight men.

20. "The temptation," he wrote, "of total negation, measuring the infinity of this attempt and its impossibility — this is the presence of the face. To be in relation with the other . . . is to be unable to kill. It is also the situation of discourse" (1996 [1951], 9).

4. *From Sacrifice to Desire*

1. For an elaboration of the concept of worlding, see Zhan (2001).

2. For a general overview on social transformations in post-Mao consumption practices, see Davis (2000). See also Evans (2000, 2001) and Gillette (2000a, 2000b) for specific discussions of gender and consumption.

3. See Zhang (2000) for an important discussion of the connections between "youth" and consumption in post-Mao China. See Yan (2003) for an insightful ethnography on related themes of love and intimacy in a rural village.

4. I have learned a great deal about how to question ideologies of globalization from my colleagues at the University of California, Santa Cruz, including Anna Tsing (2004), Jacqueline Nassy Brown (2005), and Hugh Raffles (2003), who, in recent years, have provided much creative rethinking about the cultural construction of place, space, and scale. What I say here is inspired by their work.

5. Thanks to Lydia Liu for this insight.

6. Yan Yunxiang (1997) has offered an astute ethnography of McDonald's in Beijing. He argues that McDonald's has been "localized" in its symbolic mean-

ing and cultural use by Beijing residents. This localization includes the transformation of McDonald's in China into a place of high status, where young professionals like to spend time to acquire and also display their knowledge of foreign cuisine and culture, and its use as a place for family rituals. McDonald's "style" rather than the food is the main attraction. Yan points out that McDonald's portrayal of itself as using scientific methods of food preparation also makes it a symbol of cosmopolitan modernity.

7. See Honig and Hershatter (1988) for an early discussion of these changes and Farquhar (2002) and Hershatter (1997) for an insightful discussion of sexology texts in China.

8. Yan (2003) finds in his ethnography of contemporary northern rural life that premarital sex, love, and intimacy have become the focus of courtship among rural youth. He argues that these changing expectations have been shaped by periods of migrant labor in urban areas as well as the spread of popular mass media, such as television. See also Evans (1997), who sees a continuity from earlier periods in public representations of women who engage in undomesticated sexual behavior as victims or depraved.

9. See Farrer (2002) and Farrer and Sun (2003) for descriptions of the public representations of these issues in China.

10. The four "olds" referred to old customs, old culture, old habits, and old ideas.

11. See Pun (2003) for an important discussion of tourism and labor migration as the two main forms of movement in post-Mao China.

12. But see Zhang (2001) for an ethnography that complicates this picture. Zhang examines migrant entrepreneurial families from Zhejiang province living in Beijing. They, in turn, have hired poorer migrants to work for them.

13. Ma Xiaoduo's sense of distance from her rural past is the other side of this tale of overcoming. Yan (2003) puts these views in context in his ethnography of rural life, which describes how migrant labor experiences have wrought an emergence in the countryside of an ethos of subject development, in which personal desires loom large.

5. *Legislating Desire*

All translations in this chapter are by the author.

1. See Lubman (1999) for a discussion of this point, especially chapter 9. Lubman argues that the practice of not having precedent is based on the historical flexibility of the legal system in China as well as its intimate relationship with enforcing state authority. However, recently, the highest court, the Supreme People's Court, has cautiously been trying to establish precedent by publishing carefully chosen decisions in their gazette.

2. Yanagisako (2002) argues that Hirschman's history additionally reveals how the category of "interest" became vague enough that no one felt the need to ex-

plain it. Yanagisako offers a cultural analysis of the historically specific constitution of various and sometimes competing interests in Italian family firms.

3. The negative evaluation of commerce began in China not with socialism but
    with Confucianism.

4. See Diamant, Lubman, and O'Brien (2005) for a set of essays that elaborate
    this point.

5. Microsoft sued China at the same time that Netscape and then the U.S. gov-
    ernment sued Microsoft in the United States for monopolistic practices. For
    an interesting discussion of the important role that foreign companies have
    played in China in shaping intellectual property rights, see Mertha (2005).
    Mertha delineates how these companies have aggressively lobbied the Chinese
    government to shift counterfeiting and trademark violations from civil to
    criminal offenses.

6. The information on this case comes from Ding Xiaoyin et al. (2002), from the
    Chinese Web site Lawyer-group.com (*Zhongguo Lüshi jituan*).

7. See MacPherson (1962) for the classic explication of "possessive individual-
    ism." MacPherson examined seventeenth-century English political theory to
    argue that the concept of the free individual that subtends liberal political
    theory depends on a notion of the individual as having possession of him or
    herself. This view, he argued, took for granted a model of society based on
    market relations. Marilyn Strathern (1999) has tweaked MacPherson's ar-
    guments through an anthropological interpretation of intellectual property
    rights that shows how disparate collectivities are both imagined and repressed
    in public discourse on those rights.

8. See Kraus (2004) for a lively discussion of the changing relationship between
    the state and arts production in China.

9. Jody Greene (2005) offers a marvelous historically detailed discussion of copy-
    right in seventeenth-century England that complements Rose's. She argues
    that copyright also made the person designated as author the sole figure who
    could be punished by the king and courts for politically transgressive writing.

10. Laikwan Pang's (2006) valuable discussion of copyright and globalization in
    Asia cautions us not to assume that the international legal regime of copyright
    captures all the diffuse practices of mimesis, or copying, that provide the
    creative force for cultural change.

11. *Chongqing Economic Times*, August 13, 2002.

12. *South China Morning Post*, October 13, 1999.

13. *South China Morning Post*, October 13, 1999.

14. The major Chinese Web site for debates about the case is www.gaybyte.com.
    The following quotes come from this Web site's posting of December 30,
    2001.

15. Fang Gang. 1999. As quoted on www.gaybyte.com.

6. *Desiring China*

All translations in this chapter are by the author.

1. The photo of two women shopping placed prominently in the middle of the article tells the story more pointedly, as does the caption: "Women shopping in Beijing. America has urged China to revalue its currency to make U.S. goods cheaper."

2. The specific issue was the the refusal of certain countries, especially several Latin American countries, to comply with the U.S. government's demand that they sign a waiver exempting all U.S. officials and corporate executives from lawsuits at the International Court.

3. The reigning ideology at that time was that national economies and thus the international economy thrive best under peaceful conditions — despite the fact that, of course, profit-seekers have always taken advantage of war. That idea is now defunct. See Ferguson (2004 and 2006).

4. The "primitive accumulation" by which colonizers exploited the resources of the colonized is central to the history of capitalism. This kind of accumulation continues today.

5. My analysis here is inspired by Mei Zhan's work (see especially Zhan forthcoming).

6. The language of "weed out the backwards elements" is reminiscent of Maoism, thus increasing the irony of Han's critique.

7. Perhaps it is not out of place to note here that an increasing number of young adults in China feel they should join a Christian church in order to appear to be proper global citizens.

8. As I discuss in the section on dumping, however, the category "imports from China" obfuscates the fact that these imports include products made in multinational subsidiaries or in factories subcontracting to multinational corporations. Thus, the agonistic tension between national economies that these statistics establish does not do justice to the complexity of transnational capitalist relations of production and consumption.

9. Masco's (2002) insightful analysis of the accusations against the Taiwan-born physicist Wen Ho Lee of spying for China pinpoints the United States government's need to continuously produce an amorphous sense of anxiety about espionage that fuels greater development of nuclear weapons programs. His analysis allows us to see how the Wen Ho Lee case enabled the United States to place greater demands on China in other arenas, such as accession to the WTO, even after the accusations against Wen Ho Lee were found to be baseless.

10. Johnson must have been referring to home ownership in the United States for executives, as these companies were in no position to influence housing in China.

11. Wong, Mai, and Luo, for example, state that the November 1999 trade accord between the United States and China cleared "the last major hurdle in China's accession to the World Trade Organization" (2000, 3).

12. Japan Ministry of Economy, Trade, and Industry, Asia Africa Intelligence Wire, April 12, 2004.

13. Normal value is usually calculated according to the price and cost of production in the domestic market of the exporting country. As we have seen, however, China was made into an exception on this point as well.

14. The "non-market economy" label allows those countries accusing China of dumping to use a surrogate country to measure the fair value of the goods. These surrogate countries can be chosen at random.

15. *People's Daily*, February 3, 2003.

16. *Business and Industry*, July 21, 2003.

17. Ibid.

18. Ibid.

19. Ibid.

20. *Roanoke Times and World News*, February 17, 2004, 1.

21. Global News Wire, April 10, 2003.

22. Ibid.

23. *Business Daily Update*, February 18, 2004.

24. Ibid.

25. Miranda Joseph (2002) presents a related, insightful analysis of the temporalities embedded in discourses of globalization and the construction of value in capitalism through these temporalities, which in turn pull on abstractions by analogy, such as family values.

26. Harnetty argues that the decline of the handloom industry in the area he studied, the Central Provinces, resulted from multiple factors linked to British colonialism: the extinction of native courts (a source of demand for native weavers' specialty clothing) with the rise of British power; changes in fashion following the spread of British rule; railway construction so that British products could reach the interior of India; the introduction of machine-spun yarn that burdened weavers with dependence on middlemen's financing; direct competition from British imported cloth; and the absence of tariff protection for indigenous industry until late in colonial rule. Harnetty is careful, however, to specify different divisions among weavers. He argues that urban handloom weavers survived, though with a severely declining standard of living and a circumscribed arena of work, while their rural counterparts did not. Other scholars (Breman 2004, Farnie 2004, Singleton 2004) are also careful to note the specific displacements of weavers into other aspects of the textile industry rather than their total disappearance. This displacement included the downward trend of weaving coarse cotton cloth (accompanied by a lower

standard of living for weavers) and their eventual need to enter the Indian factory mills.

27. The well-organized boycotts in China of British goods occurred between 1925 and 1927. Thereafter, they were superseded by Chinese boycotts of Japanese goods, as the nationalist movement focused on growing Japanese military domination of China. But Britain, which dominated Shanghai's International Settlement, sided with the Japanese in their protests of what they termed the illegality of the boycotts, as they included confiscation of Japanese goods that were auctioned to fund the nationalist movement. See Goto-Shibata (2005).

28. For the key Indian nationalist text, see Naoroji (1962 [1901]). For the nationalization of China's silk industry see Rofel (1999).

29. Of course, China founded its national republic in 1911, but at the time the country was still under semi-colonialism. It gained independence only with the socialist revolution.

30. See Breman (2004) for a discussion of the deindustrialization, or what he prefers to call the informalization, of the contemporary textile industry in India.

31. *Business Daily Update*, June 24, 2003.

32. BBC Monitoring Asia Pacific, November 20, 2003.

33. Thanks to Mei Zhan for this information from her fieldwork in the summer of 2005.

34. It is difficult for obvious reasons to gain an accurate picture of the numbers of rural migrants in China. Estimates range upward of 100 million (Gaetano and Jacka 2004,1).

35. See Li Zhang's (2001) and Dorothy Solinger's (1999) nuanced studies of rural migrants and their complex strategies for advancement as well as the structural constraints they face.

36. See Chan (2001) for a searing condemnation of the treatment of workers in China. She documents numerous cases of various kinds of abuse, including violations of safety and health standards, physical assault and punishment, forced labor, violations of the right to work, and violations of the right to organize. While the central government obviously colludes in these practices, Chan argues that local labor bureaus and the All-China Federation of Trade Unions are sufficiently concerned to print these stories repeatedly in their newspapers.

37. But see Pun (2005) on the cursory manner in which most factories in China handle these "contracts."

Coda

1. For another, equally compelling interpretation of this film as a rumination about labor, see Wendy Larson (2005).

Abu-Lughod, Janet. 1989. *Before European Hegemony: The World System A.D. 1250–1350.* New York: Oxford University Press.

Abu-Lughod, Lila. 1990. "The Romance of Resistance: Tracing Transformations of Power Through Bedouin Women." *American Ethnologist* 17(1): 41–55.

———. 1993a. "Finding a Place for Islam: Egyptian Television Serials and the National Interest." *Public Culture* 1993 5(3): 493–513.

———, ed. 1993b. *Screening Politics in a World of Nations.* Special issue of *Public Culture* 5(3).

———. 2005. *Dramas of Nationhood: The Politics of Television in Egypt.* Chicago: University of Chicago Press.

Adorno, Theodor W., and Max Horkheimer. 1987. *Dialectic of Enlightenment.* Translated by John Cumming. New York: Continuum.

Ahmad, Aijaz. 1987. "Jameson's Rhetoric of Otherness and the 'National Allegory.' " *Social Text* 17:3–25.

Althusser, Louis. 1971. "Ideology and Ideological State Apparatuses." *Lenin and Philosophy and Other Essays.* New York: Monthly Review Press.

Altman, Dennis. 1997. "Global Gays/Global Gaze." *glq: A Journal of Lesbian and Gay Studies* 3(4): 417–37.

———. 2001. *Global Sex.* Chicago: University of Chicago Press.

Anagnost, Ann. 1989. "Prosperity and Counterprosperity: The Moral Discourse on Wealth in Post-Mao China." In *Marxism and the Chinese Experience*, ed. Arif Dirlik and Maurice Meisner, 210–34. Armonk, N.Y.: M. E. Sharpe.

———. 1995. "A Surfeit of Bodies: Population and the Rationality of State in Post-Mao China." In *Conceiving the New World Order: The Global Politics of Reproduction*, ed. Faye Ginsburg and Rayna Rapp, 22–41. Berkeley: University of California Press.

———. 1997. *National Past-Times: Narrative, Repesentation, and Power in Modern China.* Durham, N.C.: Duke University Press.

———. 2004. "The Corporeal Politics of Quality (*Suzhi*)." *Public Culture* 16(2): 189–208.

Anderson, Benedict. 1983. *Imagined Communities: Reflections on the Origin and Spread of Nationalism.* New York: Verso.

Ang, Ien. 1985. *Watching Dallas: Soap Opera and the Melodramatic Imagination.* New York: Routledge.

Appadurai, Arjun. 1996. *Modernity at Large: Cultural Dimensions of Globalization.* Minneapolis: University of Minnesota Press.

Arrighi, Giovanni. 1994. *The Long Twentieth Century.* New York: Verso.

Barlow, Tani. 1991. "*Zhishifenzi* (Chinese Intellectuals) and Power." *Dialectical Anthropology* 16:209–32.

———. 2004a. "Socialist Modernization and the Market Feminism of Li Xiaojiang." In *The Question of Women in Chinese Feminism*, 253–301. Durham, N.C.: Duke University Press.

———. 2004b. *The Question of Women in Chinese Feminism.* Durham, N.C.: Duke University Press.

Barme, Geremie, and Bennett Lee, eds. 1979. *The Wounded: New Stories of the Cultural Revolution 77–78.* Hong Kong: Joint Publishing Co.

Barme, Geremie, and John Minford, eds. 1986. *Seeds of Fire: Chinese Voices of Conscience.* New York: Noonday Press.

Barthes, Roland. 1975. *The Pleasure of the Text.* Translated by Richard Miller. New York: Hill and Wang.

Belden, Jack. 1949. *China Shakes the World.* New York: Monthly Review.

Bello, Walden. 2001. *The Future in the Balance: Essays on Globalization and Resistance.* Oakland, Calif.: Food First Books.

Benjamin, Walter. 1977 [1963]. *The Origin of German Tragic Drama.* Translated by John Osborne. New York: Verso.

———. 1999 [1972]. *The Arcades Project.* Translated by Howard Eil and Kevin McLaughlin. Cambridge, Mass.: Harvard University Press.

Berlant, Lauren. 1997. *The Queen of America Goes to Washington City: Essays on Sex and Citizenship.* Durham, N.C.: Duke University Press.

Bernstein, Thomas P. 1999. "Farmer Discontent and Regime Responses." In *The Paradoxes of Post-Mao Reforms*, ed. Merle Goldman and Roderick MacFarquar, 197–219. Cambridge, Mass.: Harvard University Press.

Berry, Chris. 1991. "Sexual Difference and the Viewing Subject in *Li Shuangshuang* and *The In-Laws.*" In *Perspectives on Chinese Cinema*, ed. Chris Berry, 30–39. London: British Film Institute.

Bhabha, Homi K. 1990. "Dissemination: Time, Narrative and the Margins of the Modern Nation." In *Nation and Narration*, ed. Homi K. Bhabha, 291–322. New York: Routledge.

———. 1994. "Of Mimicry and Man: The Ambivalence of Colonial Discourse." *The Location of Culture*, 85–92. London: Routledge.

Bian, Wen. 1991. "*Expectation*, a TV Series in 50 Episodes." *Women of China* (May): 14–17.

Boellstorff, Tom. 1999. "The Perfect Path: Gay Men, Marriage, Indonesia." *glq: A Journal of Lesbian and Gay Studies* 5(4): 475–510.

———. 2005. *The Gay Archipelago: Sexuality and Nation in Indonesia.* Princeton, N.J.: Princeton University Press.

Bobo, Jacqueline. 1988. " 'The Color Purple': Black Women as Cultural Readers." In *Female Spectators*, ed. E. Deirdre Pribram, 90–109. London: Verso.

Bourdieu, Pierre. 1984. *Distinction: A Social Critique of the Judgement of Taste.* Cambridge, Mass.: Harvard University Press.

Breckenridge, Carol, Sheldon Pollock, Homi K. Bhabha, and Dipesh Chakrabarty, eds. 2002. *Cosmopolitanism.* Durham, N.C.: Duke University Press.

Breman, Jan. 2004. *The Making and Unmaking of an Industrial Working Class: Sliding Down the Labour Hierarchy in Ahmedabad, India.* New Delhi: Oxford University Press India.

Brinkley, Joel. 2005. "Rice Warns China to Make Major Economic Changes." *New York Times*, August 19: A9.

Brooks, Peter. 1985. *The Melodramatic Imagination: Balzac, Henry James, Melodrama and the Mode of Excess.* New York: Columbia University Press.

Brown, Jacqueline Nassy. 2000. "Enslaving History: Narratives on Local Whiteness in a Black Atlantic Port." *American Ethnologist* 27(2): 340–70.

———. 2005. *Dropping Anchor, Setting Sail.* Princeton, N.J.: Princeton University Press.

Brown, Wendy. 1992. "Finding the Man in the State." *Feminist Studies* 18(1): 7–34.

———. 2003. "Neo-Liberalism and the End of Liberal Democracy." *Theory and Event* 7(1).

Buck-Morss, Susan. 1989. *The Dialectics of Seeing: Walter Benjamin and the Arcades Project.* Cambridge, Mass.: MIT Press.

Burchell, Graham, Colin Gordon, and Peter Miller. 1991. *The Foucault Effect: Studies in Governmentality.* Chicago: University of Chicago Press.

Butler, Judith. 1993. *Bodies that Matter: On the Discursive Limits of "Sex."* New York: Routledge.

Chan, Anita. 2001. *China's Workers under Assault.* Armonk, N.Y.: M. E. Sharpe.

Chan, Anita, Richard Madsen, and Jonathan Unger. 1984. *Chen Village: The Recent History of a Peasant Community in Mao's China.* Berkeley: University of California Press.

Chatterjee, Partha. 1990. "A Response to Taylor's 'Modes of Civil Society.' " *Public Culture* 3(1): 119–32.

Cheah, Pheng. 2003. *Spectral Nationality: Passages of Freedom from Kant to Postcolonial Literatures of Liberation.* New York: Columbia University Press.

Cheah, Pheng, and Bruce Robbins, eds. 1998. *Cosmopolitics: Thinking and Feeling beyond the Nation.* Minneapolis: University of Minnesota Press.

Chen, Yuan-tsung. 1980. *The Dragon's Village: An Autobiographical Novel of Revolutionary China.* New York: Penguin.

Chou, Wah Shan. 1998. "Tongzhi/Queer: Politics of Same-Sex Eroticism in Chinese Societies." Unpublished manuscript.

Chow, Rey. 1991a. *Woman and Chinese Modernity: The Politics of Reading between East and West.* Minneapolis: University of Minnesota Press.

———. 1991b. "Male Narcissism and National Culture: Subjectivity in Chen Kaige's *King of the Children.*" *Camera Obscura* 25/26: 9–39.

Chu, Julie Y. Forthcoming. *Cosmologies of Credit: Fuzhounese Migration and the Politics of Destination.* Durham, N.C.: Duke University Press.

Chu, Yiqi. 1991. "The Mystery of 'Yearnings'' Success" (*"Kewang" Chenggongde Aomi*). *Exploration (Tansuo)* (November): 65–68.

Clifford, James. 1988. *The Predicament of Culture.* Cambridge, Mass.: Harvard University Press.

———. 1999. *Routes: Travel and Translation in the Late Twentieth Century.* Cambridge, Mass.: Harvard University Press.

Cockburn, Alexander. January 3, 2000. *The Nation,* 4.

Cohen, Lawrence. 1995. "*Holi* in Banaras and the *Mahaland* of Modernity." *glq: A Journal of Lesbian and Gay Studies* 2(4): 399–424.

Cohn, Bernard. 1996. "Cloth, Clothes and Colonialism: India in the Nineteenth Century." *Colonialism and its Forms of Knowledge: The British in India.* Princeton, N.J: Princeton University Press, 1996.

Cruz-Malavé, Arnaldo, and Martin F. Manalansan IV. 2002. *Queer Globalizations: Citizenship and the Afterlife of Colonialism.* New York: New York University Press.

Dai, Houying. 1983. *Ah, Humanity! (Ren A, Ren!).* Huacheng: Huacheng Press. Translated by Frances Wood as *Stones of the Wall.* 1985. New York: St. Martin's Press.

Dai, Jinhua. 1995a. *Jing Yu Shisu Shenhua.* (The Mirror and Common Myths). Beijing: China Radio and Television Press.

———. 1995b. *Jingcheng Tuwei: Nüxing, chanying, wenxue* (Breaking Out of the City of Mirrors: Women, Film, Literature). Beijing: Zuojia Chubanshe.

———. 2002. *Cinema and Desire: Feminist Marxism and Cultural Politics in the Work of Dai Jinhua.* Edited by Jing Wang and Tani E. Barlow. New York: Verso.

Davis, Deborah S. 2000. "Introduction: A Revolution in Consumption." In *The Consumer Revolution in Urban China,* ed. Deborah S. Davis, 1–22. Berkeley: University of California Press.

de Certeau, Michel. 1984. *The Practice of Everyday Life.* Berkeley: University of California Press.

de Lauretis, Teresa. 1984. *Alice Doesn't: Feminism, Semiotics, Cinema.* Bloomington: Indiana University Press.

Deleuze, Gilles, and Félix Guattari. 1983. *Anti-Oedipus: Capitalism and Schizophrenia.* Translated by Robert Hurley, Mark Seem, and Helen R. Lane. Minneapolis: University of Minnesota Press.

———. 1987. *A Thousand Plateaus: Capitalism and Schizophrenia.* Translated by Brian Massumi. Minneapolis: University of Minnesota Press.

Dent, Gina, ed. 1992. *Black Popular Culture.* Seattle: Bay Press.

Derrida, Jacques. 1976. *Of Grammatology.* Translated by Gayatri Chakravorty Spivak. Baltimore: Johns Hopkins University Press.

Diamant, Neil J., Stanley B. Lubman, and Kevin J. O'Brien, eds. 2005. *Engaging the Law in China: State, Society and Possibilities for Justice.* Stanford, Calif.: Stanford University Press.

Ding, Xiaoyin, Gao Ming, Zhang Mingzhe, and Song Changhong. 2002. "Shenyang: Peking Opera Music Stirs a Case." Lawyer-group.com (*Zhongguo Lüshi Jituan*).

Doane, Mary Ann, Patricia Mellencamp, and Linda Williams, eds. 1984. *Re-Vision: Essays in Feminist Film Criticism.* Frederick, Md.: University Publications of America.

Donham, Donald. 1997. "Freeing South Africa: The 'Modernization' of Male-Male Sexuality in Soweto." *Cultural Anthropology* 13(1): 3–21.

Douglas, Mary. 1992 [1966]. *Purity and Danger: An Analysis of Concepts of Pollution and Taboo.* New York: Routledge.

Elliston, Deborah. 1995. "Erotic Anthropology: 'Ritualized Homosexuality' in Melanesia and Beyond." *American Ethnologist* 22: 848–67.

Eng, David L. 2001. *Racial Castration: Managing Masculinity in Asian America.* Durham, N.C.: Duke University Press.

Eng, David L., Judith Halberstam, and José Esteban Muñoz, eds. 2005. "What's Queer about Queer Studies Now?" Special Issue of *Social Text.* Fall/Winter (84–85).

Erwin, Kathleen. 1999. "White Women, Male Desires: A Televisual Fantasy of the Transnational Chinese Family." In *Spaces of Their Own: Women's Public Sphere in Transnational China*, ed. Mayfair Hei-hui Yang, 232–57. Minneapolis: University of Minnesota Press.

———. 2000. "Heart-to-Heart, Phone-to-Phone: Family Values, Sexuality and the Politics of Shanghai's Advice Hotlines." In *The Consumer Revolution in Urban China*, ed. Deborah S. Davis, 145–70. Berkeley: University of California Press.

Evans, Harriet. 1997. *Women and Sexuality in China: Dominant Discourses of Female Sexuality and Gender since 1949.* London: Blackwell.

———. 2000. "Marketing Femininity: Images of the Modern Chinese Woman." In *China beyond the Headlines*, ed. Timothy B. Weston and Lione M. Jensen, 217–44. Lanham, Md.: Rowman and Littlefield.

———. 2001. "What Colour Is Beautiful Hair? Subjective Interventions and Global Fashions in the Cultural Production of Gender in Urban China." *Figurationen: Gender, Literature, Culture* 2:117–32.

Faier, Lieba. Forthcoming. *Contingencies of Encounter: Filipina-Japanese Marriages in Rural Japan.* Berkeley: University of California Press.

Fang, Gang. 1995. *Homosexuality in China (Tongxinglian zai Zhongguo).* Jilin: Jilin People's Press.

———. 1999. *Jing Shen Wo Xi (Psychological Self-Analysis).* Beijing: Overseas Chinese Press.

Farnie, Douglas A. 2004. "The Role of Cotton Textiles in the Economic Development of India, 1600–1900." In *The Fibre that Changed the World: The Cotton Industry in International Perspective, 1600–1990s*, ed. Douglas A. Farnie and David J. Jeremy, 395–430. Oxford: Oxford University Press.

Farquhar, Judith. 2002. *Appetites: Food and Sex in Post-Socialist China*. Durham, N.C.: Duke University Press.

Farrer, James. 2002. *Opening Up: Youth Sex Culture and Market Reform in Shanghai*. Chicago: University of Chicago Press.

Farrer, James, and Zhongxin Sun. 2003. "Extramarital Love in Shanghai." *China Journal* 50:1–36.

Ferguson, James. 2004. "Governing Extraction: New Spatializations of Order and Disorder in Neo-liberal Africa." Paper presented at Society for Cultural Anthropology conference on "Sovereignty." Portland, Ore.

———. 2006. *Global Shadows: Africa in the Neoliberal World Order*. Durham, N.C.: Duke University Press.

Ferguson, Roderick. 2003. *Specters of the Sexual: Race, Sociology, and the Conflict over American Culture*. Minneapolis: University of Minnesota Press.

Fiske, John. 1987. *Television Culture*. New York: Routledge.

Foster, Hal, ed. 1983. *The Anti-Aesthetic: Essays on Postmodern Culture*. Port Townsend, Wash.: Bay Press.

Foucault, Michel. 1977a. "What Is an Author?" In *Language, Counter-Memory, Practice: Selected Essays and Interviews by Michel Foucault*, ed. Donald F. Bouchard, trans. Donald F. Bouchard and Sherry Simon, 113–38. Ithaca, N.Y.: Cornell University Press.

———. 1977b [1971]. "Nietzsche, Genealogy, History." In *Language, Counter-Memory, Practice: Selected Essays and Interviews by Michel Foucault*, ed. Donald F. Bouchard, trans. Donald F. Bouchard and Sherry Semon, 139–64. Ithaca, N.Y.: Cornell University Press.

———. 1978. *The History of Sexuality*. Translated by Robert Hurley. New York: Random House.

———. 1979. *Discipline and Punish: The Birth of the Prison*. New York: Random House.

———. 1980. *Power/Knowledge: Selected Interviews and Other Writings, 1972–1977*. Translated by Colin Gordon, Leo Marshall, John Mepham, and Kate Soper. Edited by Colin Gordon. New York: Pantheon.

———. 1985. *The History of Sexuality, Volume 2: The Use of Pleasure*. Translated by Robert Hurley. New York: Random House.

———. 1991. "Governmentality." In *The Foucault Effect: Studies in Governmentality*, ed. Graham Burchell, Colin Gordon, and Peter Miller, trans. Colin Gordon, 87–104. Chicago: University of Chicago Press.

Fuss, Diana. 1995. *Identification Papers*. New York: Routledge.

Gaetano, Arianne M., and Tamara Jacka, eds. 2004. *On the Move: Women and*

Rural-to-Urban Migration in Contemporary China. New York: Columbia University Press.

Gallagher, Mary Elizabeth. 2005. *Contagious Capitalism: Globalization and the Politics of Labor in China*. Princeton, N.J.: Princeton University Press.

Gao, Yuan. 1987. *Born Red: A Chronicle of the Cultural Revolution*. Stanford, Calif.: Stanford University Press.

Geertz, Clifford. 1980. *Negara: The Theatre State in Nineteenth-Century Bali*. Princeton, N.J.: Princeton University Press.

Gillette, Maris Boyd. 2000a. *Between Mecca and Beijing: Modernization and Consumption among Urban Chinese Muslims*. Stanford, Calif.: Stanford University Press.

——. 2000b. "What's in a Dress? Brides in the Hui Quarter of Xi'an." In *The Consumer Revolution in Urban China*, ed. Deborah S. Davis, 80–106. Berkeley: University of California Press.

Gilmartin, Christina K., Gail Hershatter, Lisa Rofel, and Tyrene White, eds. 1994. *Engendering China: Women, Culture and the State*. Cambridge, Mass.: Harvard University Press.

Gilroy, Paul. 1987. *"There Ain't No Black in the Union Jack": The Cultural Politics of Race and Nation*. Chicago: University of Chicago Press.

Ginsburg, Faye D. 1989. *Contested Lives: The Abortion Debate in an American Community*. Berkeley: University of California Press.

——. 1991. "Indigenous Media: Faustian Contract or Global Village?" *Cultural Anthropology* 6(1): 92–112.

——. 2002. "Screen Memories: Resignifying the Traditional in Indigenous Media." In *Media Worlds: Anthropology on New Terrain*, ed. Faye D. Ginsburg, Lila Abu-Lughod, and Brian Larkin, 39–57. Berkeley: University of California Press.

Ginsburg, Faye D., Lila Abu-Lughod, and Brian Larkin, eds. 2002. *Media Worlds: Anthropology on New Terrain*. Berkeley: University of California Press.

Gledhill, Christine, ed. 1987. *Home Is Where the Heart Is: Studies in Melodrama and the Woman's Film*. London: British Film Institute.

Gold, Thomas B. 1990. "Party-State versus Society in China." In *Building a Nation-State: China after Forty Years*, ed. Joyce K. Kallgren, 125–51. Berkeley: Institute of East Asian Studies.

Gopinath, Gayatri. 2005. *Impossible Desires: Queer Diasporas and South Asian Public Cultures*. Durham, N.C.: Duke University Press.

Goto-Shibata, Harumi. 2005. "Japanese and British Perceptions of Chinese Boycotts in Shanghai: With Special Reference to the Anti-Japanese Boycotts, 1928–31." In *Japan, China, and the Growth of the Asian International Economy, 1850–1949*, ed. Karoru Sugihara, 127–44. Oxford: Oxford University Press.

Greene, Jody. 2005. *The Trouble with Ownership: Literary Property and Authorial Liability in England, 1660–1730*. Philadelphia: University of Pennsylvania Press.

Grossberg, Lawrence, Cary Nelson, and Paula A. Treichler, eds. 1992. *Cultural Studies*. New York: Routledge.

Halberstam, Judith. 2005. *In a Queer Time and Place: Transgender Bodies, Subcultural Lives*. New York: New York University Press.

Hale, Charles. 2002. "Does Multiculturalism Menace? Governance, Cultural Rights and the Politics of Identity in Guatemala." *Journal of Latin American Studies* 34: 485–524.

———. 2005. "Neoliberal Multiculturalism: The Remaking of Cultural Rights and Racial Dominance in Central America." *PoLAR: Political and Legal Anthropology Review* 28(1): 10–28.

Hall, Stuart. 1977. "Culture, the Media, and the 'Ideological Effect.'" In *Mass Communication and Society*, ed. J. Curran et al., 315–48. London: Edward Arnold.

———. 1981. "Notes on Deconstructing 'The Popular.'" In *People's History and Socialist Theory*, ed. Raphael Samuel, 227–40. London: Routledge and Kegan Paul.

———. 1985. "Signification, Representation, Ideology: Althusser and the Post-Structuralist Debates." *Critical Studies in Mass Communication* 2:91–114.

Halperin, David M. 1995. *Saint Foucault: Towards a Gay Hagiography*. New York: Oxford University Press.

———. 1998. "Forgetting Foucault: Acts, Identities, and the History of Sexuality." *Representations* 63: 93–120.

Han, Deqiang. 2000. *Peng Zhuang: Quanqiu Hua Xianjing yu Zhongguo Xianshi Xuanze* (Collision: The Pitfalls of Globalization and China's Realistic Choices). Beijing: Jingji Guanli Press.

Hangzhou Radio and Television Weekly (*Hangzhou Guangbo Yingshi*). 1991. "A Record of 'Yearnings'' Birth" ("Kewang" Dansheng Ji). January 4: 4.

Haraway, Donna. 1985. "Teddy Bear Patriarchy: Taxidermy in the Garden of Eden, New York City, 1908–36." *Social Text* 11:20–64.

Harding, Susan Friend. 2000. *The Book of Jerry Falwell: Fundamentalist Language and Politics*. Princeton, N.J.: Princeton University Press.

Harnetty, Peter. 1991. "'Deindustrialization' Revisited: The Handloom Weavers of the Central Provinces of India, c. 1800–1947." *Modern Asian Studies* 25(3): 455–510.

Harvey, David. 2000. *Spaces of Hope*. Berkeley: University of California Press.

———. 2005. *A Brief History of Neoliberalism*. New York: Oxford University Press.

Held, David, and Mathias Koenig-Archibugi, eds. 2003. *Taming Globalization: Frontiers of Governance*. Cambridge: Polity Press in association with Blackwell Publishers.

Hershatter, Gail. 1996. "Sexing Modern China." In *Remapping China: Fissures in Historical Terrain*, ed. Gail Hershatter, Emily Honig, Jonathan Lipman, and Randall Stross, 77–93. Stanford, Calif.: Stanford University Press.

———. 1997. *Dangerous Pleasures: Prostitution and Modernity in Twentieth-century Shanghai*. Berkeley: University of California Press.

———. 2002. "The Gender of Memory: Rural Chinese Women and the 1950s." *Signs* 28(1): 43–72.

———. 2004. "State of the Field: Women in China's Long Twentieth Century." *Journal of Asian Studies* 63(4): 991–1065.

Hevia, James. 1995. *Cherishing Men from Afar: Qing Guest Ritual and the Macartney Embassy of 1793*. Durham, N.C.: Duke University Press.

Hinton, William. 1966. *Fanshen: A Documentary of Revolution in a Chinese Village*. New York: Vintage.

Hirschman, Albert O. 1996 [1977]. *The Passions and the Interests: Political Arguments for Capitalism before Its Triumph*. Princeton, N.J.: Princeton University Press.

Honig, Emily, and Gail Hershatter. 1988. *Personal Voices: Chinese Women in the 1980's*. Stanford, Calif.: Stanford University Press.

hooks, bell. 1989. *Talking Back*. Boston: South End Press.

———. 1992. *Black Looks: Race and Representation*. Boston: South End Press.

Huang, Xiyi. 1999. "Divided Gender, Divided Women: State Policy and the Labour Market." In *Women of China: Economic and Social Transformation*, ed. Jackie West, Zhao Mingua, Chang Xiangqun, and Cheng Yuan, 90–107. London: Mac-Millan.

Huntington, Samuel. 1997. *The Clash of Civilizations and the Remaking of World Order*. New York: Touchstone.

Jameson, Fredric. 1986. "Third-World Literature in the Era of Multinational Capital." *Social Text* 15 (Fall): 65–88.

Hoy, David. 2004. *Critical Resistance*. Princeton, N.J.: Princeton University Press.

Jenkins, Henry. 1992. *Textual Poachers: Television Fans and Participatory Culture*. New York: Routledge.

Johnson, Kay Ann. 1983. *Women, the Family and Peasant Revolution in China*. Chicago: University of Chicago Press.

Joseph, Miranda. 2002. "Family Affairs: The Discourse of Global/Localization." In *Queer Globalizations: Citizenship and the Afterlife of Colonialism*, ed. Arnaldo Cruz-Malavé and Martin F. Manalansan IV, 71–99. New York: New York University Press.

Kang, Wenqing. Forthcoming. "Male Same-Sex Relations in Modern China." *positions: east asia cultures critique*.

Kaplan, E. Ann. 1987. "Feminist Criticism and Television." In *Channels of Discourse: Television and Contemporary Criticism*, ed. Robert C. Allen, 211–53. Chapel Hill: University of North Carolina Press.

Kipnis, Andrew. 1997. *Producing Guanxi: Sentiment, Self and Subculture in a North China Village*. Durham, N.C.: Duke University Press.

Kondo, Dorinne. 1990a. "*M. Butterfly*—Orientalism, Gender, and a Critique of Essentialized Identity." *Cultural Critique* 16 (Fall): 5–29.

———. 1990b. *Crafting Selves: Power, Gender and Discourses of Identity in a Japanese Workplace*. Chicago: University of Chicago Press.

Kraus, Richard Curt. 2004. *The Party and the Arty in China: The New Politics of Culture*. New York: Rowman and Littlefield.

Lardy, Nicholas R. 2002. *Integrating China into the Global Economy*. Washington, D.C.: Brookings Institution Press.

Larson, Wendy. 2005. "The Postman: The Workspace of a New Age Maoist." In *Gender in Motion: Divisions of Labor and Cultural Change in Late Imperial and Modern China*, ed. Bryna Goodman and Wendy Larson, 211–36. Lanham, Md.: Rowman and Littlefield.

Latour, Bruno. 1993. *We Have Never Been Modern*. Cambridge, Mass.: Harvard University Press.

Lavie, Smadar. 1990. *The Poetics of Military Occupation*. Berkeley: University of California Press.

Lee, C. K. 1998. *Gender and the South China Miracle: Two Worlds of Factory Women*. Berkeley: University of California Press.

Lemke, Thomas. 2001. "The Birth of Bio-Politics: Michel Foucault's lecture at the College de France on Neo-Liberal Governmentality." *Economy and Society* 30(2): 190–207.

Levinas, Emmanuel. 1996 [1951]. "Is Ontology Fundamental?" In *Basic Philosophical Writings*, ed. Adriaan T. Peperzak, Simon Critchley, and Robert Bernasconi. Bloomington: Indiana University Press.

Li, Tuo. 1991a. "The Politics of Literary Theory in PostMao China." Unpublished paper.

———. 1991b [1985]. *Jintian (Today)* 3/4: 59–73.

Li, Xiaojiang. 1988a. *Xiawade Tansuo (The Search for Eve)*. Zhengzhou: Henan People's Press.

———. 1988b. *Gaige he Zhongguo Nüxing qunti yishi de juexing* (Economic Reform and the Awakening of Chinese Women's Collective Consciousness). *Shehui Kexue Zhanxian (Social Science Battlefront)* 4:300–310.

———. 1989. "The Road Ahead for Women" (*Nürende Chulu*). Shenyang: Liaoning People's Press.

———. 1990. "Zouxiang Nüren" (Toward Woman). In *Nüxing Ren*, ed. Chen Yi-shih. Taipei: Shibao Chubanshe.

———. 1996. *Tiaozhan yü Huiying* (Challenge and Response). Zhengzhou: Henan People's Press.

———. 1999. "With What Discourse Do We Reflect on Chinese Women? Thoughts on Transnational Feminism in China." In *Spaces of Their Own: Women's Public Sphere in Transnational China*, ed. Mayfair Mei-hui Yang, 261–77. Minneapolis: University of Minnesota Press:

Li, Xiaojiang, and Tan Shen, eds. 1991a. *Zhongguo Funü Fenceng Yanjiu* (Research on Chinese Women). Zhengzhou: Henan People's Press.

——. 1991b. *Funü Yanjiu Zai Zhongguo* (Women's Research in China). Zhengzhou: Henan People's Press.

Li, Xiaoping. 1991. "The Chinese Television System and Television News." *China Quarterly* 126: 340–55.

Li, Ziyun. 1994. "Women's Consciousness and Women's Writing." In *Engendering China*, ed. Christina K. Gilmartin, Gail Hershatter, Lisa Rofel, and Tyrene White, 299–317. Cambridge, Mass.: Harvard University Press.

Liang, Heng, and Judith Shapiro. 1983. *Son of the Revolution*. New York: Random House.

Lin, Nan. 1995. "Local Market Socialism: Local Corporatism in Action in Rural China." *Theory and Society* 24(3): 301–54.

Lin, Yimin. 2001. *Between Politics and Markets: Firms, Competition, and Institutional Change in Post-Mao China*. Cambridge: Cambridge University Press.

Liu, Lydia. 1991 "The Female Tradition in Modern Chinese Literature: Negotiating Feminisms Across East/West Boundaries." *Genders* 12 (Winter): 22–44.

——. 1995. *Translingual Practice: Literature, National Culture, and Translated Modernity China, 1900–1937*. Stanford, Calif.: Stanford University Press.

Long, Yongtu. 1999. "Guanyü Jingji Quanqiuhua Wentide Jidian Sikao" (Some Thoughts on Questions of Economic Globalization). *Zhongguo Duiwai Jingji Maoyi Nian Jian* (Chinese Foreign Economic Trade Yearbook). Beijing: China Foreign Economic Relations and Trade Publishers House, 42–48.

Louie, Kam. 1991. "The Macho Eunuch: The Politics of Masculinity in Jia Pingwa's *Human Extremities.*" *Modern China* 17(2): 163–87.

Lü, Meiyi, and Zheng Yongfu. 1990. *Zhongguo Funü Yundong—1840–1921* (The Chinese Women's Movement—1840–1921). Zhengzhou: Henan People's Press.

Lubman, Stanley B. 1999. *Bird in a Cage: Legal Reform in China after Mao*. Stanford, Calif.: Stanford University Press.

Lukács, György. 1972. *History and Class Consciousness: Studies in Marxist Dialectics*. Translated by Rodney Livingstone. Cambridge, Mass.: MIT Press.

Luo, Zi-ping. 1990. *A Generation Lost: China under the Cultural Revolution*. New York: Avon Books.

MacPherson, C. B. 1962. *The Political Theory of Possessive Individualism: Hobbes to Locke*. New York: Oxford University Press.

Malkki, Liisa. 1992. "National Geographic: The Rooting of Peoples and the Territorialization of National Identity Among Scholars and Refugees." *Cultural Anthropology* 7(1): 24–44.

——. 1995. *Purity and Exile: Violence, Memory, and National Cosmology among Hutu Refugees in Tanzania*. Chicago: University of Chicago Press.

Manalansan, Martin F. IV. 2003. *Global Divas: Filipino Gay Men in the Diaspora*. Durham, N.C.: Duke University Press.

Mani, Lata. 1998. *Contentious Traditions: The Debate on Sati in Colonial India.* Berkeley: University of California Press.

Mankekar, Purnima. 1999. *Screening Culture, Viewing Politics: An Ethnography of Television, Womanhood, and Nation in Postcolonial India.* Durham, N.C.: Duke University Press.

Martin, Fran. 2003. *Situating Sexualities: Queer Representation in Taiwanese Fiction, Film and Public Culture.* Hong Kong: Hong Kong University Press.

Masco, Joseph. 2002. "Lie Detectors: On Secrets and Hypersecurity in Los Alamos." *Public Culture* 14(3): 441–67.

Mbembe, Achille. 2001. *On the Postcolony.* Berkeley: University of California Press.

Meng, Yue, and Dai Jinhua, 1990, *Fuchu Lishi Dibiao* (Floating up from the Surface of History). Zhengzhou: Henan People's Press.

Mercer, Kobena. 1991. "Skin Head Sex Thing: Racial Difference and the Homoerotic Imaginary." In *How Do I Look: Queer Film and Video*, ed. Bad Object-Choices, 169–210. Seattle: Bay Press.

Mertha, Andrew C. 2005. "Shifting Legal and Administrative Goalposts: Chinese Bureaucracies, Foreign Actors and the Evolution of China's Anti-Counterfeiting Enforcement Regime." In *Engaging the Law in China: State, Society and Possibilities for Justice*, ed. Neil J. Diamant, Stanley B. Lubman, and Kevin J. O'Brien, 161–92. Stanford, Calif.: Stanford University Press.

Mitchell, Timothy. 1990. "Everyday Metaphors of Power." *Theory and Society* 19:545–77.

———. 2002. *Rule of Experts: Egypt, Techno-politics, Modernity.* Berkeley: University of California Press.

Modleski, Tania. 1982. *Loving with a Vengeance: Mass-Produced Fantasies for Women.* Hamden, Conn.: Shoe String Press.

———. 1991. *Feminism without Women: Culture and Criticism in a "Postfeminist" Age.* New York: Routledge.

Morgensen, Scott. 2002. "Gay Identities in Metropolitan America." Ph.D. diss., Department of Anthropology, University of California, Santa Cruz.

Morris, Rosalind. 1997. "Educating Desire: Thailand, Transnationalism, and Transgression." *Social Text* 15(3): 53–79.

Morrison, Toni, ed. 1992. *Race-ing Justice, En-gendering Power: Essays on Anita Hill, Clarence Thomas, and the Construction of Social Reality.* New York: Pantheon Books.

Mulvey, Laura. 1989. *Visual and Other Pleasures.* Hampshire: Macmillan.

Naoroji, Dadabhai. 1962 [1901]. *Poverty and Un-British Rule in India.* Delhi: Ministry of Information and Broadcasting.

Newton, Esther. 1972. *MotherCamp.* Chicago: University of Chicago Press.

Ng, Vivien W. 1990. "Homosexuality and the State in late Imperial China." In *Hidden from History: Reclaiming the Gay and Lesbian Past*, ed. Martin Duberman, Martha Vicinus, and George Chauncey Jr., 76–89. New York: Meridian.

Nien, Cheng. 1986. *Life and Death in Shanghai*. London: Grafton Books.

Nussbaum, Martha Craven, ed. 2002. *For Love of Country?* Boston: Beacon Press.

Oi, Jean, and Andrew Walder, eds. 1999. *Property Rights and Economic Reform in China*. Stanford, Calif.: Stanford University Press.

Ong, Aihwa. 1999. *Flexible Citizenship: The Cultural Logics of Transnationality*. Durham, N.C.: Duke University Press.

———. 2003. *Buddha Is Hiding: Refugees, Citizenship, the New America*. Berkeley: University of California Press.

Pang, Laikwan. 2006. *Cultural Control and Globalization in Asia: Copyright, Piracy, and Cinema*. New York: Routledge.

Paredes, Américo. 1973 [1958]. *"With His Pistol in His Hand": A Border Ballad and Its Hero*. Austin: University of Texas Press.

Pateman, Carol. 1989. *The Disorder of Women*. Stanford, Calif.: Stanford University Press.

Peet, Richard. 2003. *Unholy Trinity: The IMF, World Bank and WTO*. New York: Zed Books.

Pomeranz, Kenneth. 2000. *The Great Divergence: China, Europe, and the Making of the Modern World Economy*. Princeton, N.J.: Princeton University Press.

Povinelli, Elizabeth A. 2002. *The Cunning of Recognition: Indigenous Alterities and the Making of Australian Multiculturalism*. Durham, N.C.: Duke University Press.

Povinelli, Elizabeth A., and George Chauncey, eds. 1999. *Thinking Sex Transnationally*. Special issue of *glq: A Journal of Lesbian and Gay Studies* 5(4).

Pratt, Mary Louise. 1992. *Imperial Eyes: Travel Writing and Transculturation*. New York: Routledge.

Pribram, E. Deirdre, ed. 1988. *Female Spectators: Looking at Film and Television*. London: Verso.

Pun, Ngai. 2003. "Subsumption or Consumption? The Phantom of Consumer Revolution in "Globalizing" China. *Cultural Anthropology* 18(4): 469–92.

———. 2005. *Made in China: Women Factory Workers in a Global Workplace*. Durham, N.C.: Duke University Press.

Rabinowitz, Paula. 1990. "Seeing through the Gendered I: Feminist Film Theory." *Feminist Studies* 16(1): 151–69.

Radway, Janice A. 1984. *Reading the Romance: Women, Patriarchy, and Popular Literature*. Chapel Hill: University of North Carolina Press.

Raffles, Hugh. 2003. *In Amazonia: A Natural History*. Princeton, N.J.: Princeton University Press.

Ren, Yin. 1991. "A 'Resolute Woman' with a Morality of Self-Perfection" (Yige Daode Ziwo Wanshande "Jiannu"). *Popular Film (Dazhong Dianying)* 2:2–3.

Rofel, Lisa. 1999. *Other Modernities: Gendered Yearnings in China after Socialism*. Berkeley: University of California Press.

Rosaldo, Renato. 1989. *Culture and Truth: The Remaking of Social Analysis*. Boston: Beacon Press.

Rose, Mark. 1993. *Authors and Owners: The Invention of Copyright*. Cambridge, Mass.: Harvard University Press.

Rose, Nikolas. 1996. "Governing 'Advanced' Liberal Democracies." In *Foucault and Political Reason*, ed. Andrew Barry, Thomas Osborne, and Nikolas Rose, 37–64. Chicago: University of Chicago Press.

———. 1999. *Powers of Freedom: Reframing Political Thought*. Cambridge: Cambridge University Press.

Ross, Andrew. 1989. *No Respect: Intellectuals and Popular Culture*. New York: Routledge.

Rowe, William, and Vivian Schelling. 1991. *Memory and Modernity: Popular Culture in Latin America*. New York: Verso.

Ryan, Mary. 1990. *Women in the Public: Between Banners and Ballots, 1825–1880*. Baltimore: Johns Hopkins University Press.

Sahlins, Marshall. 1976. *Culture and Practical Reason*. Chicago: University of Chicago Press.

Sang, Tze-lan D. 2003. *The Emerging Lesbian: Female Same-Sex Desire in Modern China*. Chicago: University of Chicago Press.

Satsuka, Shiho. 2004. "Traveling Nature, Imagining the Globe: Japanese Tourism in the Canadian Rockies." Ph.D. diss. Department of Anthropology, University of California, Santa Cruz.

Schein, Louisa. 2000. *Minority Rules: The Miao and the Feminine in China's Cultural Politics*. Durham, N.C.: Duke University Press.

Scott, Joan. 1992. "Experience." In *Feminists Theorize the Political*, ed. Judith Butler and Joan W. Scott, 22–40. New York: Routledge, Chapman and Hal.

Sedgwick, Eve Kosofsky. 1985. *Between Men: English Literature and Male Homosocial Desire*. New York: Columbia University Press.

———. 1990. *Epistemology of the Closet*. Berkeley: University of California Press.

Shou, Yuanjun. 2004. "*Half the Sky*: A Television Program for Women." In *Holding up Half the Sky: Chinese Women Past, Present, and Future*, ed. Tao Jie, Zheng Bijun, and Shirley L. Mow, 261–73. New York: Feminist Press.

Shue, Vivienne. 1988. *The Reach of the State: Sketches of the Chinese Body Politic*. Stanford, Calif.: Stanford University Press.

Silber, Cathy. 1994. "From Daughter to Daughter-in-Law in the Women's Script of Southern Hunan." In *Engendering China*, ed. Christina K. Gilmartin, Gail Hershatter, Lisa Rofel, and Tyrene White, 47–68. Cambridge, Mass.: Harvard University Press.

Singleton, John. 2004. "The Lancashire Cotton Industry, the Royal Navy, and the British Empire, c. 1700–1960." In *The Fibre that Changed the World: The Cotton Industry in International Perspective, 1600–1990s*, ed. Douglas A. Farnie and David J. Jeremy, 57–84. Oxford: Oxford University Press.

Siu, Helen F., and Zelda Stern, 1983. *Mao's Harvest: Voices from China's New Generation*. Oxford: Oxford University Press.

Solinger, Dorothy J. 1999. *Contesting Citizenship in Urban China: Peasant Migrants, the State, and the Logic of the Market.* Berkeley: University of California Press.

Somerville, Siobhan, 2000, *Queering the Color Line: Race and the Invention of Homosexuality in American Culture.* Durham, N.C.: Duke University Press.

Song, Lina. 1999. "The Role of Women in Labour Migration: A Case Study in Northern China." In *Women of China: Economic and Social Transformation*, ed. Jackie West, Zhao Mingua, Chang Xiangqun, and Cheng Yuan, 69–89. New York: MacMillan.

Spivak, Gayatri. 1999. *A Critique of Postcolonial Reason: Toward a History of the Vanishing Present.* Cambridge, Mass: Harvard University Press.

Stoler, Ann Laura. 2002. *Carnal Knowledge and Imperial Power: Race and the Intimate in Colonial Rule.* Berkeley: University of California Press.

Strand, David. 1991. "Protest in Bejing: Civil Society and Public Sphere in China." *Problems of Communism* 39(3): 1–19.

Strathern, Marilyn. 1999. *Property, Substance and Effect: Anthropological Essays on Persons and Things.* London: Athlone Press.

Strongman, Roberto. 2002. "Syncretic Religion and Dissident Sexualities." In *Queer Globalizations: Citizenship and the Afterlife of Colonialism*, ed. Arnaldo Cruz-Malavé and Martin F. Manalansan IV, 176–92. New York: New York University Press.

Su, Xiaokang, and Wang Luxiang. 1991. *Deathsong of a River: A Reader's Guide to the Chinese TV Series "Heshang."* Translated by Richard W. Bodman and Piu P. Wan. Ithaca, N.Y: Cornell East Asia Program.

Sun, Longji. 1983. *The Deep Structure of Chinese Culture (Zhongguo Wenhuade Shengceng Jiegou).* Hong Kong: Jixianshe.

Sun, Wanning. 2004. "Indoctrination, Fetishization, and Compassion: Media Constructions of the Migrant Woman." In *On the Move: Women and Rural-to-Urban Migration in Contemporary China*, ed. Arianne M. Gaetano and Tamara Jacka, 109–28. New York: Columbia University Press.

Tadiar, Neferti Xina M. 2004. *Fantasy-Production: Sexual Economies and Other Philippine Consequences for the New World Order.* Manila: Ateneo de Manila University Press.

Tan, Shen. 2004. "Leaving Home and Coming Back: Experiences of Migrant Women." In *Together with Migrants: A UNESCO Project for Poverty Reduction*, ed. UNESCO. Beijing: UNESCO Office.

Tang, Xiaobing. 1991. "The Function of New Theory: What Does It Mean to Talk about Post-Modernism in China?" *Public Culture* 4(1): 89–108.

Taussig, Michael. 1993. *Mimesis and Alterity: A Particular History of the Senses.* New York: Routledge.

Tsai, Kellee S. 2002. *Back-Alley Banking: Private Entrepreneurs in China.* Ithaca, N.Y.: Cornell University Press.

Tsing, Anna. 2005. *Friction: An Ethnography of Global Connection*. Princeton, N.J.: Princeton University Press.

Unger, Jonathan. 2002. *The Transformation of Rural China*. Armonk, N.Y.: M. E. Sharpe.

U.S. Government. 1999. *United States-China Trade Relations and the Possible Accession of China to the World Trade Organization: Hearing before the Subcommittee on Trade of the Committee on Ways and Means House of Representatives, One Hundred Sixth Congress First Session, June 8, 1999, Serial 106–8*. Washington, D.C.: U.S. Government Printing Office.

Vitiello, Giovanni. 1996. "The Fantastic Journey of an Ugly Boy: Homosexuality and Salvation in Late Ming Pornography." *positions: east asia cultures critique* 4(2): 291–320.

——. 2000. "Exemplary Sodomites: Chivalry and Love in Late Ming Culture." *Nan Nü: Men, Women and Gender in Early and Imperial China* 2(2): 207–57.

Volosinov, V. N. 1973. *Marxism and the Philosophy of Language*. Translated by Ladislav Matejka and I. R. Titunik. Cambridge, Mass.: Harvard University Press.

Volpp, Sophie. 2001. "Classifying Lust: The Seventeenth-Century Vogue for Male Love." *Harvard Journal of Asiatic Studies* 61(1): 77–117.

Von Hayek, Friedrich. 1944. *The Road to Serfdom*. London: Routledge and Kegan Paul.

Wang, Hui. 2004. "The Year 1989 and the Historical Roots of Neoliberalism in China." *positions: east asia cultures critique* 12(1): 7–69.

Wang, Jing. 1996. *High Culture Fever: Politics, Aesthetics and Ideology in Deng's China*. Berkeley: University of California Press.

Wang, Shaoguang. 2000. "The Social and Political Implications of China's WTO Membership." *Journal of Contemporary China* 9(25): 373–405.

Wang, Shaoguang, and Hu Angang. 1999. *The Political Economy of Uneven Development: The Case of China*. Armonk, N.Y.: M. E. Sharpe.

Wang, Yuejin. 1989. "Mixing Memory and Desire: Red Sorghum a Chinese Version of Masculinity and Feminity." *Public Culture* 2(1): 31–53.

Wang, Zheng. 2001. "Call Me *Qingnian* but Not *Funü*: A Maoist Youth in Retrospect." *Feminist Studies* 27(1): 9–36.

Warner, Michael, ed. 1993. *Fear of a Queer Planet*. Minneapolis: University of Minnesota Press.

——. 1999. *The Trouble with Normal: Sex, Politics and the Ethics of Queer Life*. Cambridge, Mass.: Harvard University Press.

Watson, James L., ed. 1997. *Golden Arches East: McDonald's in East Asia*. Stanford, Calif.: Stanford University Press.

Weber, Max. 1978. *Economy and Society*. Edited by Guenther Roth and Claus Wittich. Berkeley: University of California Press.

Welland, Sasha. 2006. *Experimental Beijing: Contemporary Art Worlds in China's*

Capital. Ph.D. diss., Department of Anthropology, University of California, Santa Cruz.

West, Loraine A., and Yaohui Zhao, eds. 2000. *Rural Labor Flows in China*. Berkeley: Institute of East Asian Studies, University of California Press.

Weston, Kath. 1995. "Get Thee to a Big City: Sexual Imaginary and the Great Gay Migration." *glq: A Journal of Lesbian and Gay Studies* 2(3):253–78.

Williams, Raymond. 1977. *Marxism and Literature*. Oxford: Oxford University Press.

Wolf, Margery. 1985. *Revolution Postponed: Women in Contemporary China*. Stanford, Calif.: Stanford University Press.

Wong, John, Mai Yinhua, and Luo Qi. 2000. *Sino-US Trade Accord and China's Accession to the World Trade Organization*. Singapore: Singapore University Press.

Working Party on the Accession of China. 2001. *Report of the Working Party on the Accession of China*. Geneva, Switzerland: World Trade Organization Publications.

World Trade Organization. N.d. *The World Trade Organization in Brief: 10 Benefits of the WTO and 10 Common Misunderstandings about the WTO*. Geneva, Switzerland: World Trade Organization Publications.

Wu, Yi. 2001. "Lizu Xinqidian Jianfu Xin Shiming Kaichuang Waijingji Fazhan Xinjumian" ("Base Ourselves on a New Starting Point, Shoulder a New Mission: Opening a New Phase in the Development of Foreign Economic Trade.") *Zhongguo Duiwai Jingji Maoyi Nian Jian* (Chinese Foreign Economic Trade Yearbook), 64–70. Beijing: China Foreign Economic and Trade Publishing House.

WuDunn, Sheryl. 1991. "Why So Many Chinese Are Teary: The Soap Opera Epoch Has Dawned." *New York Times*, February 1: A4.

Xie, Zhimin. 1991. *Jiangyong "Nüshu" Zhi Mi* (Enigmas of the Jiangyong "Women's Script"). Zhengzhou: Henan People's Press.

Yan, Hairong. 2003a. "Neoliberal Governmentality and Neohumanism: Organizing Suzhi/Value Flow through Labor Recruitment Networks." *Cultural Anthropology* 18(4): 493–523.

———. 2003b. "Specialization of the Rural: Reinterpreting the Labor Mobility of Rural Young Women in Post-Mao China." *American Ethnologist* 30(4): 578–96.

Yan, Yunxiang. 1997. "McDonald's in Beijing: The Localization of Americana." In *Golden Arches East: McDonald's in East Asia*, ed. James L. Watson, 39–76. Stanford, Calif.: Stanford University Press.

———. 2003. *Private Life under Socialism: Love, Intimacy and Family Change in a Chinese Village*. Stanford, Calif.: Stanford University Press.

Yanagisako, Sylvia Junko. 2002. *Producing Culture and Capital: Family Firms in Italy*. Princeton, N.J.: Princeton University Press.

Yang, Mayfair Mei-hui, ed. 1999. *Spaces of their Own: Women's Public Sphere in Transnational China*. Minneapolis: University of Minnesota Press.

Yue, Daiyun, and Carolyn Wakeman, 1985. *To the Storm: The Odyssey of a Revolutionary Chinese Woman*. Berkeley: University of California Press.

Zha, Jianying, 1992. "*Yearnings:* Public Culture in a Post-Tiananmen Era." *Transition* 57 (September): 26–51.

Zhan, Mei. 2001. "Does It Take a Miracle? Negotiating Knowledges, Identities, and Communities of Traditional Chinese Medicine." *Cultural Anthropology* 16(4): 453–80.

——. 2005. "Civet Cats, Fried Grasshoppers, and David Beckham's Pajamas: Unruly Bodies After SARS." *American Anthropologist* 107(1): 31–42.

——. Forthcoming. *Other Worldly: Relocating Traditional Chinese Medicine Through Encounters*. Durham, N.C.: Duke University Press.

Zhang, Chengzhi. 1990. *The Black Steed*. Translated by Stephen Fleming. Beijing: Chinese Literature Press.

Zhang, Li. 2001. *Strangers in the City: Reconfigurations of Space, Power, and Social Networks within China's Floating Population*. Stanford, Calif.: Stanford University Press.

Zhang, Xianliang. 1986. *Half of Man Is Woman*. Translated by Martha Avery. New York: W.W. Norton.

Zhang, Zhen. 2000. "Mediating Time: The 'Rice Bowl of Youth' in Fin de Siècle Urban China." *Public Culture* 12(1): 93–113.

Zhong, Xueping. 2000. *Masculinity Besieged? Issues of Modernity and Male Subjectivity in Chinese Literature of the Late Twentieth Century*. Durham, N.C.: Duke University Press.

Zhu, Hong, ed. 1988. *The Chinese Western*. New York: Ballantine Books.

Zito, Angela. 1994. "Silk and Skin: Significant Boundaries." In *Body, Subject and Power in China*, ed. Angela Zito and Tani E. Barlow, 103–30. Chicago: University of Chicago Press.

——. 1997. *Of Body and Brush: Grand Sacrifice as Text/Performance in Eighteenth-Century China*. Chicago: University of Chicago Press.

generational difference, articulations of, 4, 125–27

global economy: anti-colonial struggles and, 193; British imperialism and, 192–93; China's integration into, 162, 194; historical perspective on, 191, 194, 195. *See also* neoliberalism

globalization: anthropological approaches to, 114; capital flow and, 11–12, 163; theory of, 25, 90–91, 93, 113, 159, 195. *See also* cosmopolitanism; neoliberalism

Guattari, Félix, 198, 211–13 n. 43

Hall, Stuart, 214 n. 5, 221 n. 12

Harding, Susan, 160

Harvey, David, 210–11 n. 38

Hong Kong: capitalists in, 18; gay culture in, 100; in mainland Chinese imagination, 109

humanism, 35, 52–53; post-Mao, 73

human rights, 169–70, 196

India, 56, 193, 226 n. 26

intellectual property rights law, 140; historical origins of, 143, 224 n. 9; postsocialism and, 140–44

intellectuals, 37, 46, 49–52, 53, 54, 73, 215–16 n. 19, 216 n. 23

International Monetary Fund (IMF), 162

June 4th movement, 8, 9–10, 34, 119, 214 n. 4

labor conditions, in U.S. and China, 170

language, 160, 216 n. 28

Maoist socialism, 7, 12, 65, 139, 206 n. 12; class relations and, 174; class struggle and, 209 n. 30; everyday life and, 205 n. 1; feminism and, 13; modernity and, 13, 67; narration and,

49; rejection of, 43; spatial arrangements and, 128

Marx, Karl, 211 n. 41

masculinity, 60, 73, 104, 217–18 n. 35, 218 n. 41; art and, 74; national identity and, 130, 218 n. 42

May 4th movement, 193

melodrama, 32, 47–48, 50, 215 n. 13; desire and, 33; facticity and, 51; political content of, 33, 213 n. 2. See also *Yearnings*

Mercer, Kobena, 53–54

Microsoft, 140, 224 n. 5

museums: anthropological critiques of, 69; colonialism and, 220 n. 10; subalterity and, 79. See also women's museum

national identity, 33, 37, 38, 48, 130; allegories of, 217 n. 32; consumerism and, 126; cosmopolitanism and, 197; masculinity and, 60–61; sexuality and, 100–101; women and, 56–57, 62, 83

narrative style, socialist, 174–76

neoliberalism, 2–3, 13, 19, 110, 145–46, 159–62, 166, 170, 182, 184, 205 n. 7, 206 n. 8, 206 n. 17; aspirations and, 196; Christian proselytizing and, 169; cosmopolitanism and, 112, 133–34; creation of capitalist subjects and, 184; governmentality and, 15, 17, 176, 195; government policies and, 15; intellectual property rights and, 143–44; law and, 140; Maoist socialism compared to, 209–10 n. 32; national projects and, 20; possible futures and, 200–204; public morality and, 154; theories of, 15–20, 176, 197–200, 210 n. 38; United States and, 167–68. See also World Trade Organization

concerning China's entry into WTO and, 167–69; textile industry decline in, 194; trade organizations in, 186–87, 194

universals, theories of, 210 n. 37

urban life. *See* rural and urban areas

Wedding Banquet, The, 98

Welland, Sasha, 74

women's liberation, 70–71

women's museum, 67–69, 71–72, 74–78, 80–83, 220 n. 10

World Bank, 162

world systems theory, 191

World Trade Organization (WTO), 12, 158, 160–62, 177; China's entry into, 29, 140, 143, 157–92, 194–96; consumer fundamentalism and, 164; educating the public about, 174; historical amnesia and, 194; mission statement of, 190–91, 195; negotiations over textiles and, 191–94; orientalism and, 182–83

Xiaojiang, Li, 27–28, 66–74, 80–83

Yanagisako, Sylvia, 23, 210 n. 37, 223 n. 2

yearnings, 5, 32

Yearnings (Chinese soap opera), 26, 27, 31, 41, 42–63, 215–16 n. 12, 216 n. 23; masculine fantasy and, 217 n. 34; political allegory and, 57–61, 214 n. 11; U.S. media interpretation of, 32, 213 n. 2; viewers' reception of, 32–33, 58–60. *See also* melodrama

Yi, Wu, 173–76

Zhengzhou, 68–69

Zi'en, Cui, 103, 109, 200

LISA ROFEL is a professor of anthropology at the University
of California, Santa Cruz. She is the author of *Other Modernities: Gendered
Yearnings in China after Socialism.*

Library of Congress Cataloging-in-Publication Data

Rofel, Lisa.
Desiring China : experiments in neoliberalism, sexuality,
and public culture / Lisa Rofel.
p. cm. — (Perverse modernities)
Includes bibliographical references and index.
ISBN-13: 978-0-8223-3935-9 (cloth : alk. paper)
ISBN-13: 978-0-8223-3947-2 (pbk. : alk. paper)
1. China — Social conditions — 21st century. 2. Sex — Social aspects — China.
3. Popular culture — China. 4. Culture and globalization — China. 5. Cosmopolitanism — China. 6. Post-communism — China. 7. Neoliberalism — China.
8. National characteristics, Chinese. I. Title.
HN733.5.R67 2007   306.70951'090511 — dc22
2006033807